US–JAPAN TRADE FRICTION

US–Japan Trade Friction

Its Impact on Security Cooperation in the Pacific Basin

Edited by

T. David Mason

*Associate Professor of Political Science and Co-Director of the
Japan Program of the Center for International Security and Strategic
Studies, Mississippi State University*

and

Abdul M. Turay

*Professor of Economics and International Trade
Mississippi State University*

Foreword by Janos Radvanyi

*Director of the Center for International Security and Strategic Studies
Mississippi State University*

M
MACMILLAN

First published 1991

Published by
MACMILLAN ACADEMIC AND PROFESSIONAL LTD
Houndmills, Basingstoke, Hampshire RG21 2XS
and London
Companies and representatives
throughout the world

Printed in Hong Kong

British Library Cataloguing in Publication Data
US–Japan trade friction : its impact on security
cooperation in the Pacific Basin.
1. United States. Foreign relations with Japan   2. Japan.
Foreign relations with United States
I. Mason, T. David   II. Turay, Abdul M.
327.73052
ISBN 0–333–49067–3

Contents

vi   *Contents*

List of Tables

Foreword

Over the course of the past decade, the fundamental web of relations between Japan and the United States has remained strong, and government-to-government relations have continued to be productive. The personal relations between the leaders of the two nations are marked by shared concern for common problems. However, mass media attention to the mounting US trade deficit with Japan has triggered new measures in Congress aimed at further opening of Japanese markets to American imports and a greater sharing by Japan in the US defence burden in the Pacific region.

While most Americans view Japan favourably, few recognize how valuable Japanese–US ties are and how important are Japan–US security interests. The two-way trade represents a yearly $112 billion, with Japan importing twenty per cent of all US agricultural products and fifteen per cent of American-made commercial aircraft. Military bases in Japan host 60 000 American military personnel, and Japan is paying 40 per cent of this annual expense – $6.2 billion, more than any other NATO ally's contribution to common defence. The over $25 billion in Japanese direct investment in the United States is creating approximately 200 000 jobs, and Japanese investment is financing about one-third of the US national deficit. 500 000 Americans visit Japan annually; while over 2 million Japanese tour the United States yearly. 20 000 Japanese students study in American universities, and 1800 Americans study in Japanese institutions of higher education.

Despite these mutual benefits, however, complaints from each shore of the Pacific can be heard. Americans maintain that Japan's market and business practices still hinder foreign competition. The trade disputes even produced an American hit-list of unfair trade practices on which Japan was listed as one of the major violators. On the other hand, the Japanese are convinced that the era of American stewardship over Japan has ended and Japan must emerge as a nation with a major role to play on the international scene.

The challenge for both nations is real and the issues to be solved are sensitive; yet both countries recognize that their relationship is the most important for maintaining prosperity and peace in the Pacific Basin. Thus, continued US–Japanese friction over trade issues needs to be eliminated not only for economic reasons but also for the continuation of beneficial security relations. At a time when the contours of a new Soviet policy are emerging in the Far East and President Mikhail Gorbachev of the USSR and China's Deng Xiaoping are patching up differences and normalizing Sino–Soviet relations, a strong US–Japan economic and security cooperation is more imperative than ever.

The general premise of the present volume reflects these sentiments and emphasizes the importance of the need to promote closer ties and greater understanding between the United States and Japan.

The Center for International Security and Strategic Studies (CISS) at Mississippi State University is honoured to sponsor this anthology which has come into being through the long efforts of Senior CISS Fellows, Dr. T. David Mason and Dr. A.M. Turay. Warmest appreciation also goes to the Japan–United States Friendship Commission without whose support this study would not have been possible. Last but not least, we would like to thank the contributors, whose chapters offer us enlightenment on the issues involved in US–Japan trade friction and the political and security dimensions of the US–Japan relationship.

JANOS RADVANYI
Director of the Center for International
Security and Strategic Studies
Mississippi State University

Acknowledgements

This volume is the product of a research symposium entitled 'US–Japan Trade Friction: Geopolitical and Security Considerations in the Pacific Basin'. The symposium was held in Jackson, Mississippi, in the autumn of 1986 under the sponsorship of the Center for International Security and Strategic Studies (CISS) at Mississippi State University. We, the editors of this volume, are indebted first and foremost to Dr Janos Radvanyi, Director of CISS, for his tireless work on the conception of the project and the direction of this symposium. Without his initiative and persistence, this project and the book that follows would not have materialized.

We are also indebted to the Japan–US Friendship Commission and its Executive Director, Lindsey Sloan, for their generous grant which made it possible to bring together this collection of scholars for the symposium. The Japan National Oil Corporation also contributed its support, as did a number of local supporters of CISS, and we cannot overstate our appreciation of the assistance, financial and otherwise, that we received from McRae's Department Stores, Deposit Guaranty Bank, Mississippi Power & Light Company, Irby Construction Company, and from Paul Latture, Executive Director of the Jackson Chamber of Commerce.

A number of people have provided invaluable assistance in the preparation of the final version of the manuscript. Grady Johnston scrutinized the entire manuscript with considerable care in search of typographical and transcription errors and was most helpful to the editors in pointing out passages that were in need of clarification and updating. Catherine Vellake and Tan Tsai handled much of the logistical arrangements for the symposium and assisted in the transcription of the original drafts of the author's papers. Tom Davis and Chris Campany assisted in the preparation of a number of the tables and figures and in the research required to update some passages. Lisa Aplin and Cindy Blackwell were of immeasurable help in the preparation of the final draft of the manuscript, in the transcription of several chapters and in handling much of the correspondence with the publishers.

Finally, we are indebted to Simon Winder and Belinda Dutton, our publishing editors, for their willingness to publish this volume and for their patience with us in its preparation, and to Keith Povey for his painstakingly thorough editorial work on the final draft of the manuscript. Of course, we and the individual chapter authors remain responsible for any errors in fact and interpretation contained in the chapters that follow.

T. DAVID MASON
ABDUL M. TURAY

Notes on the Contributors

Tsuneo Akaha is an Associate Professor of International Relations at Bowling Green State University in Ohio. He holds degrees from both American and Japanese universities, including a PhD in International Relations from the University of Southern California. He is the author of *Japan in Global Ocean Politics* (1985). His other works have appeared in *Asian Survey, Pacific Affairs, Coastal Zone Management Journal,* and *Marine Policy Reports.*

James E. Auer is the Special Assistant for Japan in the Office of the Secretary of Defense. He served in the US Navy from 1963 to 1983 in a number of positions, many of them in Japan. These included political advisor to the Commander of US Naval Forces in Japan, visiting student at the Japan Maritime Self-Defence Force Staff College (equivalent of the US Navy War College) in Tokyo, and commanding officer of a guided missile frigate homeported in Yokosuka. He holds an AB degree from Marquette University and a PhD from the Fletcher School of Law and Diplomacy, Tufts University. His thesis, *The Postwar Rearmament of Japanese Maritime Forces 1945–1971,* was published in England by Praeger Publishers and in Japanese translation by the Jiji Press under the title *Yomigaeru Nippon Kaigun.*

Scott C. Flanagan is a Professor of Political Science at Florida State University. He is the author of numerous journal articles on Japanese parties, political culture and mass political behaviour. He is also the co-author of *Japanese Electoral Behavior: Social Cleavages, Social Networks and Partisanship* (1977) and *Politics in Japan* (1984), and co-editor of *Crisis, Choice and Change: Historical Studies of Political Development* (1973), *Political Opposition and Local Politics in Japan* (1980) and *Electoral Change in Advanced Industrial Democracies: Realignment or Dealignment* (1984).

Yasuo Imai is the General Manager, Washington Office, Japan National Oil Corporation. He is a graduate of Tokyo University Faculty of Law. Previously, he has served in the Ministry of International Trade and Industry (MITI), Japan, and has held the posts of Economic Attache of the Japanese Embassy in Tehran, Iran; Deputy

Director, Steel Division, Minister's Secretariat, MITI; and Deputy Director, General Coordination Division, Energy Agency, MITI.

Joseph G. Kvasnicka is Vice-President and Economic Advisor at the Federal Reserve Bank of Chicago, and received his graduate training in economics at Wayne State University. He joined the Bank in 1964 as an economist, eventually rising to his present position as the Head of the Research Department's International Section. He also held the position of Senior Staff Economist on the President's Council of Economic Advisors in the administrations of Presidents Nixon and Ford while on a leave-of-absence from the Bank. He has served as a part-time and Visiting Professor at Indiana University, University of Wisconsin Graduate School of Banking, University of Cape Town, and DePaul University. He is the editor of the Bank's *International Letter* and has published numerous articles in the field of international finance.

T. David Mason is an Associate Professor of Political Science and Associate Director of the Center for International Security and Strategic Studies at Mississippi State University. He is a specialist in comparative politics (non-Western political systems) and security studies, and his research has focused on the politics of civil violence and instability and on Sino–Soviet relations. His research has appeared in the *American Political Science Review, Asian Affairs, Political Behavior, Comparative Political Studies,* and other journals and anthologies.

Ronald A. Morse is Assistant Secretary for Development and Secretary of the Asia Program at the Woodrow Wilson International Center for Scholars in Washington, DC. He received his PhD from Princeton University. Before joining the Wilson Center, he served in the Departments of Defense and Energy. He has been an advisor and consultant to numerous government agencies and private organizations and is a founding member of the US National Committee for Pacific Energy Cooperation. He is the author of numerous books, articles and anthologies, including: *The Limits of Reform in China, US–Japanese Energy Relations: Cooperation and Competition, Blind Partners: Japanese and American Responses to an Unknown Future,* and *Japan and the Middle East in Alliance Politics.*

Janos Radvanyi is a Professor of History and Director of the Center for International Security and Strategic Studies at Mississippi State University. He received his training in International Law and Economics at the Graduate School of Diplomacy, Budapest and entered the Hungarian Diplomatic Service in 1954, serving in a number of capacities in Turkey, Switzerland, France and Syria. In the home office he was appointed to head the Asian Division and also served as Chief of Protocol. His last post was Washington, DC, where he was Chief of the Hungarian Mission until 1967. From 1968 to 1978 Ambassador Radvanyi was a Scholar in Residence at the Hoover Institute on War, Revolution and Peace at Stanford University. He received his PhD from Stanford in 1971 and joined the faculty of Mississippi State University that year. He has written several books and articles and has lectured widely on international security affairs.

Abdul M. Turay is a Professor of Economics and International Trade at Mississippi State University and Adjunct Professor of Economics at the University of Oklahoma. He is Editor of the *Journal of Economics and Finance* and has published works on such topics as Japanese voluntary restraints on automobiles, the internationalization of the Japanese yen, and other areas of international trade. His works have appeared in such journals as *Journal of World Trade Law, Economic Planning, Midsouth Journal of Economics and Finance,* and *Revista Internazionale di Scienze Economiche e Commerciali.*

Martin E. Weinstein is a Professor of Political Science at the University of Illinois at Champaign-Urbana. He received his PhD from Columbia University and has served as Special Assistant for Political Planning to the US Ambassador in Japan, as a Research Associate at the Brookings Institution, and as a Researcher at the International University of Japan. He has published numerous books and articles on Japanese defence policy, including *Japan's Postwar Defense Policy, Northeast Asian Security after Vietnam,* and *Japan: the Risen Sun.*

1 Introduction: The Strategic Context of US–Japan Trade Friction

T. David Mason

Since 1980, the fabric of relations between Japan and the United States has been strained by tensions arising from a variety of longstanding and recently intensifying bilateral issues. In particular, tensions have been heightened by the rapid escalation of the bilateral trade imbalance, and this development has added fuel to the longstanding debate over defence burden sharing that has percolated just below the surface of US–Japan relations since the early 1950s. Public concern and political tensions over these two closely inter-twined issues have been further intensified by fundamental shifts under way in the economic and strategic environment of the Asian–Pacific region. China's domestic reforms and its increasing involvement in the international economy, the rise of the 'Four Tigers' (South Korea, Taiwan, Singapore, and Hong Kong) as industrial powers in world markets, and the evidence of 'new thinking' in Gorbachev's more accommodative approach to Asia generally and China and Japan specifically all combine to present the US–Japan partnership with the prospect of dramatic shifts in the structure of the strategic environment that defines the *raison d'etre* of their longstanding security alliance.

On the surface, government-to-government relations between the two allies have remained cordial and strong during the 1980s, owing in no small part to the amicable personal relationship and shared political views of President Ronald Reagan and Prime Minister Yasuhiro Nakasone. The two former leaders' mutual respect for each other, their shared concern for common problems challenging the US–Japan alliance, and their compatible views on the proper policy response to the challenges facing the alliance have led the two chief executives to join in resisting domestic pressures (in both nations) for policy changes that might, in the long run, jeopardize the stability and primacy of the trade and security ties between the two powers. Indeed, their leadership abilities were sorely tested in the process.

1

However, both Nakasone and Reagan were able to bequeath to their successors a US–Japan relationship that was largely unblemished by any substantial new trade restrictions or alliances revisions. With the accession to the Prime Ministership of Noboru Takeshita, followed by Sosuke Uno and, in August of 1989, Toshiki Kaifu, and the transition to the Bush administration in Washington, we are led, quite naturally, to wonder whether these mounting pressures within their respective domestic constituencies to seek drastic remedies for the mounting trade imbalance and the defence burden sharing issue can be so effectively contained by new leaders who lack both the personal popularity to resist hostile public sentiments and the strong personal relationship to co-operate in this endeavour. The major catalyst for the recent surge of tensions in US–Japan relations has been the mounting trade imbalance. Trade issues have triggered heated debates in both houses of the US Congress and played a prominent role in the presidential campaign of 1988 (at least during the primaries). Quite naturally, many Americans fear that competition from Japanese industries is costing Americans their jobs. This concern is heightened by the widespread perception that Americans are losing in a competition that is not fair because, allegedly, Japan restricts the access of American goods to its markets. From time to time, the US Congress has responded to these sentiments by introducing legislative proposals containing various protectionist and retaliatory measures, all of which are intended to compel Japan to rectify the trade imbalance or face restrictions on its access to US markets. To date, no such legislation of any significance has made it through both houses of Congress or past the veto pen of the President. And Representative Richard Gephardt met with little success in rallying voters to his presidential candidacy that had trade protection as the centrepiece of his campaign message. Meanwhile, ominous macroeconomic problems, such as the spiralling budget deficit, that, arguably, are the more significant underlying causes of America's global trade deficit, remain beyond the political will of the Congress or the President to address. The failure of political leaders in both nations to redress the trade imbalance through policies that are mutually beneficial allows the trade problem to worsen to the point that the stability of other elements in bilateral relations – most notably the longstanding security cooperation between Japan and the US – are jeopardized by the mounting public discontent over trade issues. It is to this issue – the possibility that tensions over trade issues might threaten the stability of US–Japan security cooperation in the Pacific Basin – that this volume addresses itself.

What is often ignored in much of the public debate over trade issues is not only the fact that US–Japan economic relations are, in the broader context, of fundamental importance to both nations' economies but also the possibility that continued friction over short term trade issues could eventually erode the equally essential and mutually beneficial security relationship that has existed between the two nations since the close of the Second World War. Indeed, the emergence of growing friction over US–Japan trade problems has served to intensify tensions over the proper distribution of strategic responsibilities and financial burdens inherent in the two nations' security relationship. More critically, these tensions over mutual security relations have emerged at precisely the point in time when the two nations are faced with perhaps their greatest shared security challenge since the Korean War: the steady buildup of Soviet military forces in Asia to the point that the Soviet Union has deployed in Asia what amounts to an independent war-fighting capacity. Despite ominous evidence of the severity and potential volatility of this threat (witness the KAL-007 incident), large segments of the American public seem more concerned with the argument that the US is shouldering an inordinate portion of the costs of shared defence against this threat and that Japan has exploited this situation by shifting resources that would otherwise be devoted to defence into the modernization of their industrial base, thereby further enhancing their competitive advantage over US industries. As with the trade issue, elected officials in the US, fearing the political consequences of bucking the tide of popular sentiment on burden sharing issues, have remained more inclined to exploit these issues for short term advantage, especially in election years, than to argue for the critical importance to US security of a continued relationship with Japan.

Despite public concern with trade friction and security cost sharing, US relations with Japan remain a cornerstone of the United States' economic health and national security. As the leading trading partner of the US, Japan purchased $25 billion worth of US goods in 1983 and the figure rose to over $29 billion by 1986. This constituted 23 per cent of all Japanese imports and was more than double the value of goods Japan imported from all the EEC nations combined. For the US these figures represented over 12 per cent of all exports and likewise exceeded combined US exports to France, West Germany, and the United Kingdom. Japan remains the major customer for US agricultural goods, purchasing between six and seven billion dollars worth each year, a figure that also exceeds the total purchases of US commodities by the European Community. In addition, the proportion of US non-fuel exports to Japan that are manufactured goods has continued to rise, reaching 46 per cent in 1984 as compared to 38 per cent in 1973. Furthermore, capital flows from Japan have increased in recent years, to a total of over $40 billion in 1984. Thus, much of the dollar flows out of the US that result from the trade deficit are finding their way back into the US economy. In part, they are returning in what amounts to Japanese financing of US budget deficits. But a considerable volume of these flows have taken the form of Japanese direct investment in production facilities in the US, much to the benefit of American workers.

Still, the imbalance in bilateral trade accounts is so large that one cannot easily deny the existence of barriers, largely of the non-tariff variety, to Japanese markets, and several chapters in this volume discuss these. As the trade deficit has mounted, Japan's political leadership has become increasingly sensitive to this matter and has taken steps to allay US concerns and at least moderate the magnitude of the imbalance. The Plaza Accord among the G-5 nations in September 1985 resulted in a sharp appreciation in the value of the yen against the dollar, from approximately 250 to one to current levels of about 140 to one. This has had the effect of making US goods cheaper in Japanese markets, although to date without substantially reducing the size of the trade deficit. During his visit to Washington in January 1988, Prime Minister Takeshita pledged to pursue the recommendations of the Maekawa Report, which called for strong stimuli to Japanese domestic demand in order to increase imports and reduce its trade deficit with the US. Although the projected ten billion dollar reduction in the trade deficit would still leave an imbalance of over $50 billion, Takeshita's pledge at least indicated his intention to continue the efforts of his predecessor to take active remedial measures on bilateral trade problems.

Equally disturbing in the debate on US–Japan defence burden sharing has been the lack of public attention to the critical strategic importance of this alliance in the Asian–Pacific context. Over the course of the last two decades, the Soviet Union has deployed over 50 divisions of combat troops in Asia, some 2000 combat aircraft (some of which are nuclear capable), a number of SS-20 intermediate range ballistic missiles, and a Pacific fleet that is now the largest and most powerful in the Soviet navy. With basing facilities at Cam Ranh Bay, the Soviets have gained power projection capabilities that, in a crisis, could threaten vital sealanes in the Indian Ocean as well as the Pacific. In recent years the threat that Soviet forces pose to

Japan – and hence to US military assets stationed there – has increased with their deployment of combat troops and aircraft on at least two of the Kurile Islands that Japan claims as its territory. Recent trends toward a lessening of tensions between China and the Soviet Union further intensify the gravity of the Soviet threat in that, with Sino–Soviet rapprochement, the US and Japan could no longer count on China as a mainland counterweight to the Soviet Union in the event of a crisis. Thus, despite the marked decline in rhetorical hostility under Gorbachev, the dimensions of the military challenge facing the US–Japan alliance have, if anything, become potentially more serious.

The gravity of the Soviet threat has not been lost on the Japanese, as opinion surveys have consistently confirmed the Japanese public's overt hostility towards the Soviet Union. The historically grounded dispute over the Northern Territories – the four southernmost Kurile Islands that Japan claims as its territory but which the Soviet Union occupies – has in recent years only intensified as a result of incidents such as the downing of KAL-007. Despite US complaints about the low level of Japanese defence spending, Japan has in fact surpassed the often-cited ceiling of one per cent of GNP and currently ranks sixth in the world in military spending. Efforts to upgrade the capabilities of the Self-Defence Forces (SDF) are documented in greater detail in later chapters of this volume. Still, in the absence of a defence force capable independently of countering the Soviet presence in Asia, Japan recognizes that it will remain heavily dependent upon US security guarantees. To stabilize these ties, Japan has since 1978 increased its contribution to the cost of providing and maintaining facilities for US forces stationed in Japan.

Equally important though less often recognized or understood has been Japan's contribution to mutual security interests through its trade and aid policies toward other nations in Asia. By actively assisting in the development of the strong, growing, and prosperous economies in ASEAN and other nations of the Pacific Basin, Japan has promoted a degree of prosperity and political stability that has, in effect, inoculated these nations against the threats and appeals of the Soviet Union and its proxies in the region. Indeed, one could even argue that the general economic dynamism of the Asian–Pacific region, stimulated in no small part by Japanese trade and aid policies, has encouraged the tendencies towards 'new thinking' in Soviet foreign policy by presenting Mikhail Gorbachev with an Asia full of opportunities for advancing his agenda of domestic economic reform and revitalization, rather than a region full only of threats that require further militarization of Soviet policy in Asia. US security interests have thus been enhanced by the preservation of governments that are favourably disposed to the Western alliance and relatively immune to penetration by Soviet influence.

Still, public attention and debate in the United States tend to focus almost exclusively on the size of Japan's defence budget and the limited capabilities of its Self-Defence Forces. This tendency is heightened by the growing public discontent over trade imbalances. The danger is that, by focusing on these aspects of US–Japan relations, public debate in the US ignores the more subtle and significant implications of any deterioration in US–Japan security cooperation. For instance, given Japan's geopolitical vulnerability to the Soviet Union and its near total dependence on imports of energy and raw materials, it is conceivable that a Japan that was independent of US security guarantees might be inclined to reduce its strategic and economic vulnerability not by attempting to match Soviet military might in the region but by cultivating greater economic interdependence with its mainland neighbour. This seems all the more likely under present conditions, given Gorbachev's apparent desire to use international trade as a major element of his efforts to reform and modernize the Soviet economy. On energy matters alone, Japan's dependence on imported oil has introduced an element of strain in its relations with the US, as Japanese support of US positions on Middle East conflicts has placed at risk the security of its supplies of Middle East oil. Even here, US perceptions of Japan's role in the Middle East are dominated by the notion that US military efforts to secure the flow of oil from the Persian Gulf and elsewhere have benefited mainly Japan (and Western Europe), not the US.

Thus, it is evident that economic and security concerns are inextricably intertwined in the web of US–Japanese relations. To the extent that trade frictions are allowed to intensify, we run the risk that these strains in bilateral relations will catalyze a parallel erosion in the structures of security cooperation that bind the two nations' strategic interests in the region. It is the purpose of this volume to explore the nature and significance of both economic and security ties between Japan and the US, to explore the extent to which conflicts in one arena can disrupt or intensifies conflicts in the other, and to assess the prospects for the future of security relations between the two as they face the challenge of a rapidly changing strategic and economic environment in the Asian–Pacific region.

2 The Economic Dimensions of US–Japan Trade and Trade Frictions
Abdul M. Turay

INTRODUCTION

Successful international trade policies such as those of Japan have once again proven that trade can be an 'engine of growth', but can also create trade frictions with major trading partners. What is trade? Why is trade one of the most sensitive issues of this decade and beyond? Why has trade between the US and Japan created so much friction? What are the causes of these frictions? What are the specific areas of trade friction? It is the objective of this chapter to attempt to answer these and other questions underlying the economic dimensions of US–Japan trade friction. It is important to point out that there are many political, cultural and social factors that may contribute to trade frictions between the two countries. These factors, however, are addressed in other chapters in this volume.

This chapter will be divided into four sections. The first section will provide some definitions which would be essential to the discussion of trade and trade frictions. The second section will examine the historical perspective of the US–Japan trade problems. The third part will examine the theoretical foundation of the trade friction. The areas of trade friction between the two countries will be addressed in the fourth section.

PRELIMINARY DEFINITIONS AND CONCEPTS

Since one of the objectives of this chapter is to help readers understand the issues which contributed to trade and trade conflict between the US and Japan, it is useful to clarify some of the basic concepts used in this debate. In discussing the trade relations between the two countries, economists generally consider the macroeconomic and microeconomic factors that influence the trade relations between the two countries. What is international trade? International trade is generally referred to as the exchange of goods and services across international boundaries. Countries trade, therefore, to reap the benefits or gains from the exchange. International trade may be affected by macro and microeconomic factors. Macroeconomics is concerned with the economy as a whole or some segment of it, such as the rate of savings, the level of investment, rate of unemployment, changes in price levels, and the ways in which a government raises revenues (taxes) and spends (expenditures).

When related to international trade, the macroeconomic aspect of international trade deals with the balance of payments and adjustments of a nation. The balance of payments measures a nation's total payments and total receipts from the rest of its trading partners. Microeconomics, on the other hand, is concerned with individual economic units and specific markets. Thus, the microeconomic aspect of international trade deals with the basis for trade, the gains from trade, and the reasons for and the results of obstruction to free flow of trade called commercial policies.

The current trade problems between the two countries can be traced to the traditional issue of 'saving-investment imbalance'. This issue will be discussed later. However, in the macroeconomic sense, savings represent that portion of income not used for consumption, while investment refers to spending by both the private and public sectors on job-creating and income producing goods. Savings are traditionally higher in Japan than in the US. This has resulted in a saving–investment imbalance between the two nations. In the 1980s, the gross private savings of Japan was about 30 per cent of its GNP, and approximately 17 per cent of the GNP of the American economy.

The trade conflict between the two countries has also been related to the business practices of both nations, which block the entry of each other's products in their respective markets through the use of tariff and non-tariff barriers. Tariffs are taxes on imported goods. An import tariff is the most commonly used form of trade restriction. Another form of tariff is the export tariff, which is prohibited by the US constitution, but is used extensively in other countries as a source of revenue.

Non-tariffs, such as a quota, are a direct quantitative restriction on imports. In Japan, the most common type of non-tariff barriers are standard and testing requirements, government procurement practices, and customs procedures, to name just a few. When tariffs and non-tariff barriers are used, we refer to the practice as 'protectionism'. In other words, these are measures to protect or insulate a domestic industry from foreign competition. This issue, of course, is at the centre of the debate as the US Congress battles with the problem of the persistent trade deficit with Japan.

A trade deficit occurs when imported goods exceed exports, and the opposite will represent a trade surplus. During the 1980s, several hundred Bills have been introduced in the US Congress to deal with the persistent trade deficit. Despite the popularity of protectionism as a response to the US trade deficit, it is an ineffective trade policy.

In sum, these are just a few of the conceptualizations that lend themselves to the discussion of trade conflict between the US and Japan. To ensure that the reader understands the issues, I will continue to define and explain other terms throughout this discussion.

US–JAPAN TRADE: AN HISTORICAL PERSPECTIVE

This section of the chapter will set the stage for the discussion of historical events which have influenced trade relations between US and Japan. History has a way of helping to shape current and future events. US–Japan trade frictions can be traced back to the 1850s when the US and some Western European nations stripped Japan of its authority to impose tariff. This action was known as the 'unequal treaties'. In 1854, the US and Japan signed the Kangaroo Treaty calling on Japan to open its ports to US ships. Despite these difficulties, trade between the US and Japan continued to grow throughout the nineteenth and twentieth centuries. This growth was disrupted in the 1930s with the Smoot–Hawley Tariff Act of 1930 at the outbreak of the Second World War. The Smoot–Hawley Act raised US tariffs on imports by more than 50 per cent. Some economists argued that this action was partly responsible for fuelling the 1929 Great Depression.

During the 1940s, US–Japan trade relations moved to more difficult times. When President Roosevelt imposed an export control on such items as petroleum products and scrap metal being sold to Japan, the imposition of the export control by the US government was in retaliation for Japanese militarism during the Second World

War. At the end of the war, trade relations between the two countries was centred around the reconstruction of the Japanese economy under the Marshall Plan. This phase of the economic relationship between the two countries came to an end in the 1950s, as Japan imposed 'Voluntary Export Restraints' (VERs) on US products in retaliation for US pressure on labour-intensive Japanese products such as cotton textiles, bicycles, bolts, nuts, etc.

In the 1960s and 1970s, the bilateral trade problem between the US and Japan was attributed mainly to exchange rate fluctuations and the economic growth rate in both economies. Exchange rate is the domestic currency price of a unit of the foreign currency – meaning the number of dollars required to purchase Japanese yen. Therefore, a currency can appreciate or depreciate in value against other currencies. When the value of a currency appreciates it means its price has risen against others. For example, in 1973 the Japanese yen appreciated against the US dollar, which started a period of economic turmoil between the two countries. Consequently, Japan's exports to the US were expensive while US exports to Japan were less expensive. However, in 1973 the Japanese government was more concerned with export controls than the appreciation of the yen. The US government in that same year imposed export controls on soybeans in Japan, and the Oil Producing Export Countries (OPEC) imposed their oil embargo. These two measures had a much broader effect on the Japanese economy than the appreciation of the yen. Between the summer of 1973 and autumn 1974, oil prices increased from three dollars per barrel to $11.65 per barrel. As a result, Japan's oil bill rose from $6.7 billion in 1973 to about $21 billion in 1974. However, this was not unique to the Japanese economy. The US economy also suffered from the oil embargo as the US oil import bills increased from eight billion dollars in 1973 to $26 billion in 1974.

The 1970s were marked by the introduction of a 'New US Economic Policy' by President Nixon. The policy called for the suspension of all conversions of the dollar and a 10 per cent surcharge on imports. Even though this policy was not directed specifically towards Japan, its intent was clear. It was a move against Japan for failing to revalue its currency and its unwillingness to open its markets. Revaluation of a currency means resetting the exchange rate at a higher level than the current one. The opposite of revaluation is devaluation which refers to setting the exchange rate below its current level. The revaluation of the yen was significant because the low value of the yen makes Japanese goods and investments more attractive to US residents and makes US goods and investments unattractive to Japanese residents. The result was that the US continued to experience a trade deficit with Japan.

In the 1980s, the persistent US trade deficit with Japan dominated the bilateral trade issues between the two countries. Japan argues that economic conditions in the US, and not trade related issues, are the causes of a weak yen. On the other hand, the US position is that sluggish consumer spending in Japan and differences in production between the two countries are the key factors responsible for the Japanese trade surplus with the US. Japan, in turn, insists that the failure of US businessmen to understand the Japanese market is another reason for the trade friction. US businesses, therefore, argue that the Japanese trade surplus is a result of Japanese business practices which blocked the entry of US products by the use of non-tariff barriers.

In 1981, the US presented the Japanese government with a list of 'market access shopping lists', which include some items as computers, plywood, leather, autoparts, and agricultural products. The US government requested that the Japanese government streamline its customs procedures to help resolve the problems surrounding Japanese standards for imported products. In 1982, Japan announced its trade liberalization policies including 'standards issues'. These standards were defined in terms of design specifications. However, the US rejected Japan's liberalization measures on the grounds that they were already in place and did not represent any significant progress toward resolving bilateral trade conflicts between the two nations.

In 1983, however, the US–Japan trade relations showed some sign of progress as the two nations cooperated in the field of high technology, and the US was successful in getting Japan to lift some of its non-tariff barriers. The year ended with a summit between President Ronald Reagan of the US and Japanese Prime Minister Nakasone. Both agreed to create a committee to find ways to liberalize Japanese rules on foreign investment to internationalize the Japanese yen, to further cooperate in the field of high technology, and to further open Japanese import markets.[1] However, 1984 was a difficult year for US–Japan bilateral trade relations, because both economies had to deal with significant domestic economic and political issues which had an influence on international policies. This led to trade talks in 1984 to settle some of the major issues separating the two nations. At the end of the talks Japan agreed to liberalize some farm imports, agreed on a dollar–yen stabilization programme, and the revision of the non-tariff trade agreement of 1982. However, the frustration on both sides about trade issues continued in the 1980s. For example Japan's continuing trade surplus with the US prompted the introduction of several protectionist bills in the US Congress. The US deficit was about $156 billion in 1986, and increased to $171 billion in 1987. It is important to point out that the US trade deficit with Japan has been offset by capital inflow from Japan into the US, which helped to keep US interest rates relatively low. In 1986, however, the threat of protectionism continued to dampen the US–Japan bilateral trade relations as the US merchandise trade deficit reached an historical high of $59.1 billion. This represented an increase of 27 per cent over the previous year. As a result of the threat of protection, Japan agreed to continue the 'market-oriented' sector-selective Moss Talks with the US government for the purpose of eliminating certain tariff and non-tariff barriers in Japan on such items as auto parts and accessories. The reason the US is interested in auto parts and accessories is because Japan has used Foreign Trade Zones (FTZ) successfully to accumulate a substantial trade surplus with the US in these markets. The US trade deficit with Japan on auto parts and accessories in 1986 amounted to $4.3 billion. An FTZ is a trade area where imported goods are stored, inspected, repackaged, or combined with components made in the country where the FTZ is located. For the Japanese producers of auto parts, FTZ enables them to accelerate their export status for purposes of excise tax rebates and customs drawbacks, in that manufacturers of auto parts are generally required to pay excise taxes when the parts are produced and exported. But in an FTZ, the taxes are rebated if the items are exported. This advantage enables Japanese firms to export more auto parts to the US market, which was partly responsible for the US trade deficit (including trade in auto parts and accessories).

The 'Moss Talks' of 1985 also covered another industry, that is the telecommunication industry. However, the negotiations in this industry were much better than previous ones because the discussion shifted from discussion to monitoring producers and suppliers for violations such as dumping of their products in third-country markets. Dumping refers to the act of selling a product in a foreign market at a price below what the same product is selling for in the domestic market. However, by the summer of 1986, the most dominant issue in US–Japan trade relations was the dumping of semi-conductor products by Japan in third-country markets such as Hong Kong and Singapore (this issue will be developed in detail later in another section).

Other issues that separated the two nations in 1986 and 1987 ranged from machine tools to the Kansai International Airport Construction. For example, in 1986 Japan accounted for about $1.3 billion worth of metal working machine tools imported into the US. This figure prompted calls for action to protect the American industry. To avoid any form of trade restriction, both the US and Japan signed a Voluntary Export Restraints agreement limiting Japanese exports to the US. The Kansai International Airport construction added further strain on US–Japanese trade relations in 1986. Many US companies were shut out of the bidding process for the project and, therefore, demanded retaliation on Japan.

In conclusion, it seems that the bilateral trade relations between the US and Japan have been dominated by economic forces. In particular the recent loss of the US competitive edge and the fluctuation of the dollar and the yen in foreign exchange markets are the underlying economic factors responsible for much of the bilateral trade conflict between the two countries. A high dollar price prior to 1985 made imports more attractive in the US and US exports less attractive in foreign markets. This contributed to the persistent trade deficit the US experiences with Japan. However, we should not forget the cyclical factors or business cycles, such as recession, which tend to be more severe in the US than in Japan and tend to influence trade. The 1981–82 recession had less impact on Japan than the US. As a result, Japanese producers and suppliers maintained a high level of investment compared to their counterparts in the US. Consequently, Japan was in a much better position to increase its exports to the US at the end of the recession in 1983 and 1984, accelerating the US trade deficit with Japan further and further. Thus, the attention paid to the trade problems between the two nations is a clear sign of the US frustration with Japan and her failure to help reduce the US trade deficit.

THE THEORETICAL FOUNDATIONS OF US–JAPAN TRADE FRICTION

This section of the chapter will examine in detail some of the theoretical foundations for US–Japan trade frictions. As was stated in the previous section, the underlying factor in the US–Japan trade and trade friction has been the US trade deficit or Japanese trade surplus. The reason for the deficit and the surplus have been based on how each country views the causes of trade imbalance. What are the factors responsible for the trade imbalance? Some of them include: (a) savings–investment imbalance; (b) exchange rate; and (c) protectionism.

Savings–Investment Imbalance

Savings is that part of income not spent on consumption; and investment is defined as spending by business firms to add or replace its non-human productive assets such as plant equipments or spending by firms on new job-creating and income producing goods. The conflict over Japan's large trade surplus with the US has been attributed to the imbalance between domestic savings and investment in both countries. To understand the role savings and investment play in a country's trade surplus or deficit, let us examine what has and is still happening in both countries.

The US economy in the last two decades has experienced huge financial shortfalls caused by the persistent budget deficit. This shortfall has been accompanied by tight monetary policies in the US which, in turn, have caused US interest rates to rise, thus attracting more foreign capital. It has kept domestic capital at home in the form of private savings. However, one negative aspect of the inflow of foreign capital into the US economy is that it causes the value of the dollar to rise as foreign investors convert their domestic currencies into dollars. Thus, demand for dollars increases and the value rises. This is not the only factor responsible for the rise in the dollar. There are other factors such as economic growth accompanied by low inflation which may also cause the value of the dollar to rise. When foreign investments are made in a prosperous economy there is an increase in the demand and the value of the currency. The value of the dollar relative to the Japanese yen remained high during the period 1980–1984. This had an effect on US competitiveness in Japan and other foreign markets. US goods became less competitive because they were very expensive relative to others, thus adding to the growing decline in the US savings–investment balance when compared to Japan's. This also has had an effect on the growing bilateral trade deficit of the US and the surplus in Japan.

In sum, investment is an injection into an economy since it adds to total expenditure of a given economy and stimulates production. Savings represent a leakage out of the economy because it is that part of income generated but not spent. Therefore, an equilibrium level of income in an economy will occur where savings equal investments $(s=I)$.

In Japan, high savings rates represent income generated but not spent on imports from the US, while in the US, the low savings rates represent income generated and spent on imports from Japan. Since savings should equal investment, the lower savings ratio in the US would mean lower investment and lower productivity for exports. At the same time, higher savings in Japan mean higher investment and productivity for exports to the US market; and thus the trade deficit will continue to worsen between the two countries. Also, as long as the US savings are less than Japan's, the more the former will spend on its rival's imports. Therefore, when the US imports are greater than exports, the US will experience a trade deficit.

Exchange Rate

Exchange rate is the value of one currency in respect to another. The exchange rate, along with the economic growth rate in both economies, has represented the most dominant macroeconomic factor used to explain the trade conflict between the two nations. How do the exchange rate and economic growth contribute to the understanding of the trade conflict between Japan and the US?

In an effort to liberalize its exchange control structure, the Japanese authorities passed the 'New Foreign Exchange and Foreign Trade Control Law' in December 1980. The new law made foreign exchange transactions and direct foreign investment in Japan freer, whereas this type of transaction had been prohibited unless ordered by ministerial ordinance.

Furthermore, the new law gave Japanese consumers and firms an unlimited freedom to convert yen into other foreign currencies, especially US dollars. The unrestricted exchange rate provision gave Japanese firms the opportunity to increase their investment activities in the US and, at the same time, ease the restrictions on foreign ownership of Japanese securities.

Liberalization of Japanese exchange controls could have important long run implications on the bilateral trade conflict with the US. For example, in recent years capital movement from Japan to the US in response to exchange rate flexibility has amplified the savings in the value of the dollar–yen exchange rate. Furthermore, the liberalization of the Japanese exchange rate has also influenced interest rate movement, which is partly responsible for large swings in the value of the yen in the late 1980s. Rising interest rates in Japan have increased the demand for yen-denominated assets, particularly from OPEC investors.

Also during the early 1980s, the dollar was grossly overvalued which resulted in excessive US imports and weak exports. Between 1980 and 1984, the dollar appeciated by about 20 per cent against the Japanese yen. The appreciation further worsened the US trade deficit as Japanese imports became more attractive in the US and US exports less attractive to Japan. The deficit remained at a high plateau through 1987. However, since 1985, the dollar has depreciated against the yen, but US imports from Japan continue to far exceed US exports to Japan. That means the US trade deficit continues to persist, even though it declined in the first quarter of 1988.[2] There are several reasons the US trade deficit has not declined proportionally with the depreciation of the US dollar: (1) the strong performance of the US economy; (2) the US federal budget deficit; and (3) the declining competitiveness of certain US industries.

In conclusion, the New Foreign Exchange and Foreign Trade Control laws have reduced tensions in the area of investments as investors on both sides can now participate more freely in each other's financial markets.

Protectionism

As a policy instrument, protection of domestic industries has emerged as an issue which has overshadowed the bilateral trade relations between the US and Japan. Protectionism is a policy to restrict imports in order to protect a chosen domestic industry from foreign competition. In the US concern over the trade deficit has promoted hundreds of restrictive Trade Bills to be introduced in the US Congress, and in Japan the government has introduced several restrictive measures to protect its industries. What is the level of protection in both countries and how has it contributed to the trade conflict?

Table 2.1 shows the nominal tariff rates for both the US and Japan for selected industries. The figures in parentheses show the rankings from the highly protected industry to the lowest. The Table also

Table 2.1   Nominal tariff rates for various industries in the US and Japan – 1984

US Nominal Tariff		Industries	Japan Nominal Tariff	
2.20	(18)	Agriculture, Forestry, and Fishing	18.40	(2)
6.30	(10)	Food, Beverages, and Tobacco	25.40	(1)
14.40	(2)	Textiles	3.30	(14)
27.80	(1)	Wearing Apparel	13.80	(4)
5.60	(11)	Leather Products	3.00	(15)
8.80	(5)	Footwear	16.40	(3)
3.60	(16)	Wood Products	0.30	(21)
8.10	(6)	Furniture and Fixtures	7.80	(6)
0.50	(22)	Paper and Paper Products	2.10	(17)
1.10	(21)	Printing and Publishing	0.20	(22)
3.80	(14)	Chemicals	6.20	(10)
1.40	(19)	Petroleum and Related Products	2.80	(16)
3.60	(15)	Rubber Products	1.50	(18)
9.10	(4)	Non-metallic Mineral Products	0.60	(20)
10.70	(3)	Glass and Glass Products	7.50	(7)
4.70	(13)	Iron and Steel	3.30	(15)
1.20	(20)	Non-Ferrous Metals	6.90	(9)
7.50	(8)	Metal Products	6.90	(9)
5.00	(12)	Non-Electrical Machinery	9.10	(5)
6.60	(9)	Electrical Machinery	7.40	(3)
3.30	(17)	Transport Equipment	6.00	(12)
7.80	7)	Miscellaneous Manufacturers	6.00	(11)

Source   Alan V. Deardorff and Robert M. Stern 'The Effects of the Tokyo Round on The Structure of Protection', in R.E. Baldwin and A.O. Kruegor, eds., *The Stucture and Evolution of Recent US Trade Policy* (Chicago: University of Chicago Press, 1984), pp. 370–373.

shows that Japan's average tariff on industrial products are generally lower than those in the US. However, the Table also reveals that high tariffs in Japan tend to be in the processed food, beverage and tobacco industries, while in the US high-tariff industries are the textile and clothing industries. Other highly protected industries in Japan and the US are footwear and glass and glass products, respectively. On the average, US tariff rates are much higher than those in Japan. Therefore, the reduction or elimination of all tariffs would be more beneficial to Japan than the US.

Tariffs are not the only means used to protect industries in both countries. Today the most dominant forms of protection used by both countries are what is referred to as non-tariff barriers (NTBs). NTBs are tools used to restrict the flow of goods and services across national boundaries. Other restricting tools include: quotas, voluntary export restraints (VERs), and technical, administrative and other regulations. NTBs can also come in the form of international cartels, dumping, and export subsidies.

Table 2.2   Import quotas in the US, Japan and other major trading countries

Countries	Number of import quotas	Import quota on agriculture	Import quota on industry	Discriminatory restrictions against Japan
United States	7	1	6	
Japan	27	22	55	
United Kingdom	3	1	2	
France	46	19	17	22
West Germany	4	3	1	3
Italy	8	3	5	35
Canada	5	4	1	

Source   Gary R. Saxonhouse, 'The Micro and Macroeconomics of Foreign Sales to Japan', 261 Copyright 1983 Institute for International Economics. Reprinted by permission from *Trade Policy in the 1980s* by William R. Cline.

As shown in Table 2.2, the most commonly used type of NTBs in Japan are import quotas. Of the 27 import quotas used in Japan, 22 are applied to the agricultural industries and the remaining five are applied to the manufacturing industry.

Both nations have also used 'intangible' non-tariff barriers to protect their respective industries, having an impact on US–Japan bilateral trade relations. An example of intangible protections would be governmental regulations which prevent foreigners from participating in domestic procurements. The Nippon Telephone and Telegraph (NTT) has been cited as an example of a Japanese agency that excludes American firms from participating in its procurement. Other intangible protective measures include: (a) widespread regulations and red tape used by both governments; (b) the oligopolistic behaviour of businesses in both countries in which a number of firms dominate a specific market and create barriers to entry by foreign firms. For example, the Japanese government has encouraged what are called 'recession cartels'. The idea is to recognize failing industries and limit imports in that industry in order to protect the domestic industry from failure as a result of a recessionary pressure. Another example of how oligopoly is used to restrict the flow of goods in Japan is through the distribution system. The distribution system in Japan is controlled by a few firms which exclude foreign competitors. An example would be the 'Keiretsu' conglomerates consisting of manufacturers, financial institutions, and industrial targeting. Industrial targeting, when used as a form of protectionism, can be in the form of export subsidies or tax incentives for a particular industry. Export subsidies are in the form of government payments to a firm to export a commodity. The US, at one time or another, can unilaterally impose duties on imports to nullify foreign subsidies, especially in the case of subsidized goods originating from Japan.[3]

In conclusion, the issue of protectionism has emerged in the 1980s as the most dominant issue in US–Japan trade relations. This is partly due to the concern over the record trade deficit of the US. Hundreds of protectionist Bills have been introduced in current sessions of the US Congress, including the 1988 Trade Bill.

AREAS OF TRADE FRICTION

Thus far, the chapter has examined the fundamental issues which have had some impact on the US–Japan trade friction. In this section, an examination of the key areas of trade frictions between the US and Japan will be undertaken. This section will be divided into three areas of trade friction. These are (a) industry, (b) trade policies, and (c) economic policies.

Industrial Cases

In examining US–Japan bilateral trade frictions, it is sometimes difficult to separate the industrial issues from the trade and economic issues because they are all related in some way. However, in this section an attempt will be made to separate these issues. Industrial cases that have played a vital role in the US–Japanese bilateral trade conflict are agriculture, automobiles, steel, semi-conductors, and machine tools.

1. *Agriculture*:   Since the end of the Second World War, Japan has continued to be the major importer of agricultural products from the US. In 1982, for example, 42 per cent of Japan's total agricultural

imports came from the US, and for individual products such as corn, wheat and soybeans. In 1983, fifteen per cent of the US total world exports of agricultural products was sold to Japan. As Table 2.3 shows, the total US agricultural exports to Japan were $37,813 million in 1984. However, Japanese trade restriction on agricultural products helped to reduce US exports in 1985. As Table 2.4 shows, Japan consistently raised its quotas to protect its agricultural industry from 1984 to 1987. These quotas have remained the major source of tension between the two countries.

Table 2.3   Exports and imports of agriculture to Japan, 1981–5
(in millions of dollars)

		Exports					*Imports*		
1981	1982	1983	1984	1985	1981	1982	1983	1984	1985
43 338	36 623	36 108	37 813	29 242	18 590	16 975	18 104	21 522	22 020

Source   US–Japan Economic Relations Yearbook 1984–5

Table 2.4   Japan's import quotas for certain agricultural products 1984 (*in metric tons*)

Year	Beef	Oranges	Orange Juice
1984	37 700	92 500	7000
1985	44 600	103 500	6500
1986	51 500	114 500	8000
1987	58 400	270 500	8500

Source   US Trade Representative.

Japan has also used other forms of trade restrictions to protect its agricultural sector, namely price supports and food control laws. In 1982, 78 per cent of the value of Japan's agricultural products received some form of price support[4] as compared to 49 per cent of the US. Other than price support, Japan has also used food control laws to protect its agricultural sector. Food control laws have similar effects as quota on certain items. For example, wheat, barley and rice imports were greatly restricted by the food control laws.

Why is Japan's agricultural sector highly restrictive? The answer has little to do with international trade, but lies in the political and cultural realms. In an effort to preserve the rural family and village culture and in conjunction with the strong political influence of the Japanese farmer, the government of Japan has chosen to protect the agricultural sector from foreign competition. The US response has been to pressure Japan to remove some of the trade barriers in agriculture.

2. *Automobiles*: The conflict over Japanese trade surplus of auto- mobiles with the US came to a head in 1981 when the Reagan administration imposed Voluntary Export Restraints (VERs) on Japanese cars (see Table 2.5).

VERs gave Japan the opportunity to increase auto production in the US which led to increased imports of auto parts from Japan. This, of course, further fuelled the trade conflict between the two countries because it had a negative impact on the US auto part industry. To soften the impact and appease both US parts producers and US

Table 2.5 Unofficial quota allocations on Japanese car imports into the US, 1981–5 (in units)

Exports	1981–3 Quota	1984 Quota	1985 Quota	Increase 1984–5 (in Percentage)
Toyota Motor Corp.	516 659	551 792	620 800	12.5
Nissan Motor Co., Ltd	456 030	487 040	547 900	12.5
Honda Motor Co., Ltd	348 61	372 338	428 600	15.1
Mazda Motor Co., Ltd.	159 282	173 468	229 700	32.4
Mitsubishi Motor Corp. (including sales to Chrysler Corp.)		122 612	186 200	51.9
Fuji Heavy Industries Ltd	112 584 70 014	76 250	117 200	136.6
Suzuki Motor Co., Ltd. (for sales to GM)	0	17 000	52 000	208.9
Total*	1 680 00	1 850 000	2 300 000	24.3

* Not included in these figures are the separate quotas on exports of four-wheel drive vehicles, station wagons and mini vans and on shipment to Puerto Rico. These quotas were estimated at 112 900 units and 95 700 units, respectively for 1985.
Source US–Japan Economic Relations Yearbook 1984–1985.

Congressional critics, Japanese authorities urged its US-based auto makers to increase their demand for US-made parts. In response to the pressure from Congress and the administration, the Japanese government eliminated tariffs on 38 auto parts categories. VERs will continue to be a major trade policy as the US and Japan compete for shares of the US market. This is because VERs are agreements negotiated between an importer and the exporter. Moreover, VERs would be a more acceptable choice to the Japanese as they often face the choice of agreeing to the VERs or facing a tariff on its exports. VERs, therefore, may be the most ideal long term arrangement for both countries as they continue to look for solutions to the trade conflict.

3. *Steel Industry*:   In the last twenty years, the American steel industry has found itself under increasing competition with foreign producers, especially Japan. In 1968, the industry received protection in the form of VERs on carbon steel. Earlier in 1976, the US government imposed import quotas on so-called 'specialty steel' (such as stainless steel sheet and plate) because imports were causing serious setbacks to the US industry. In accordance with Article XIX of the GATT (General Agreement on Tariff and Trade) rules, Japan asked for compensation in response to the US import quotas on steel, on the grounds that they exercised self-restraint on prices and the amounts exported to the US. This conflict led to a negotiation which produced a formal 'Orderly Marketing Agreement' (OMA) in 1983. OMA is very similar to VERs because they both represent a negotiated agreement between two or more nations to limit the exports of specific goods to an importing country. The agreement (OMA) reduced the import of 'specialty steel' from Japan but gave them a larger share of the US market which represented approximately 60 per cent of the US market by 1984.

However, the trade imbalance in steel continued with the implementation of the OMA. In an effort to reduce Japan's trade surplus in steel, both nations reached a compromise which called for Japan to limit its exports to 5.8 per cent for a five-year period from 1985–1990. Why have US policy makers shown such a strong interest in protecting the steel industry? The answer can be found in the structure of the industry, in that firms which make up the industry are rather inflexible in responding to competitive shocks.

The OMA put an end to the steel trade conflict between Washington and Tokyo. But it left the Japanese steel industry still concerned about the wave of protectionism in the US. To avoid further protectionism in the industry, there has been a movement toward more joint ventures, as evidenced by the Klheding–Pittsburgh steel joint venture on the establishment of a seamless pipe mill. Finally, as a defensive motivation against protectionism, Japanese steel firms are increasing their investment in the US.

4. *Semi-conductors*:   The US frustration with Japan over the semi-conductor industry reached its climax in 1987 when the US nego-tiators claimed that Japan was dumping computer chips in third-country markets such as Hong Kong, Singapore and Taiwan at below 'fair market prices'. The conflict is over the definition of fair market value, which is obviously different in both countries. The US definition includes administrative and marketing costs, plus an eight per cent mark-up for profit. While Japan's definition of fair market value is based on the GATT which is based on the higher of either production cost or price in the house market.

The dispute is over two key computer chips, the 64k Dynamic Random Access Memory (DRAM) and the Erasable Programmable Read Only Memories (EPROM). In 1985, Japan announced a two-part plan to settle the trade dispute in the semi-conductor industry. Under the plan, the Japanese government was to establish a floor price (or minimum price) for DRAM and EPROM chips, and encourage Japanese firms to increase imports of US made circuits or chips. In return, the US government would drop any discussion about sanctions or trade barriers. The issue was not resolved, and by February 1987, the US announced a 100 per cent *ad valorem* tariff on certain products imported from Japan.[5] The reaction from Japanese officials was that retaliatory measures of their own were necessary.

In conclusion, the semi-conductor trade conflicts between the two countries had some effect on US–Japanese negotiations and other trade issues. Also, the political fallout from the US actions was apparent in Japanese local elections as the US tariffs became the political issue in the campaign.

5. *Machine tools*:   Since the early 1980s, the Japanese penetration in the US machine tools market has increased steadily. In 1983, for example, 37 per cent of US imports of machine tools were Japanese.[6] By 1986, Japanese industries accounted for approximately 47.5 per cent or $1.3 billion dollars of imports of metal working machine tools in the US. This growth in Japanese penetration of the US market continued to increase the trade tension between the two countries. As early as 1982, the major American machine tool producer, Houdaille Industries had petitioned the US Trade Representative

asking for protection against Japanese imports of machine tools under the Revenue Act of 1971. The Houdaille Industries petition was based on the grounds that the Japanese government unjustifiably restricted US commerce by tolerating an international cartel. This policy by the Japanese government called for the protection of Japanese industries from foreign competition and tax subsidies to make the industry internationally competitive.

In 1983, the US Machine Tool Industry Association sought and received voluntary export restraints on machine tool imports from Taiwan, West Germany, Switzerland; and Japan called for the limitation of exports to the US of the following items: machining centres, numerically controlled and non-numerically controlled leather punching, shearing machines and milling machines. Like most trade restrictions, the VERs on machine tools gave the American industry time to boost its capacity utilization, accelerate their modernization programmes, and help to regain their competitive status at home and abroad.

Trade Policy

US–Japanese bilateral trade conflict partly stems from the difference in trade policies of the two countries. This section will, therefore, attempt to shed some light on the differences in trade policies between the two countries. What is trade policy? A trade policy is sometimes referred to as commercial policy. Trade policies are forms of restrictions and regulations on the free flow of international trade. The most commonly used is a tariff. A tariff, which is a form of tax, may be an import tariff or an export tariff. An import tariff is a tax or duty on imports, while an export tariff is a similar duty on exports. While the US Constitution prohibits the use of export tariffs, many countries, especially developing countries, use export tariff as means to raise revenues.

In contrast, many industrial countries such as the US and Japan use import tariffs to protect some industries. There are specific types of tariffs such as ad valorem, specific or compound tariffs. An *ad valorem* tariff would be a fixed percentage of the value of the traded good, while specific tariff is expressed as a fixed sum on the traded good. A compound tariff consists of both *ad valorem* and specific tariff.

In the last decade, most of the trade policies adopted by either the US or Japan have been in response to two problems perceived as significant to their trade position in relation to the other. For example, the Japanese VERs discussed earlier were requested by the US government because of the concern about the deterioration of the US auto industry. Another instance is that in 1981, Japan responded to complaints from major trading partners by adopting a five-point trade policy to ease frictions. They are: (1) procedures for testing imports. The purpose of the programme was to reduce non-tariff barriers such as testing, certification procedures and customs practices which tend to restrict the export of goods to Japan; (2) import restrictions. Under the programme, Japan promised to examine its import quota policy for agriculture and leather products. This examination will hopefully lead to some reduction in import quota; (3) stocking policy. Japan would stockpile certain strategic minerals such as oil, rare metals and foreign grain. The object of this programme has been to increase imports of these items, and thus answer foreign complaints about restrictive acess to the Japanese market; (4) export policy. The Japanese government encouraged procedures to avoid surges of sensitive products such as semi-conductors and steel to name a few; (5) industrial cooperation. The Japanese government promised to promote industrial cooperation with major trading partners in such areas as investment, technology exchange, joint research and development projects.

Other policy changes came in 1981 when major trading partners complained that their domestic banks had been forced to operate at a competitive disadvantage in Japan. The Japanese government announced that foreign banks would be given similar treatments as domestic Japanese banks.

In 1983, Japan once again announced a series of trade policies to further defuse trade frictions with the US and other major trading partners. These policies included: (1) the removal of regulatory barriers within its standards certification system, thereby allowing US and other foreign producers to be treated in the same manner as Japan's with respect to health, safety and performance standards; (2) improvement of the marketing and distribution of imported tobacco products by the Japanese government; (3) restrictions on semi-conductor materials to encourage more imports; (4) internationalization of the Japanese yen to reduce the demand pressure on the dollar and open Japanese capital markets to foreign investors; and (5) reducing administrative barriers, such as labelling requirements and border taxes, in order to increase imports from the US.

However, what is surprisingly true is that Japanese trade policies are more guided towards dealing with current and prospective problems than those of the US. Periodically, the US has negotiated bilateral agreements with Japan to limit export of such products as steel and automobiles into the US market. The US government considers such agreements as preferable substitutes to an all out imposition of a tariff or a quota. However, as shown in Table 2.6, the US used non-tariff barriers as part of its overall trade policy, especially in the automobile market. Not shown in the table is the recent reclassification of cab chassis as light trucks with the resulting 25 per cent tariff rates.

Table 2.6   Trade barriers in the auto markets of the US and Japan

Trade barriers	US	Japan
Tariff	3%	None
Local Content	None	None
Quantitative Restrictions	None	None
Value-Added Tax	None	None
Non-tariff Barriers:	(1) Strict safety, emission and fuel economy standards (2) Fuel economy standards embodied in Energy Policy and Conservation Act of 1975, differentiate between North American-made (75% or more value added in US and foreign made vehicle in computing corporate average fuel economy	(1) Strict emission control standards (2) Difficult compliance procedures (3) complex distribution system (4) 15–20 % commodity tax on all cars, varying with size and weight, and (5) high dealer margins on luxury US cars

Source   US International Trade Commission

In general, both nations rely on non-tariff barriers, but differ in terms of specifics. For example, the US linked trade policy to its foreign policy objective, while Japan considered its trade policy as an integrated part of its long term industrial policy. This strategy has enabled the Japanese to realize a surplus in its balance of trade and balance of payments with the US, thus creating the trade conflict.

Economic Policy

As in the case of trade policy, the differences that exist in the economic policies of the US and Japan have contributed to the conflict in bilateral trade relations. Economic policy is defined as a statement of objectives and outline of methods which might be used to achieve those objectives by a government, political party or a business enterprise. Examples of areas covered by an economic policy could be concern for the achievement of full employment, a high rate of economic growth and economic stability with a low inflation rate. On the other hand, some of the methods or policy instruments used to achieve these policy objectives are fiscal policy (taxation and government expenditures) and monetary policy (expansion or contractions in the money supply to achieve price stability or to dampen swings of business cycles). Thus, one could say the economic policies of the two nations have been the natural outgrowth of different economic and political situations. Therefore, the following discussion will focus on the influence of economic policy on trade and trade conflict between the two nations.

The US Economic Policy: Specific economic policies aside, the US government, like most Western governments, has broad economic objectives which include 'seeking and maintaining an economic environment in which private sector (individuals and corporations) can pursue their various economic interests in an atmosphere of general growth and stability. In order to support these general economic objectives, the US government, at one time or another, has used such economic instruments as fiscal or monetary policies.

Table 2.7 US Federal budget deficit and current account deficit 1981–5 (billions of dollars)

Federal budget deficit (1981–5)	$797.32
Balance-of-payment deficit (1981–5)	$273.60

Source IMF International Financial Statistics

As Table 2.7 documents, a large balance of payment deficit followed a major US fiscal policy in the early 1980s when the US reduced federal tax rates and increased defence spending.

Most of the Japanese surplus delivery during the period 1981–1985 was used for the purchase of US government securities. In that case, Japan was financing the US budget deficit.

Equally important, the US monetary policy has had an indirect effect on its international position with Japan. For example, during the period 1978–1985, the monetary growth rate averaged 7.8 per cent per year, while in Japan it averaged at 5.5 per cent. US monetary policy was far more expansionary than Japan's. As the US spent more on imports, its trade deficit increased.

Japan's Economic Policy: Japan's economic policies have had a direct influence on their international trade position. In 1986, in response to an appreciated yen, the Japanese government instituted various monetary and fiscal policies to deal with the overvalued yen. The government proposed (a) a less restrictive monetary policy by reducing the interest rates. This action encouraged more domestic consumption, shifting the Japanese economy to a domestic-led economy; (b) increased government spending, especially on public work projects. The objective here was to stimulate demand for imports and to reduce its surplus with the US; (c) the reduction of utility rates and price of imported goods; and (d) the provision of assistance to small depressed businesses with the intention to make them more competitive domestically and internationally.

The Japanese government also used such economic policies such as structural adjustment policies to assist firms hurt by international factors such as dollar–yen exchange rate fluctuations. One such action was the institution of a subsidized loan programme called the 'yen-impact' programme. The programme called for a moratorium on interest and principal payments for firms experiencing falls in export revenues as a result of the yen appreciation.

In summary, we have seen that both the US and Japan face different economic objectives and, therefore, demand different economic actions. However, if the trade conflict is to be resolved, economic policy in Japan will have to focus on 'homegrown' growth. Such a focus will increase consumption and investment in Japan and thus help to reduce its surplus with the US.

CONCLUSION

This chapter has attempted to address some of the trade issues that separate the US and Japan and which have contributed to the trade friction. It is clear that with the US facing huge budget and trade deficits, and Japan with its big surplus, that the conflict is likely to continue because of the differences in economic policies. The US economic policies are mainly domestically-oriented even though its international trade position is affected. Japan's economic policies are designed to have an impact on the international trade position of Japan's economy. Thus, lasting stability in US–Japanese trade relations will only come about with basic changes in both countries' trade and economic policies.

To resolve the issue of trade friction between the two countries, solutions must be found for such issues as saving–investment imbalance, protectionism and other issues that separates the two nations. As pointed out in an earlier section, both nations use various forms of non-tariff barriers to protect their respective industries. However, one thing is clear: the differences in protection between the two are not so great to justify reciprocity. Whatever differences exist can be resolved in order to avoid an acceleration of the trade conflict between the two countries.

Notes

1. For further discussion, see Edward Leslie 'Trade Gap With Japan to Widen Despite Higher US Exports in '83', US Department of Commerce, *Business America*, 20 February, 1984, pp. 38–39.
2. This situation can theoretically be explained with the use of the so-called J-curve effect. The J-curve effect explains why the trade deficit worsens (or improves) in the short term immediately following a depreciation (or appreciation) of a currency.
3. Some of the goods referred to are: iron and steel, machinery, electronics, petroleum and automobiles. For details, see Gary F. Saxonhouse, 'What Is All This About Industrial Targeting In Japan?' *The World Economy*, Vol. 6, September 1983, pp. 253–74.
4. Japanese Minister of Agriculture, Forestry and Fisheries, *Annual Report on Agriculture: 1982*, July 1983, p. 28.
5. Japanese products affected by the February 1987 US *ad valorem* tariff are small colour and black and white television sets, control processing units for computers, computer tapes and disks, and combination radio and tape players.
6. See US International Trade Commission, *Competitive Assessment of the US Metal-Working Machine Tool Industry*, USITC Publication 1428, September 1983.

3 The Political and Cultural Dimensions of the Trade Friction between the United States and Japan
Scott C. Flanagan

Over the course of the 1980s relations between Japan and the United States have entered a difficult phase of adjustment. Growing strains have emerged whose rise in intensity has seemed to parallel the rising US deficit in its bilateral trade balance with Japan. When we reflect on these developments, it is striking how recent they are in origin. Japan and the United States entered the decade of the 1960s with a strong and untarnished relationship. The United States still saw itself as playing the big brother, protector role and Japan was content to remain securely tucked under the American nuclear umbrella, to follow the American lead in international affairs, and to focus its energies on building its economy. These were compatible roles and perceptions, and the relationship was by and large a harmonious one. Japan was just entering the second stage of its economic reconstruction, its industrial sector still had a reputation for producing shoddy goods, and the US still had the image of the world's supreme and invincible economic power.

Clearly this picture has changed dramatically in a very short amount of time. I will begin by discussing the causes of change that have introduced new strains into the US–Japan relationship. I will then turn to a discussion of how the two sides have tried to adjust to the new reality and the ways in which behaviours on both sides have unnecessarily aggravated the situation and given rise to a substantial perception gap. Unfortunately in politics, perceptions, no matter how incorrect or distorted they may be, often become the reality, the basis on which nations act. The exercise here will not be to try to assess blame on whichever side is the more responsible for the trade imbalance, but rather to better understand the cultural and psychological sources of friction. If this exercise is successful in pointing out some of the causes of friction, it may also be able to point the respective partners towards more constructive approaches to resolving the problem.

AN INTERDEPENDENT RELATIONSHIP

The starting point of any discussion of the growing strains in the US–Japan relationship is a recognition of the central importance of the relationship to both partners. Japan and the United States share an enormous stake in maintaining peace and stability around the world and preserving an open free trade system. The United States and Japan are the two largest economies in the non-communist world and by some accounts the two largest economies in the entire world. Together these two countries account for one-third of total world production and consume one-third of the world's annual production of raw materials (Yamamura, 1983).

The Japanese and American economies are also highly intertwined. The United States has been Japan's largest trade partner for many years. Not only has the United States remained the biggest market for Japanese goods for over most of the post Second World War period but Japanese dependency on the American market for its exports has grown dramatically during the 1980s. Between the years 1974 to 1976, the American market absorbed between twenty and 23 per cent of Japanese exports. That figure ranged between 24–26 per cent in the years 1977 to 1982 and thereafter rose rapidly, reaching 35 per cent in 1984 and 38 per cent in 1986. The United States has also been Japan's largest single source of imports over virtually the entire postwar period, but the picture here is more one of stability rather than rising market share. Indeed American exports dropped below twenty per cent of total Japanese imports in 1976, reached a low of 17 per cent in 1980 and did not again attain the 20 per cent mark until 1986 when American products captured 23 per cent of the Japanese import market.

Given the above figures, it should come as no surprise to find that Japan has been a leading source of imports into the American market over the past decade, standing second only to Canada until 1986, when Japanese imports rose to first place. During most of the 1970s, Japanese exports accounted for around 12 per cent of total American imports and then rose rapidly after 1980, reaching 22 per cent of total American imports in 1986. What may be a little more surprising to some is that Japan has also been a major market for American goods, ranking second only to Canada over the last decade. While the figures are somewhat more modest here, there has been a gradual growth in the share of American exports going to Japan, rising from 9 per cent in 1975 to 12 per cent in 1986.[1]

These figures clearly demonstrate the important and growing interdependence between the Japanese and American economies. At the same time, however, these numbers also point to two major asymmetries in the US–Japan trading relationship. First the United States has been and remains a significantly more important market for Japan than Japan is for the United States. Japanese exports to the US have risen much more rapidly than the reverse trade flow, such that by 1986 the share of total Japanese exports going to America was over three times as large as the share of total American exports sent to Japan. Moreover foreign trade is a significantly larger factor in the overall Japanese economy than in the American economy. Thus exports as a proportion of GNP stand at 11 per cent for Japan but only 5 per cent for the US. To make the comparison more concrete, Japanese exports to the United States in 1986 amounted to 4.1 per cent of Japan's total GNP, whereas American exports to Japan represented only 0.6 per cent of the US GNP, making Japan nearly seven times more dependent on this bilateral export trade than the United States.[2]

The second source of asymmetry in the US–Japan trade relationship is of course the trade imbalance. As the data in Table 3.1 make clear, the alarming rise in the American balance of trade problem over the last decade has been paralleled by a growing imbalance in the US bilateral trade with Japan. Actually the United States began running a negative balance of trade with Japan in 1969, but this bilateral trade imbalance and the American overall trade imbalance did not reach serious levels until the late 1970s, rising steadily since then. Table 3.1 shows that the US trade with Japan has been the single largest contributor to the American trade deficit, accounting by itself for over 50 per cent of the deficit in two years and falling below 31 per cent in only one year during the 1976 to 1986 period. Across these eleven years, then, America's trade with Japan has accounted on average for nearly 40 per cent of the total US trade deficit. It is little wonder, then, despite the fact that US trade has been running a deficit with virtually every region of the world, that Japan has been singled out by American policy makers and the general public as the principal target of criticism and blame in

Table 3.1   The Japan–US merchandise trade balance from 1975–1986 (in US$ million)

Year	Total US imports from Japan	Total US trade balance	US trade balance with Japan	Percentage total US trade deficit attributable to Japan	Total Japanese trade balance
1975	11 257	8903	−1690	–	−2110
1976	15 531	−9483	−5335	56	2426
1977	18 565	−31 091	−7999	26	9686
1978	24 540	−33 947	−11 580	34	18 200
1979	26 260	−27 536	−8631	31	−7640
1980	31 216	−25 481	−10 410	41	−10 721
1981	37 597	−27 978	−15 801	56	8740
1982	37 683	−36 444	−16 989	47	6900
1983	41 306	−62 013	−19 629	32	20 534
1984	57 135	−107 838	−33 560	31	33 611
1985	68 783	−132 130	−46 152	35	46 099
1986	81 911	−152 657	−55 029	36	82 743

Note   The Japanese trade data reported in the last column was computed in US dollars on a customs clearance basis, while the remaining American data excluded military transfers.
Source   Keizai Koho Centre, 1988

discussions of the trade problem. Moreover, while up through 1980 Japan was fighting hard to maintain a favourable balance of trade, and was therefore using its positive trade advantage with the United States and other countries to purchase needed raw materials, mainly oil, in recent years the Japanese balance of trade has moved sharply in its favour, further fuelling American criticism of Japan.

Given the central importance of the overall US–Japan relationship to both countries, it is quite regrettable that increased trade-related friction has arisen to threaten the confidence of both sides in the future stability and reliability of the relationship. Clearly not all the trends are negative. Recent years have witnessed increased areas of cooperation – joint ventures, Japanese investments in the US, technical exchanges, etc. While there certainly are optimistic signs on some fronts, the potential for emotional confrontations and punitive counter-measures remains. We will turn first, therefore, to an analysis of the origins of this bumpy period in US–Japan relations.

SOURCES OF STRAIN

The sources of strain in the US–Japan relationship are of rather recent origin and can be attributed to two rapid, major changes and one dramatic non-change. The first change is the striking rate of growth in the Japanese economy which in large part has been fuelled by the expansion of Japanese exports. Foreign trade has played perhaps a unique role in the economic development of Japan. Early in the industrialization process in recognition of the Japanese islands' limited endowments in certain kinds of natural resources, the idea seems to have become firmly implanted in the Japanese psyche that Japan must export to survive. Between 1880 and the First World War, Japan's exports grew twice as fast as world trade volume, and during the interwar period ten times as quickly, giving rise to widespread charges in the international community at that time of export dumping. From the end of the Second World War to the late 1960s, the growth of Japanese exports again greatly exceeded the expansion of world trade volume, this time by a factor of three (Ohkawa and Rosovsky, 1973). Such rapid rates of expansion gave rise to the notion in some quarters that Japan was a model of 'export-led growth'.

During the first three decades following the end of the American occupation, the Japanese leadership followed an almost single-minded pursuit of a growth-at-any-cost developmental strategy. While the standard of living of the Japanese population increased substantially over this period, government spending on welfare, social services, health, the environment, and other quality of life expenditures lagged. In addition, the tax and consumer credit structures encouraged saving and the postponement of major purchases. Japan was rapidly becoming an economic super-power, but its people were still living in 'rabbit hutches'. Open sewers, honey-bucket trucks, over-crowded streets, subways and stores, air and noise pollution, poorly maintained and aesthetically ugly universities and other educational facilities, cramped living quarters, long working hours, extremely low per capita ratios of parks and green space, over-crowded and grossly inadequate leisure facilities – these are not the characteristics that we normally associate with an advanced industrial stage of development.

Many of these kinds of enduring quality of life problems – which were especially pronounced in Japan's urban areas and continued to persist in the face of growing national affluence – gave rise to a number of social and political changes in the late 1960s and early 1970s. These politically significant developments included changes in mass values and expectations, the rise of a new issue agenda and the emergence of progressive local governments. In a period during which the ruling Liberal Democratic Party was suffering the loss of control of the government administrations in many important urban cities and prefectures and its majorities in both houses of the National Diet were being reduced to a razor thin edge, the government finally took some long overdue steps. These included legislating strict pollution control measures, substantially increasing welfare spending levels in a number of areas related to health care, the elderly and children, and directing more government spending to the alleviation of some kinds of urban problems.

In the midst of these changes in public mood and government policies, it was predicted in a 1972 report by the Japan Economic Research Centre (Nihon Keizai Kenkyukai Centre) that Japan's economy would become increasingly internationalized as a result of a major expansion of the domestic market. Japanese consumers would increasingly demand and get larger homes, more consumer goods and a rapidly rising standard of living. Among other things, this change was expected to draw into Japan larger imports of manufactured goods.

Whether or not these predictions would have been realized is open to debate. In any case the OPEC oil shock which quadrupled oil prices in the 1973–74 period and the second spurt in oil prices triggered by the Iranian revolution in 1979, brought these internal pressures for increased consumer spending into check. In the face of Japan's mounting oil bill, with oil imports rising from 20 per cent to 50 per cent of imports after the first oil shock, the Japanese economy was redirected down a familiar path – increasing production for the export market (Saxonhouse, 1986). Convinced by the runaway inflation and product shortages in 1974 of their worst fears about Japan's fatal weaknesses and vulnerability, voters began drifting back to the conservative party fold by the end of the decade and resigned themselves to another round of austerity measures and belt tightening.

It is most interesting to compare the effects of the two oil crises on the Japanese and American economies. The first oil crisis had a devastating effect on Japan, especially psychologically. In 1974 the growth rate of the Japanese economy in real terms was minus 1.2 per cent compared to minus 0.6 for the American economy. This economic downturn in Japan was much sharper than that experienced in the United States, given the fact that up to 1973 Japan had been enjoying annual double digit increases in its GNP in real terms for over a decade. However only the psychological effects of the first oil shock were long lasting in Japan. Not only did Japan recover more rapidly than the United States, but, most significantly, when the second oil shock hit in 1979, it hardly caused a ripple in the growth performance of the Japanese economy. Thus during the economically difficult years of 1979 though 1982, the American economy grew at an average annual rate of only 0.3 per cent while the Japanese economy was growing at an average rate of 4.1 per cent (Keizai Koho Centre 1988).

The Japanese success formula during these difficult years was derived from a combination of domestic austerity and foreign trade expansion. On the domestic front between 1976 and 1982, wages were kept low, so that unit labour costs remained virtually flat (at a time when they were rising by 50 per cent in the United States), investment in residential housing dramatically declined and private consumption increased at a rate of only about half of the annual increase in GNP (Saxonhouse, 1986; Suzuki, 1981). At the same time Japanese government expenditures increased only modestly as a result of budget cutting and administrative reform campaigns aimed at trimming the size of government.[3] This pressure for cutting government spending also meant reducing some of the increased benefits that had been offered to certain sectors of the public during the early 1970s and further restricting investments in social infrastructure. Regardless of how one might assess the costs of these measures, the results were extremely low rates of growth in government expenditures, especially when compared to the growth of the American budget during this same period, and relatively high personal savings rates and low interest rates and wage increases. While all of this served to enhance the volume and competitiveness of Japanese products in the international market it also meeant that the Japanese dream of reaching parity with the United States in living conditions was again postponed. That it was politically possible for the party in power to implement this austerity programme and to more or less steadily gain support in the polls from the late 1970s down to the election of July 1986 is undoubtedly one of the great competitive advantages that the Japanese derive from their social fabric and political culture.

This austerity programme at home was coupled with an aggressive expansion of the export market that was sustained by heavy investments in new plant equipment.[4] During the six years from 1975 through to 1981, Japanese exports grew by an average annual rate of over 18 per cent. This was followed by a couple of sluggish years and then another burst of growth from 1983 to 1986 when total Japanese exports realized an average annual gain of nearly 13 per cent. Over the entire period from 1975 to 1986 Japanese exports grew by 275 per cent. This at a time when American exports were growing by only 89 per cent and Japanese imports by only 118 per cent. While it can be argued that these new Japanese exports were largely paying for Japan's increased oil bill during the 1973–76 period, that was less true by the end of the 1970s and not true at all after 1982 (see Table 3.1). Once set in motion, then, the economic programmes that Japan developed in response to the first oil shock assumed a life of their own, which was shielded from public pressures for more domestic spending and unaffected by changes in the status of Japan's current accounts balance or multi-lateral balance of trade. The result of this set of government and corporate policies has been an enormous growth in Japanese exports over the last decade which foreign markets have had to absorb.

THE CHANGING STRUCTURE OF JAPANESE EXPORTS

The second major change that has intensified the friction between the United States and Japan stems from changes in the kinds of products that Japan is exporting and their destination. Over the postwar period, there has been a steady rise in the proportion of Japan's exports going to the advanced industrial societies of North America and Western Europe. For example, if we look only at the United States and the European Community nations, the proportion of total Japanese exports going to these nations increased between 1975 and 1986 from 30 to 53 per cent. If we break down the growth of Japanese exports over this same period by region of destination, we find that exports to the United States and European Community nations increased by 622 and 441 per cent respectively, while smaller but still substantial increases of 233 and 200 per cent were realized respectively with the southeast Asian and the communist nations.[5] In comparison, Japanese exports grew at the low rates of 99 and 61 per cent respectively for the Latin American and Middle Eastern nations and actually declined by 36 per cent for the African nations (Keizai Koho Centre, 1988).

At the same time that the destination for Japan's growing export trade was increasingly being channelled towards the advanced industrial democracies, and most especially the United States, the content of these exports was also changing. Japan's progression from the earlier phases of industrialization to advanced industrialism have been extremely rapid. Up to the early 1960s the Japanese economy still stressed labour-intensive industries such as textiles and supported their development in part through borrowing from abroad. From the mid-1960s to mid-1970s Japan shifted to the capital-intensive phase of development and became highly competitive in heavy industries (shipbuilding, steel, etc.) and manufacturing (radios, hi-fi equipment, watches, cameras and optical equipment, bicycles, motorcycles, sports equipment, musical instruments, etc.). During this phase Japan's current accounts moved into the black and it began paying off its foreign debt. Beginning in the mid-1970s Japan began to make the transition towards a knowledge-intensive phase of industrialization, realizing that its manufacturing goods would increasingly come under severe competition from the newly industrialized countries (NICs) of Asia. During this period Japan's current account balances have not only remained in the black but Japan has become the leading creditor nation in the world, with sizeable foreign investments earning income from abroad.

These changes in Japanese industry and its pattern of exports have made Japanese exports into the United States progressively politically more sensitive because they have been associated with a growing number of industrial deaths in the United States as industry after industry has been wiped out or mortally wounded by Japanese competition – radios, televisions, hi-fi and other audio equipment, tape recorders, motorcycles, farm equipment, etc. Even more importantly, the Japanese challenge has increasingly been aimed not at America's declining industries but at those very industries on which US policy makers believe their country's economic future depends – computers, data processing, communication and other advanced electronic equipment, semi-conductors, computer assisted tool casting etc.

Beyond the economic realities of the Japanese challenge, there is a symbolism associated with some Japanese industrial successes which engenders a particularly sensitive response from some portions of the

American public. Not only has the Japanese export campaign during the 1980s severely damaged a number of important American industries, but in several cases the challenge has been directed at industries that are as American as apple pie – such as cars and even baseball equipment! Probably the Japanese automotive invasion has had the most profound effect on American perceptions of the foreign threat to American industry. Partly it is the suddenness of the Japanese success coupled with the highly visible loss of American jobs in the automobile industry which has riveted and magnified perceptions in this case, as the Japanese share of the American automobile market rose from 6 per cent in 1973 to nearly 23 per cent by 1982 (Keizai Koho Centre, 1988). But also in part it is the symbolism of the car as an American invention and the centrepiece of the American way of life that has made this particular loss carry much more emotional baggage than say the loss of jobs in the textile industry.

In another sense, the timing of the Japanese challenge has intensified the American response in excess of what might be warranted on a purely economic basis. The period of this rapid advance of Japanese goods into the American market from the mid-1970s to mid-1980s happened to coincide with a period in which the American ego was reeling from a multitude of assaults and bruises from the international environment. This was a time when the American people and their leaders were trying to adjust to their diminished role in the world'– the aftermath of Vietnam, the collapse of the role of the US dollar as the world's standard currency and its decline in value against other currencies, American impotence in the face of the OPEC oil cartel, the Iranian hostage incident, world terrorism, and communist expansionism in Afghanistan and Nicaragua.

Given the major changes in the volume of Japanese exports to the United States and their more threatening content, it is not surprising to find that the American public has begun to increasingly associate US economic difficulties with Japan. Indeed NYT/CBS national surveys of the American public in 1985 and again in 1986 have shown that by a very large margin, Americans indentify Japan as the main source of economic threat. When asked to mention any country out of a long list that posed a serious threat to the United States' position in international trade, 29 per cent failed to mention any country (none, DK–NA). Among those naming any country, however, 65 per cent named Japan. The next highest frequency of mentions was 31 per cent for Taiwan, followed by 24 per cent for China and Hong

Kong and seventeen per cent for South Korea and West Germany. Only 6 to 7 per cent mentioned France or Britain.[6] The rising tide of Japanese exports followed the first Arab oil shock in 1973, therefore, has become increasingly politically sensitive in the United States giving rise to growing domestic pressures for protectionist legislation and other kinds of counter-measures.

THE OTHER SIDE OF THE TRADE BALANCE PROBLEM

The third major cause of increased trade friction between the United States and Japan is a dramatic non-change – the continuing failure of American products to penetrate the Japanese market. Indeed the Japanese import market continues to appear relatively closed, not just to American products but to the manufactured products of all of the nations of the world.

In this regard, Japan emerges as an anomaly or deviant case when compared to the economies of all of the other advanced industrial democracies. The universal pattern found in Western Europe and North America is for continued economic growth to be associated with higher levels of integration of their domestic economies into the world economy. In stark contrast to this pattern, Japan's total imports as a percentage of her GNP have remained constant at the 10 per cent level over the last 30 years.[7] Even more surprising is the fact that its imported manufactured goods as a percentage of GNP have also remained level at around 2 per cent (Yamamura, 1983). This is even more puzzling since it is known that consumption patterns shift increasingly away from basic commodities and towards value added manufactured goods as standards of living increase. In other words it appears that the flat growth of manufactured imports has been achieved by unnatural, artificial means.

The guiding principle governing Japanese trade is 'import raw materials, export finished goods'. As a result Japan ranks lowest among all the OECD (Organization for Economic Cooperation and Development) countries in terms of the percentage of manufactured imports as a proportion of total imports. This figure has stood at about 20 per cent for Japan. If we cite some comparative data for 1986 the aberrant nature of this low figure becomes immediately apparent. In that year manufactured goods accounted for only 22 per cent of Japanese imports, but 38 to 40 per cent of total imports for the United States, West Germany, France and Britain. Another way to look at these figures is to compare the amount of manufactured goods a nation imports to those that it exports. In 1986, Japan imported only 21 per cent of the dollar amount of manufactured goods that they exported. The closest major advanced industrial nation to Japan was Germany whose imports of manufactured goods in that year totalled about 60 per cent of manufactured exports, while Britain and France had nearly balanced import and export levels and the United States was importing nearly twice as much manufactured goods as it was exporting (Keizai Koho Centre, 1988).

The fact that the Japanese government and business community have been so successful in enforcing this principle on her domestic market is a continuing source of frustration not just to America and the other advanced industrial societies, but to the newly industrializing nations as well. Countries like Korea, Singapore, Taiwan, Hong Kong, Malaysia and Thailand are able to manufacture steel, cars, televisions, refrigerators, and other household appliances more cheaply than the Japanese can due to low wages and dedicated, hard-working labour forces. These countries have encountered great success in penetrating the American market and that of other advanced industrial nations, but they have had comparatively very little success into the Japanese market.

In trying to correct this problem, beginning back in the 1960s, the first line of attack was against Japan's tariff barriers which were erected in the early postwar period to facilitate the rebuilding of the Japanese economy, but by the late 1960s were clearly unequal and inappropriate. After successive painstaking rounds of tariff reduction negotiations, Japan's average tariffs, standing at a little under three per cent since 1980, are now slightly lower than those for the European Community or the United States (Keizai Koho Centre, 1088). The fact that the tariffs are gone but the problem remains has redirected attention to various kinds of non-tariff barriers. While in some areas, factors such as product cost, quality or appeal to Japanese taste undoubtedly has some impact on market access, examples too numerous to cite demonstrate that high quality, low cost, appealing foreign products encounter similar problems in gaining a foothold in the Japanese domestic market (US Trade Representative, 1982). Further evidence of the artificial non-market barriers to the expansion of American imports into Japan can be seen by the fact that despite the dramatic fall in the value of the dollar relative to the yen, from about 240 yen to the dollar in 1985 to around 140 by April of 1987 and nearly 120 by April of 1988, there has been no major expansion of American imports into Japan, at least in the short term, and in many cases no significant decline in the retail prices being charged in Japan for American goods. As will be argued below, the explanations for this phenomena and the remaining barriers that block the access of foreign goods to the Japanese market are largely cultural rather than economic or legal.

The combination of all three of these above factors – the dramatic rise in Japanese exports in response to the energy crisis, the dispro-portionate shift of these exports towards the American market and their more challenging content, and the continuing failure of many American products to gain a substantial foothold in the Japanese market – has led to increasing frustration and charges of unfairness on the US side. Recent NYT/CBS national surveys of the American public mood reflect this sense of unfairness and high levels of support for protectionist counter-measures directed against Japanese pro-ducts.[8] While significant majorities of Americans still seem to feel that on the whole foreign trade helps the American economy, 45–48 per cent felt that trade with Japan was bad for the American economy compared to only 35–37 per cent who felt it was good. In addition 53 per cent of the American public felt that the Japanese government restricted the sale of American goods in Japan and that those restrictions were unfair, compared to only 30 per cent who either felt that there were few restrictions or that there were significant restric-tions but that they were fair. Moreover large majorities of 66-68 per cent felt that the Japanese government had not done enough to correct the trade imbalance, compared to only 13 to 16 per cent who felt that the Japanese have done enough. Finally 71 per cent of the American public felt that something should be done about the trade imbalance and of those 69 per cent felt that the United States should impose a substantial tax on Japanese products while 77 per cent agreed that the US should impose quotas on Japanese products.

In a second set of nationwide surveys conducted in March and June 1986, over 70 per cent of the American public believed that the US economy is being more hurt than helped by existing trade relations, 45 per cent said that imports are negatively affecting their own local community and one-third said they knew someone personally who had lost his or her job due to foreign competition.[9] Not only does this show that Americans are personalizing the foreign imports issue but large majorities were shown to support protectionist counter-measures. For example, two-thirds felt that imports should be limited if they were simply priced lower than American goods while 78 per cent felt that the government should limit imports from countries found to engage in unfair trading practices. Finally most Americans felt that the positive benefits of protectionism – helping American industries, saving American jobs, etc, – outweighed the costs of protectionism – inflation, less efficient and competitive American industries, reduced consumer access to high-quality Japanese goods, etc. The only comfort that Japanese policy makers could derive from these surveys was that the trade deficit issue still ranked fairly low in salience and priority for most Americans in 1986. On a more ominous note, however, a March 1988 ATS nationwide poll found that nearly 60 per cent of the American people believed that economic competitors like Japan pose more of a threat to US security than traditional military adversaries like the Soviet Union.[10]

Not only is an anti-Japanese attitude beginning to crystallize around the trade issue within the American public, but important attitude changes are also beginning to take shape at the elite level. In January 1988 the annual Gallup Poll of American opinion leaders conducted for the Japanese Foreign Ministry found that 61 per cent felt Japan had not fulfilled its international duties at all and while 85 per cent said that most of Japan's major obstacles to foreign imports still remain.[11] In addition 40 per cent said that Japan's emergence as one of the world's largest economic powers was a threat to the United States, the highest proportion ever reported in the sixteen-year history of the poll. Since the Second World War, the mass public has always been more ready to invoke protectionist measure than American elites, who typically have been ideologically wedded to free trade principles. There are increasing signs, however, that this elite level support for free trade is beginning to crack in the face of the Japanese challenge. While President Reagan staunchly supported free trade throughout his presidency, during the later years he encountered growing difficulties in mustering sufficient support in Congress to prevent overrides of his vetoes of protectionist measures.

THE MANAGEMENT OF THE TRADE PROBLEM

To some degree the problems that have beset the US–Japan relationship have been inevitable. Both economies have been experiencing rapid changes and large dislocations in the face of increased foreign competition within certain major but declining industries (steel, shipbuilding, for example). Both economies have been buffeted by changing world economic conditions – from recession to inflation to the energy crisis – that has created a defensive mood in each capital. Whenever there are rapid, major changes in import levels concentrated in a few highly visible product lines, there are bound to be problems of adjustment which will require time to work through.

At the same time, to a significant degree the problems in the relationship have been worsened by the way in which they have been handled. A high degree of emotionalism has characterized the negotiations on both sides with each feeling wronged and unfairly treated. Bruised feelings, frustrations and emotional outbursts have done more to damage relations than the objective problems, all of which creates ill will, suspicions and distrust and makes each side feel less inclined to compromise and more inclined to believe in the absolute truth of its own arguments and discredit the arguments of the other.

The result is a communications gap with each side presenting sharply contrasting explanations for the causes of the US trade imbalance. According to the Japanese view, the problem is of America's own making. American industry has become complacent and uncompetitive. American workers have consistently demanded wage hikes that their increases in productivity and attention to product quality have not warranted. American managers have been too short-sighted, looking only for short term profits rather than long term growth and increased market share. Thus they have been unwilling to sacrifice short term profits for the sake of staking out a larger market share or for investing in new plant equipment that won't pay off until several years down the road. More immediately, the rapid recent growth of the trade imbalance is attributed to Reaganomics which tried to revitalize the domestic American economy by stimulating consumption through tax cuts. Not only did this policy fail to invigorate American industry but it also created a demand for a flood of imports and increased budget deficits, both of which can be directly related to American's growing trade balance problem (Osamu, 1987).

In regard to the problem of access to their market, the Japanese say that Americans have not invested sufficient time or energy in learning to understand their market – few American businessmen have bothered to learn Japanese, or learned the unique ways of doing business in Japan, and American products typically have not been redesigned to meet the needs and tastes of the Japanese market (cars with steering wheels on the wrong side, appliances too large for

Japanese homes or stores, and so on). The Japanese market is open, but it is a highly competitive one, frequently characterized by cut-throat, nearly suicidal price slashing wars in desperate struggles for increased market share in which bankruptcies are a common occurrence. Those who have not adequately prepared themselves to do battle in this market have no chance.

The Japanese further argue that Americans should realize that Japan is still in many respects a weak and vulnerable country that must export to survive. Americans should also admit that it is the multi-lateral worldwide trade balances that count not the bilateral balances and should factor in service exports, which is an area of invisible trade in which the United States holds a substantial lead over Japan. Finally, the Japanese note that when the American economy is going well, US leaders ignore these problems, but when things go badly for the American economy, these leaders vent their anger on Japan as a convenient scapegoat. The Japanese are then forced under extreme emotional threats to make concession after concession. But in essence nothing that the Japanese do will make the Americans happy, because nothing the Japanese can do will solve the problems which are essentially of America's own making. In sum, the Japanese feel that they are being punished for their success by a lazy American bully (Cohen, 1985).

The American view stands in stark contrast to the above picture. US policy makers feel that Japan has over-exaggerated its need to export and greatly over-played the 'weak little Japan' theme. They see Japan as a great economic power that has consistently taken a narrow self-interested view. They feel that Japan has been deficient in recognizing its responsibilities for contributing to foreign aid, international security and the maintenance of orderly world markets (Vogel, 1984). America has generously opened its factories, universities and research organizations and the Japanese have appropriated American financed scientific findings and technology in an effort to either compete with new American products or beat American companies into the market place with new products.

The Japan Incorporated collusion between the Japanese government, big business and the financial community, and the practice of industrial targeting which provides certain favoured Japanese industries with tax breaks, subsidies, investments, liberal loans and protective, cartel-like arrangements gives Japanese products an unfair advantage in foreign world markets. At the same time the Japanese have employed a wide array of unfair devices, from obscure regulations to lengthy licensing procedures to informal quotas to greatly limit access to their own market. In sum, the Americans view the Japanese as arch-mercantilists run amok with little concern for what their single-minded pursuit of an ever widening favourable balance of trade is doing to the economies of the rest of the world (Cohen, 1985).

Not only are the perceptions of both sides at sharp variance with each other but, in addition, both sides have further aggravated the situation by their negotiating behaviour. On the American side the situation is aggravated by too little expertise on Japan at the highest levels of government. In general it has been noted that there is a marked information gap between the two societies. The Japanese have invested heavily in studying the American language, culture, politics and market, but the American media, institutions and policy makers still seem to be oriented towards Western Europe. This is reflected in the training received in government, business and American universities. Also the American penchant for unilateral actions has unnecessarily ruffled feathers across the Pacific.

Two examples illustrate these American insensitivities in its dealings with Japan. The year 1971 was a watershed year of change in the Japanese–American relationship. This was the year of the two Nixon shocks discussed below which rudely awakened Japan from its comfortable reliance on the United States. The Japanese saw these incidents as Pearl Harbour in reverse, as they found their protector suddenly turning on them. Voices in Japan began questioning the American commitment and whether the United States would really come to Japan's aid if attacked.

Our example here is the first Nixon shock in July 1971, when Nixon, without consulting or notifying the Japanese in advance, announced he would visit China. Like a good and loyal retainer, Japan had for many years been toeing the US line, which severely restricted economic and political relations with mainland China, at some political and economic cost. Suddenly they found themselves deserted, alone and abandoned in an uncomfortable position not of their own making. When they tried to follow the US lead in abject pursuit, China had all the leverage. Thus the Japanese found themselves with no other tenable policy than to seek accommodation with China on China's terms. The Chinese made it clear than no accommodation was possible while Eisaku Sato remained Prime Minister, hinted that certain other LDP (Liberal Democratic Party) successors might also be unacceptable and generally drove a hard bargain. The impact of this unilateral move was further heightened by two other events in 1971: the second Nixon shock in August when Nixon announced his New Economic Policy, adding a ten per cent surcharge on all existing US tariffs and taking steps to devalue the dollar, measures that were interpreted as being aimed primarily against Japanese imports; and secondly the conclusion in the autumn of the US–Japan textile dispute under the direct threat that the United States would unilaterally impose a quota exclusively on Japanese textile imports under the provisions of the 'Trading with the Enemy Act'.[12]

A second and more recent example of American insensitivities to the Japanese cultural and political context can be seen in Reagan's performance at the twelfth Seven Nation Economic Summit held in Tokyo, 4–6 May, 1986. Nakasone, whose tenure as Japan's Prime Minister began in 1982, was the first Prime Minister in many years that the Americans really felt comfortable with. Most Japanese leaders are by training masters of ambiguity, because the leader in Japan, to be effective, is expected to be a neutral negotiator and mediator among conflicting views and personalities rather than a initiator or advocate of positions. Thus Americans often find the Japanese negotiating style baffling, as Japanese hide their true preferences while seeking some area of accommodation. When we add to this the Japanese distaste for open conflict and penchant for resorting to subtle ways of communicating unwelcome information to preserve surface harmony and rapport, it is little wonder that bilateral negotiations, even at the highest levels, have often engendered more confusion than light. Thus on several occasions American negotiators have been convinced that they heard a 'yes', when they were really being told 'no'. Inevitably this confusion later results in feelings of betrayal and deceit on the US side, when the firm promises and concessions that the American negotiators felt they had elicited do not materialize in changed Japanese policies.

Nakasone was a new type of Japanese leader, more in the American mould. He was an accomplished public debater, forthcoming and persuasive in presenting his views, comfortable and skilled in using the media and desirous of leading Japan in some fundamentally new directions. Moreover Nakasone's vision for Japan in most respects coincided nicely with American interests, particularly his desires to increase Japanese military spending, adopt a more active and visible role for Japan in strategic and international affairs, and 'internationalize' Japan by making Japanese institutions more open and compatible with those of the rest of the world and by stimulating domestic consumption to draw in more imports (Pyle, 1987).

Nakasone had been very successful in enhancing his own public popularity and that of his party by playing on his special relationship with President Reagan and his ability to interact with foreign leaders on a more equal basis than his predecessors, and hence forcefully make Japan's case in an international atmosphere of mounting Western criticism against Japanese trade practices. However his second two-year term as party president was coming to an end in the autumn of 1986 and factional rivals within his party were trying to enforce the party rule limiting leaders to two terms to force him out of the party presidency and Prime Ministership. In an American political context, Nakasone's party would have been clamouring to keep him at the helm, because of the major impact his personal popularity had had on increasing the LDP's support in the public opinion polls. In Japan, however, party factional interests are often at odds with the interests of the party as a whole. In the face of these obstacles, Nakasone hoped to parlay a series of media triumphs in the spring of 1986 – including the announcement of the Maekawa Report in April (calling for a fundamental re-direction of the Japanese economy away from the export-led model and toward a domestic market orientation), hosting the Economic Summit in May and the state visit of the Prince and Princess of Wales – into a major electoral victory for his party in the double election in July. Such a scenario he hoped would win him a third two-year term as party president and Prime Minister.

What Nakasone needed from President Reagan was some public demonstration that the vaunted 'Ron–Yasu' special relationship could be counted upon to provide Japan with reassurances at a time when the rapidly rising value of the yen against the dollar was already causing serious economic hardships for numerous export-oriented Japanese companies. Nakasone bent over backward to accommodate Reagan and insure a successful meeting, even to the point of signing a joint communique which named Libya in a statement on terrorism, an action for which he was highly criticized at home. One might have expected that American policy makers would have realized that it was in America's long term interests to help Nakasone in this situation by at least appearing to be understanding and sympathetic towards the Japanese problem. But Reagan refused to do anything in the way of offering even symbolic assurances regarding the further devaluation of the dollar. This was viewed as a serious defeat for Nakasone by the Japanese press (Pharr, 1987).

American insensitivities to the Japanese cultural and political context are compounded on the Japanese side by a pluralistic, consensual style of governmental decision making which make it difficult for Japanese leaders to move their government in any clear direction (Campbell, 1984). This often results in the practice of Japanese leaders making promises which they later cannot fulfil, creating an impression of insincerity and untrustworthiness. In some cases, realizing their own inability to get all the various necessary actors in the Japanese decision process on board, Japanese leaders have secretly asked their American counterparts to resort to public bullying tactics, in order to create a crisis atmosphere in which domestic support for the desired change could be secured. Since the Japanese invitation to apply such a tactic remains secret, the Japanese press has a heyday depicting American arrogance, with great cost to Japanese feelings of goodwill towards the United States (Vogel, 1982; Cohen, 1985).

On the other hand when the United States does take some action, even a fairly modest one that will not have a major economic impact on Japan, the Japanese often over-react in a strongly emotional way. For example in April 1988, the US House of Representatives passed a Trade Bill which included sanctions against the Toshiba Corporation for illegally selling US military secrets to the Soviet Union, tougher anti-dumping measures, and a reciprocal measure which authorized barring any country's firms from directly participating in the US securities market which did not open its securities market to US firms. Immediately strong indignation was widely expressed by Japanese government and industry leaders, with Hajime Tamura, the Minister of International Trade and Industry, declaring the US House to be 'guilty of racial discrimination and anti-Japanese sentiment' (Simons, 1988; Curtis, 1988). This despite that fact that this Bill was far milder than the earlier failed Gephardt Amendment which called for mandatory retaliation against countries running excessive surpluses with the United States and despite the fact that it was widely known that there was not enough support in the Senate for even this watered down Trade Bill to override an expected presidential veto.

All of this has given rise to the following typical negotiation scenario. America identifies a new problem it has with Japan – some new American industry under threat or a new focus on a problem with a particular product's access to the Japanese market – and initiates negotiations. Japanese negotiators promise to take measures to correct the situation, but appear to do little or nothing. The

Japanese ask for patience and make largely symbolic responses. As repeated negotiations meet with the same apparently stalling responses, the American representatives push harder, the Japanese promise more, and little or nothing happens. This goes on until the Americans lose patience and begin to make serious threats. As the Japanese feel themselves being pushed to the wall, they tell the Japanese public and affected business interests that they will have to give in. Some compromise is made within the Japanese policy making system and they tell the US they cannot do more. Typically this is not enough to satisfy the Americans, but just enough to defuse the crisis, at least temporarily.

The American learning experience from this repeated scenario tends to instil a conviction that it is necessary to threaten and intimidate the Japanese in order to get any action. It appears that on occasion some American negotiators have tried to cut the process short by coming in yelling and threatening on the first day. In turn, the Japanese become defensive and interpret this behaviour as an affront to their national sovereignty. The Japanese are highly sensitive (indeed one might say over-sensitive) to any hint of this kind of treatment, because it reinforces their cultural self-image as being unique and isolated from the international community of nations and under attack from the outside.

Ultimately the American approach is not only negative but self-defeating, because once American actions have confirmed Japanese suspicions that the Americans are bent on unfairly punishing Japan, the game is lost. As we have found, the Japanese are very adept at making concessions that have the appearance of change but in effect yield no real change. In the Japanese cultural context, it is necessary for negotiators to establish personal rapport before they can deal effectively with the substantive issues at hand. Without proper attention to building personal trust and confidence first, there is little hope that anything can be accomplished through negotiations outside of the unilateral action/forced response scenario. The United States–Japan relationship is too important for both sides to allow cultural misperceptions and emotional over-reactions to get out of hand and create unnecessary problems.

UNDERSTANDING JAPANESE BEHAVIOUR

The crux of the debate is that the United States charges that Japan has been engaging in unfair trade practices, charges which the

Japanese deny. It is, of course, difficult to verify such claims in a completely unambiguous manner, especially those charges that the Japanese government and business co-operation unfairly advantage Japanese exports in foreign markets. Still the fact that numerous 'made in Japan' products can be found selling for less in America than in Japanese retail outlets gives the appearance that something is not quite right.

Charges of unfairness in the area of access to the Japanese market, however, are harder to dismiss, because enough concrete examples have been identified to make a convincing case that foreign companies have in many instances encountered unusual barriers in trying to sell their products in Japan. For example in some cases, when foreign companies have submitted detailed plans of a new product to apply for a licence to sell it in Japan, Japanese regulations have been specifically re-written to exclude it. In other cases the product has been rejected on the grounds that it does not meet Japanese standards, without informing the foreign company of what the standards are or what is needed to conform to those standards. Moreover on a number of occasions shortly after being denied access, an almost identical product has appeared under a Japanese company label, suggesting to some that the Japanese government may have turned over these rejected foreign company plans to Japanese companies. Even when permission to market a product is attained, foreign companies regularly meet with a host of other barriers in the forms of marketing cartels which agree to limit their purchase of a foreign product to the informal quotas set by MITI, excessively enforced regulations which add delays and expense, bizarre advertising and marketing restrictions, limited access to retail outlets and a byzantine distribution system which mysteriously inflates the prices of imported goods to such astronomical levels that they are inevitably relegated to the small luxury market (Vogel, 1982; Kaufmann, 1982; Kraar, 1983: Ingersoll, 1985–86; Rohlen, 1985–86).

Regardless of what the foreign complaint is, the Japanese have tended to take a minimalist response, giving the appearance that they are dragging their feet and determined to make the fewest changes possible. From one perspective, this behaviour might be explained in terms of narrow self-interest, since undeniably the present arrangements greatly benefit Japan. But in another sense, such an approach seems very short-sighted and ultimately self-defeating, because it is transforming the debate over mutual interests and relative advantage from a rational to an emotional level and raising the spectre of a possible extremist American response. Why the Japanese would take these risks and flirt with disaster is difficult to explain when, as many have pointed out, they have much more to lose from moves which would further limit their access to the American market than they do from a further opening of their own. Indeed many suspect that removing all the barriers to market access in Japan that Americans claim are 'unfair' would still leave Japan with a sizeable trade surplus. The Japanese themselves seem to recognize this by frequently invoking the argument that conceding to this or that specific American complaint would only amount in dollar terms to a drop in the ocean, which would do little to overcome the American trade balance problem. This then becomes a Japanese argument for not doing anything. In this regard they fail to grasp the symbolic value of these 'fairness' measures. The point is not the dollar value of these changes but rather that these changes should have been made some years ago, and the longer that removing these problems is resisted, the more they will fester and breed resentment all out of proportion to their monetary importance to either side (Yamamura, 1987).

How then do we explain this seemingly self-defeating Japanese behaviour? Several different answers can be found in the literature. Firstly, many political scientists who have written about Japanese decision making have developed or subscribed to a model of the policy making system as one which is fragmented and compartmentalized, lacking central control and direction, and conducted at the sub-governmental level in ways that raise serious problems of coordination and consensus building when decisions span across differing institutional jurisdictions (Campbell, 1984; Pempel, 1987; Fukui, 1987; Haley, 1987). This conceptualization of the Japanese policy making process in turn is linked to an evaluation of the process as prone to failure and immobilization when it involves issues and actors in the international environment that are external to Japan (Hellmann, 1969; Angel, forthcoming).

Secondly, as Campbell (1984) has argued, the Japanese decision making process is based on a consensual rather than a majoritarian model, such that even a weak actor, if intensely opposed, can veto any change in policy. The more institutional actors and jurisdictions involved in a decision, therefore, the more difficult it is to reach any decision, making hard decisions and real change most difficult to implement, except at times of crisis when all parties can be convinced that they must sacrifice their own interests for the common good. As Campbell further argues, this system works best when decisions are made at the sub-government level within the confines of a single agency or jurisdiction where strong in-group feelings prevail. When multiple institutions and actors are involved, it is often necessary to resort to a contrived consensus, which is typically achieved either by vertical integration, where a neutral go-between of higher status than the disputants mediates a solution, or by the creation of a pseudo-uchi, a contrived intimate, home-like environment, which is accomplished by involving representatives of the disputants in a prolonged, face-to-face group context so that they are able to develop a strong rapport and sense of group commitment and shared responsibility. It is important to note that neither of these methods of reaching a contrived consensus are typically available or practical in an international setting.

From this perspective, the typical scenario described above of unfulfilled promises and repeated delays are not the result of deceit or bad faith but rather the inability of a Japanese negotiator, even when he is the Prime Minister himself, to forge a consensus around his concessions back home. This conceptualization of Japanese decision making has given rise to the notion that without foreign pressure (*gaiatsu*), changes in Japanese behaviour cannot be expected. Thus foreign pressure, sometimes applied at rather intense levels, becomes an essential ingredient in the Japanese decision making process, such that without it, many decisions, even those that are in Japan's as well as America's long term interest, cannot be realized.

This view, however, is not a universal one. Indeed a number of Japanese observers reject the *gaiatsu* argument and contend that the Japanese are supremely capable of acting in their own interest. They feel that all the harping on the unique aspects of Japanese culture is simply a convenient mask of ambiguity and inscrutability to hide behind when it is in the Japanese interests to forestall foreign demands. When it is in Japan's interests to make changes, even rather dramatic changes, it seems to be able to do so with both comprehensiveness and dispatch, as can be seen for instance in Japan's domestic policy changes in the face of the first oil shock in 1974. There may well be some truth in this view and I would have to say that what strikes me as being the most unique feature about Japanese society is the degree to which so many Japanese seem to emphasize the importance of their own cultural uniqueness.

Many card-carrying 'Japan bashers' amplify this view by claiming that Japanese behaviour is cynically designed to maintain and maximize every marginal benefit for as long as possible at all costs. This is the view of Japan as the supreme economic animal concerned with nothing but bottom line economic profits and unwilling to take action that cannot be directly linked to or does not serve that goal. As evidence for this view this school of thought points to the enormous lobbying and information gathering activities that the Japanese have mounted in the United States. In 1988 the Japanese are expected to spend $310 million on 'soft-side' activities in the United States, including $50 million on Washington lobbying, $45 million on public relations, and many other activities aimed at buying up Washington influentials, buying off politicians, buying into American basic scientific research and compromising potential scholarly critics by funding and shaping the acceptable parameters of their research (Holstein, 1988). A number of successes are claimed for these activities, including defeating Congressional efforts to impost harsh sanctions on the Toshiba corporation for peddling US secrets to the Soviets, watering down those elements of the 1988 US Trade Bill that the Japanese found objectionable, ferreting out information on proposals for US government actions against Japanese interests and leaking them to potential allies in other parts of the American government, and blocking the promotions of 'Japan bashers' in the Commerce Department.

According to this view, the Japanese use their PR efforts to focus American attention on the domestic causes of the trade imbalance problem and when that fails use their listening posts in Washington and fifteen consulates and seven JETRO (Japan External Trade Organization) offices scattered around the United States to take a very sensitive reading of the American pulse. In that way, the Japanese can essentially ignore or deflect with empty promises the rising crescendo of American rhetoric and threats regarding a particular issue until that moment when the American decision making process is finally mobilized and poised to take action. At that point the Japanese calculate the minimal action necessary to forestall American sanctions and escape once again with the lowest possible costs to Japanese interests.

Another view can be found in the work of Chalmers Johnson (1987), who while also rejecting the *gaiatsu* explanation, attributes Japanese behaviour more to miscommunication and misunderstanding than to calculation and deceit. He argues that for much of the last decade, Japanese and American negotiators have been talking *past* each other, often using the same words but with different meanings. Johnson asserts that for historic developmental reasons, the Japanese and American concepts of the 'market' and the role of government in economic affairs is very different. For this reason American charges have often appeared to the Japanese as unfounded and simply a reflection of American sour grapes over the Japanese success. At the same time, those holding the American conception of the market will always and inevitably perceive policies pursued in accordance with the Japanese conception of the market as inherently unfair (1987: 423).

The problem here is not one of mistranslation or miscommunication. The Japanese understand well what is being asked of them. However in their view of the function of the market and the legitimate role of government they are not doing anything wrong. Far from it, their whole developmental experience sanctions the wisdom of their present course and counsels against abandoning what has brought them so far, simply to placate the unreasonable demands of their trading partners. The idea that Japan could survive and prosper by shifting from an export-led to a domestic-led market is a new and untested one and the Japanese are not given to radical departures.

Johnson believes that the release of the Maekawa Report in 1986 demonstrates that at least some Japanese now understand and accept American complaints and are ready to direct the Japanese economy down a new path. However there has been substantial criticism of the Maekawa Report in Japan and some evidence to suggest that it was a consciously unbalanced analysis, which deleted the authors' felt criticisms of the United States so as not to 'further upset the Americans' (Iida, 1987). If in fact the report was written mainly for external consumption and filled with empty platitudes to placate American and European criticism of Japan and ensure the success of the 1986 Tokyo Summit, it may not be the turning point that American negotiators are looking for. Thus Johnson's summary evaluation of the Maekawa Report's findings may not necessarily reflect the views of the writers, but it certainly makes his own position very clear. He writes (1987:426):

The authors of the report recognize that a nation that does not import any of the things it exports, that refuses to give its workers the leisure time and wages they deserve, that lends a good part of its trade surplus back to Americans so that their government can continue on its spending binge, and that refuses to open its markets to neighbouring states that only a few years ago were among the most revolutionary on earth is not a success story but a supply-side monster.

Finally there is a fourth explanation that we might add to the above as another kind of cultural explanation. This view would argue that the Japanese market is relatively closed to foreign competition not so much by government design but because Japan itself is still to a large extent a closed society. To the extent that the problems of access to the Japanese market are influenced by widely held social norms and traditional values, the trade problem can be viewed as largely beyond the realm of government to influence one way or the other. Japan is a holistic society that places great emphasis on maintaining group harmony and solidarity and does so, in part, by exaggerating the threat from the outside. When the group is a company, like Toyota, then group members are expected to demonstrate their loyalty to the group by neither owning a Nissan or considering working for Nissan and by not doing anything that could be considered as weakening the competitiveness or survivability of Toyota relative to Nissan or its other competitors. When the group becomes Japan, then foreign nations become the enemy and it is only a small step to the conclusion that importers of raw materials are national heroes and importers of finished goods are traitors.

As Rohlen notes (1985–6: 36), the Japanese have a deep-seated tendency to see the world as dichotomized between 'Japanese' and 'outsiders'. The almost inevitable result of these cultural perceptions is the tendency to feel uncomfortable around foreigners and an instinctive desire to want to keep them at arm's length. These perceptions feed into the poor, vulnerable, threatened Japan self-image which in turn leads to excessively defensive and over-emotional responses to any foreign action perceived as being aimed against Japanese interests. Almost any action which does not benefit Japanese interest tends to be construed as 'anti-Japanese' in a racial discriminatory sense rather than simply in an objective profit and loss sense.

These extreme Japanese sensitivities to being surrounded and threatened by outsiders can be seen, for example, in the Japanese media's reaction when IBM increased the number of American employees in its Tokyo office a few years ago. Headlines warned of a new American 'invasion' (Rohlen, 1985–6). Yet the Japanese are completely insensitive to the impact their invasion of America might be having. The Japanese are presently investing far more in the United States each year than is any other nation, much of it in real estate. According to recent reports Japanese investments now control 11 per cent of the commercial property in downtown New York, 20 per cent in Houston and 23 per cent in Los Angeles.[13] If anything like that was happening in Japan it would cause a national scandal and mobilize a campaign to legally bar further foreign investments. The only place where Japanese investments have become an issue in the United States is Hawaii, where in Honolulu Japanese investors have entered the single-family home market in a massive way, buying up large numbers of homes at extremely inflated prices. Moreover, the complaint in Honolulu is an economic not a racial one, as these overseas Japanese investors are pricing residents in need of housing out of the home market.

Another aspect of Japanese culture also greatly advantages Japanese insiders *vis-à-vis* foreign outsiders in the domestic Japanese market. Japan is still in many ways a particularistic society. It is particularistic in the sense that rules are not universally enforced. Often the legal and customary rules governing economic activity may be very stringent, but implementation depends on the personal relationship between the enforcer and the enforcee. The closer the relationship the more leniency and allowances that are made. Japan is also a particularistic society in the sense that individuals, whether entrepreneurs, retailers or customers, prefer to do business with those with which they have a longstanding personal relationship. In this sense the Japanese are not the exclusively economic animals that they are often pictured as being. In many cases they are willing to pay more to maintain a long term, trusted relationship than to transfer their dealings to new partners for the sake of a short term economic gain.

This preference for the tried and true works against all newcomers in the Japanese market, whether they be native or foreigners. And indeed the Japanese system often comes down hard on domestic newcomers in an established market or those that try to buck the system and gain profits from foreign sources at the expense of domestic producers. Still foreigners, by definition, encounter difficulties in Japan because no matter how much energy they invest in building rapport with relevant Japanese officials and counterparts, they will always be less preferred than Japanese partners due to the exclusiveness of Japanese society. These particularistic preferences help to explain the 'disappearing market' phenomenon in Japan (Cohen, 1985: 168). American products that have no direct competitor in the Japanese market often do very well. If they do extremely well, however, they are likely to trigger the emergence of domestic competition. What is so amazing is how quickly the Japanese market deserts the foreign producer once a domestic supplier emerges. In part, as Rohlen (1985–6) explains, this is because the foreign producer is typically not in a position to supply the personalized attention and around-the-clock service that Japanese buyers expect.

Regardless of the mix of pragmatic and emotional elements in the above cultural norms and practices, they clearly serve to limit the accessibility of the Japanese market to foreign producers. Rohlen (1985–6) calls them 'invisible barriers' because they are difficult to detect, impossible to quantify in any way and cannot be removed by a simple policy change or new law. While they remain, however, they will be a major contributor, not only to the trade imbalance, but to emotional cries of foul by American and other foreign businessmen.

WHERE DO WE GO FROM HERE?

The Japanese are not doing themselves any favours by their single-minded approach to becoming the number one economic power in the world. By moving rapidly toward super-power status without taking on the responsibilities of a super-power, they have put themselves in a vulnerable position. Japan is vulnerable because, while depending on the United States for its security, it has consistently resisted playing a larger role in maintaining international peace and security. The American image that Japan is a free rider that is gaining an unfair economic advantage by refusing to assume a fair portion of the defence burden is only amplified by Japanese leaders' recent penchant to lecture their US counterparts of the dangers of weakening American's vigilance against the Soviet menace in the face of Gorbachev's campaigns for a new openness and reform (Curtis, 1988). Unfortunately Japan continues to project the image that it is indifferent to all global problems which do not bear directly on Japan's own well-being. To overcome this, Japan must begin to play a much larger role in giving back to the world something of which it is extracting. If Japan is not going to carry a large defence spending burden, and there are good arguments for accepting that position, then it certainly could afford to take *the* leading role in developing new, constructive programmes to benefit the welfare and stability of Third World nations. Only in this way can Japan overcome the image it projects as a predator who simply views the rest of the world as a resource to exploit.

Japan is also vulnerable because it has made itself too convenient a target by its policy of unrestrained advance into foreign markets while failing to open up its own markets in a reciprocal manner. As the polling data cited earlier demonstrate, negative feelings against Japan are beginning to crystallize within the American public and leadership. Japan's real fear should not be the adoption by the American Congress of retaliatory trade measures or even protectionism but rather development of a pervasive Japan phobia, a deep-seated fear and hatred of Japan. Lobbying, PR and philanthropy will only carry the Japanese so far if not matched with actions. In this regard, whether by design or inertia, the Japanese are playing a risky game in which time is running out. The Gephardt campaign in 1988 was only a symptom of the problem, as were some of the comments Mondale made in the 1984 presidential campaign.[14] Since 1982 the US economy has been doing fairly well and that has muted criticism of Japan. But the potential for an anti-Japanese backlash is there and may flower overnight when the next recession hits the American economy. In this regard it is well to keep in mind that the American decision making system contrasts sharply with the conservative, deliberate, slow-moving system we find in Japan. The American system is prone to dramatic, abrupt change which cannot always be easily anticipated.

What is ironic in all of this is that what has been Japan's greatest strength – its exclusive, homogeneous, close-knit society and culture – is increasingly becoming its greatest weakness. A nation which depends on foreign trade for its survival cannot continue to exclude foreigners as extensively as Japan has – from its schools and education system, from employment in its companies, from participation in its financial markets, from ownership of private property and commercial enterprises, and from citizenship or even residence. Increasingly more Japanese are realizing this and we hear calls for the 'internationalization' of Japan with growing frequency. Much of this, however, is still just window-dressing, another PR effort aimed at placating foreign criticism. The Japanese have not yet really come to grips with what internationalization would mean – the loss of their sense of homogeneity and uniqueness. How can the Japanese internationalize without diluting their national character? Are they willing to give up the comfort and security of their exclusivistic culture? Are they willing to work and live beside foreigners and watch their sons and daughters intermarry? We might picture Japan as a reluctant inn-keeper, who needs outsiders' business to survive, but is unwilling to invite them in for fear that they will re-arrange the furniture and destroy the blissful comfort of his dwelling.

In the long run, of course, internationalization will come to Japan. But in the short run, to alleviate the friction and avoid emotional confrontations, Japanese policy makers would do well to become more sensitive to the problems caused by the rapid conquest of foreign markets. More orderly and gradual invasions will provoke less opposition and allow more time for adjustments. Japanese policy makers also need to make allowances for the special problems that foreign producers have in gaining and maintaining a foothold in the Japanese market. Just as in the United States, affirmative action programmes have been set up for minorities in recognition of the inherent inequalities built into the marketplace which are biased against their success, so too may the Japanese government have to step in with short term proactive programmes designed to overcome some of the built-in cultural biases against foreign access. Finally, Japan must realize that their heavy dependency on the United States for exports and high levels of investment in American securities, capital equipment and real estate gives them a high stake in the continued health of the American economy. In the view of some, that economy – with its huge trade deficits and government budget imbalances and volatile stock market – is an accident waiting to happen. In this light, Japanese policies which further destabilize the US economy for the sake of short term profits are short-sighted indeed.

There are lessons in all of this for US policy makers as well. Of course the US–Japan trade problems cannot be solved purely by unilateral action by the Japanese. In many respects America's economic problems are of its own making and US leaders should not use Japan as a scapegoat to escape focusing on the difficult decisions that need to be made to put their own house in order. To the extent that Japanese policies and practices remain blatantly unfair, however, what can be done?

Above, four differing explanations of Japanese behaviour were provided. If we discount as excessive the Japan bashers' view of Japanese behaviour as a highly co-ordinated national conspiracy orchestrated by MITI, all three of the remaining explanations, each of which undoubtedly contains some kernel of truth, counsel against expecting a quick solution to the US–Japan trade friction. Whether one believes that the Japanese decision makers are immobilized and incapable of action, pragmatically motivated to resist outside pressures to abandon successful Japanese formulas for what they see as failed Western economic policies, or simply unable to effect, through official policies and legislative bills, what are essentially culturally rooted practices, one should not expect the Japanese to change very fast of their own volition.

Philosophically the Japanese mind is not accustomed to striking out in new directions, but is very adept at adjusting to changes in the external environment. Only when changes appear inevitable are they likely to be fully embraced (Richardson and Flanagan, 1984: 156–9). Thus, American negotiators would do well to maintain the pressure on Japan, but with decorum and composure. The United States should not enter negotiations expecting that the Japanese will understand the fairness and logic of the US position and accede to American demands. Rather the US should enter negotiations prepared to take unilateral steps designed to encourage an appropriate Japanese response. Thus, they should present the American position and negotiate first, and if that fails to elicit a compromise, then move ahead quickly, without rancour or inflammatory rhetoric, to enact policy changes of a reciprocal nature which will begin to close off parts of the American market unless the Japanese open up parts of theirs. These American measures should not be primarily punitive in nature but rather contain high incentives for the Japanese to change their behaviour to bring it in line with the rest of the world. An excellent example of this would be the measure contained in the House Trade Bill passed in April 1988 which simply stated that the Federal Reserve of New York would forbid foreign-owned securities firms from acting as primary dealers in US government securities, unless their home country granted a similar privilege to US companies (*Japan Times*, 29 April 1988: 12).

Another mechanism which the Japanese well understand are quotas, as they not only have an elaborate system of informal quotas in place but also occasionally work out similar arrangements to artificially guarantee domestic competitors a 'fair share' of the market. This concept of fair share is much more important to the Japanese than the American concept of fair play, and, hence, they readily understand and accept measures to control market share so long as they are not arbitrary and stand in some relationship to market forces. Thus, there is a need for flexible quotas to allow for orderly market change.

The Japanese will respond most favourably to these sorts of approaches if American policies are clearly defined, consistent and based on long term, stable objectives, with desired changes plotted out well in advance and phased in slowly. In the long run this consistent nudging will not only resolve some of the American problems with the bilateral US–Japan trade but work to the benefit of the Japanese as well. The Japanese people deserve better than their government is giving them. The ruling party and big business in Japan essentially have been able to take advantage of a non-competitive political situation to focus government tax and spending policies single-mindedly on economic growth policies which have long post-poned or restrained spending on housing, parks, education, welfare and other quality of life measures. The Japanese people need to be disabused of the idea that their high savings rate is necessary and need to begin demanding that their government do more for them, or at least change the tax and financial polices to encourage and enable the people to do more for themselves instead of simply hoarding their money for some future expected rainy day.

We end where we started, noting that the United States and Japan are mutually dependent on each other for their economic prosperity and security. Both sides recognize this and yet are given from time to time to unfortunate outbursts which undermine the good will and trust which are so vital to maintaining the health and strength of the relationship. I have suggested here there are more constructive approaches that both sides could take that can defuse the tension and misunderstanding while moving the relationship towards a more viable, long term trade pattern.

Notes

1. The above figures are computed from data reported in the Keizai Koho Centre, 1988. This publication consists entirely of a most useful compilation of raw data tables. The trade data for Japan was reported in US dollars on a customs clearance basis, while the trade data for the United States excluded military transfers.
2. The above figures were computed from data presented in the Keizai Koho Centre, 1988. All the Japanese numbers refer to 1986, but all the American numbers were based on 1985 data, the last year reported.
3. Actually the size of the Japanese government in terms of the numbers of government employees and the size of the public sector relative to the population was already quite small by Western standards prior to the administrative reform efforts in the early 1980s. Indeed in per capita terms the public sector is only about half the size in Japan that it is in the United States, Britain and Germany (Richardson and Flanagan, 1984).
4. Saxonhouse (1986) reports that during the six-year period 1979–1985 Japanese investment in new plant equipment increased at an average annual rate of seven per cent, roughly three-quarters of which was

designed for production for the export market. It seems ironic that while the Japanese were rapidly expanding their industrial capacity, American big business was in many cases using the Reagan tax breaks for something other than their intended purpose of enabling US industry to become more competitive through modernizing its plant equipment. Instead we find many corporate giants and money men using these tax breaks to capitalize on opportunities to achieve quick paper profits, through a cycle of company buyouts, squeezing the profit out of these new acquisitions by not reinvesting in upgrading their equipment and finally tax write-offs for plant closings and subsidiary bankruptcies when such acquisitions begin to become unprofitable and uncompetitive. Such predatory behaviour is bad economics for America and would be unheard of in Japan where executives have an enduring commitment to their companies and are more concerned with its market share and long term survivability than near term profits. Bankruptcies and plant closings are certainly not at all unheard of in Japan, but in the Japanese case executives do not profit from their failures but rather go down with the ship.

5. The percentage figure given here for the rise in exports to the European Community nations is somewhat inflated, because the total reported exports for 1975 were based on nine EC countries, while the 1986 figure included twelve EC countries as a result of the admission of Greece, Spain and Portugal into the European Community during the interim. In all cases, the reported percentages were computed by comparing the 1975 and 1986 export figures. In most cases the growth in exports has been almost perfectly monotonic, and so this procedure provides an accurate picture of export trends. However, in the case of the Middle East and Africa, exports peaked in 1981 and have declined somewhat thereafter. (Keizai Koho Centre, 1988).

6. These two nationwide American surveys were conducted by the New York Times and CBS News in July of 1985 and April of 1986 in conjunction with parallel national surveys conducted by the Tokyo Broadcasting System in Japan. These two American surveys realized 1569 and 1601 completed interviews respectively. Here the reported question above was found only on the 1986 survey.

7. Saxonhouse, 1986. We find essentially the same result if we compare the ration of Japanese total imports to GDP. From 1977 through 1985 this proportion varied from 8.2 to 12.3 per cent and averaged 10.6 per cent. However in 1986 this figure dropped to 6.4 per cent, demonstrating clearly that the sharp fall in the US dollar relative to the yen was not matched by a rise in the volume of US exports into Japan (Keizai Koho Centre, 1988).

8. See note 6.

9. These two nationwide surveys on American attitudes about international trade were conducted in March and June of 1986 by Mathew Greenwald and Associates and The Government Research Corporation. As reported in Greenwald and Teixeira, 1986.

10. This Americans Talk Security (ATS) poll was one in a series being conducted co-operatively by four polling organizations including Mar-

tilla and Kiley of Boston and Market Opinion Research of Detroit. This poll was a national telephone survey conducted 22–27 March and realizing 1004 completed interviews. As reported in *The Japan Times*, 30 April 1988: 4.

11. This Gallup survey conducted annually since 1972 is based on a mailed questionnaire sent to 5000 professionals selected at random from *Who's Who in America*. In the 1988 survey 1550 of these American opinion leaders responded. As reported in *The Japan Times*, 29 April 1988: 1.

12. Cohen, 1985. The psychological symbolism of threatening to designate Japan as America's 'enemy' was clearly destructive of mutual trust and in retrospect seems excessive in light of the fact that textiles were at the time clearly a declining American industry and Japanese imports of man-made textile products accounted for only two per cent of American consumption.

13. Reported in the television documentary, *Inside Japan*, produced by the Georgia Public Television Network and first broadcast 12 July, 1988.

14. Mondale warned that the 'next American generation might be destined to clean up around Japanese computers' (Nacht, 1983).

References

Angel, Robert C. (1988), 'Explaining Policy Failure: Japan and the International Context in 1969–1971,' *Journal of Public Policy* (April-June): 175-94.

Campbell, John Creighton (1984), 'Policy Conflict and Its Resolution within the Governmental System', in Ellis S. Krauss *et al* (eds), *Conflict in Japan*, (Honolulu: University of Hawaii Press).

Cohen, Stephen D. (1985), *Uneasy Partnership: Competition and Conflict in US–Japanese Trade Relations*, (Cambridge, Mass: Ballinger Publishing Co).

Curtis, Gerald L. (1988), 'Japan's Arrogance of Power', *The New York Times* (8 May): E-29.

Fukui, Haruhiro (1987), 'Too Many Captains in Japan's Internationalization: Travails at the Foreign Ministry', *The Journal of Japanese Studies* 13 (Summer): 359–382.

Greenwald, Mathew and Ruy Teixeira (1986), 'Storm Warnings on the Trade Front', *The JAMA Forum* 5 (Number 1): 14–23.

Haley, John O. (1987), 'Governance by Negotiation: A Reappraisal of Bureaucratic Power in Japan', *The Journal of Japanese Studies* 13 (Summer): 343–58.

Hellman, Donald C. (1969), *Japanese Domestic Politics and Foreign Policy: The Peace Agreement with the Soviet Union*, (Berkeley: University of California Press).

Holstein, William J., *et al* (1988) 'Cover Story: Japan's Influence in America',*Business Week* (11 July): 64–75.

Iida, Tsuneo (1987), 'Decline of a Superpower', *Japan Echo* 14 (Autumn): 22–23.

Ingersoll, Robert S. (1985-6), 'Japan's Industrial Challenge to America', *Asian Affairs* 12 (Winter): 6–18.
Johnson, Chalmers (1987), 'How to Think About Economic Competition from Japan', *The Journal of Japanese Studies* 13 (Summer): 415–28.
Kaufmann, S. J. (1982), 'What Really Bothers Foreign Businessmen in Japan', *The Japan Times* (3 April): 5.
Kraar, Louis (1983), 'Japan Blows Smoke about US Cigarettes', *Fortune* (21 February): 99–105.
Keizai Koho Centre (1988), *Japan 1988: An International Comparison*, (Tokyo: Keizai Koho Centre).
Nacht, Michael (1983), 'The American Mood', pp. 9–16 in Philip B. Jones, *US–Japan Relations: Towards a New Equilibrium*, (Cambridge: The Program on US–Japan Relations, Harvard University).
Ohkawa Kazushi and Henry Rosovsky (1973), *Japanese Economic Growth: Trend Acceleration in the Twentieth Century*, (Stanford: Stanford University Press).
Osamu, Shimomura (1987), 'The "Japan Problem" is of America's Making', *The Japan Echo* 14 (Autumn): 24–6.
Pempel, T. J. (1987), 'The Unbundling of "Japan, Inc.": The Changing Dynamics of Japanese Policy Formation', *The Journal of Japanese Studies* 13 (Summer): 271–306.
Pharr, Susan J. and Kishima Takako (1987), 'Japan in 1986: a Landmark Year for the LDP', *Asian Survey* 27 (January): 23–34.
Pyle, Kenneth B. (1987), 'In Pursuit of a Grand Design: Nakasone Betwixt the Past and Future', *The Journal of Japanese Studies* 13 (Summer): 243–70.
Richardson, Bradley M and Scott C. Flanagan (1984), *Politics in Japan*, (Boston: Little Brown).
Rohlen, Thomas P. (1985-86), 'Invisible Barriers: American Companies in the Japanese Marketplace', *Asian Affairs* 12 (Winter): 35–50.
Saxonhouse, Gary R. (1986), 'Structural Adjustment in Japan in the 1980s,' Paper presented at the Conference on Japan in the 1980s, VI, Southern Center for International Studies, Atlanta, Georgia, 1–2 May.
Simons, Lewis M. (1988), 'House Trade Bill Racism-Motivated,' *The Honolulu Advertiser* (23 April): B–5.
Suzuki, Yoshio (1981), 'Why is the Performance of the Japanese Economy So Much Better?' *The Journal of Japanese Studies* 7 (Summer): 403–13.
US Trade Representative (1982), *Japanese Barriers to US Trade and Recent Japanese Government Trade Initiatives* (November) (Washington DC: US Government Printing Office).
Vogel, Ezra F. (1982), 'American Perceptions of Japan: Growing Sense of Unfairness', in Philip Jones, ed., *US–Japan Relations in the 1980s: Towards Burden Sharing*, (Cambridge: The Program on US–Japan Relations, Harvard University).
Vogel, Ezra F. (1984), 'New Attitudes for a New Era', pp. 207–14 in Richard B. Finn, ed., *US–Japan Relations: New Attitudes for a New Era*, (Cambridge: The Program on US–Japan Relations, Harvard University).
Yamamura, Kozo (1983), 'Managing US–Japan Relations: An Overall

View', pp. 47-57 in Philip B. Jones, *US–Japan Relations: Towards a New Equilibrium*, (Cambridge: The Program on US–Japan Relations, Harvard University).

Yamamura Kozo (1987), 'Shedding the Shackles of Success: Saving Less for Japan's Future', *The Journal of Japanese Studies* 13 (Summer): 429–56.

4 Energy Cooperation and the Future of US–Japan Security Relations
Ronald A. Morse

The lessons of US–Japan energy and energy security ties are rather straightforward and reflect trends in the bilateral relationship more generally. It is also probably accurate to state that bilateral energy relations have never been smooth when it comes to issues outside of narrow research or technical exchange matters.

Historically there have been two areas of potential conflict in the energy area: (1) trade in resources, and (2) foreign policy issues. In the resource area, when the United States was competitive in coal, natural gas and oil exports, there was little US aggressiveness in seeking foreign markets. As US energy exports became less competitive, US efforts to seek Japan's cooperation in importing resources became more political, more protracted, and a part of overall trade tensions.

Energy is also a geopolitical consideration and is part of any foreign policy strategy. When the US expected Japan to support US energy and energy security objectives in the 1970s, Japan, because of its own domestic political and strategic priorities, extended modest but not enthusiastic cooperation to US positions. This was especially true when the security of Middle East oil supplies was at issue.

If there have been tensions and differences in US–Japan energy and energy security relations, they relate to quite different historical, economic and political forces that shape the domestic agenda in the two countries. The degree to which the leaders in the United States and Japan can overcome these domestic forces and shape a more cooperative relationship in the future is the key issue. Past experience, however, does not make one optimistic about significant 'cooperation' in the decades ahead. Indeed, as US and Japanese 'energy relations' shift into competition in high technology energy applications and nuclear power plant production, there will be even more trade competition.

BACKGROUND

In the same way that basic energy supply and demand issues have changed both within the United States and Japan, the international security context within which these policies operate has also changed. Some of these issues and differences between Japan and America have historical roots. For example, one would expect policy makers in Japan and the United States to have very different perceptions about global security issues simply as a result of their relative national strengths and international responsibilities after the Second World War. For nearly four decades the United States has assumed the role of global policeman and guardian of free world security interests. Japan, until quite recently, has generally resisted including any military considerations in its foreign policy formulations and has preferred to characterize itself as a middle-sized power operating quietly in the shadow of American strategic policy. The United States has more or less accepted this division of effort and has consistently encouraged Japan to pursue its specific economic interests, keeping its military activities limited to coordination with US interests in the Asian–Pacific region. This situation has set the context for a variety of other global relationships and is important in the consideration of energy security issues.

The main challenges to US–Japan energy cooperation in the foreign policy context were greatest in the 1970s, especially during the two oil shocks of 1973 and 1979. During these years 'energy security', as the concept was used, was another way of referring primarily to the relationship between energy matters and Middle East issues. Since the early 1980s the focus on energy issues has changed dramatically, with energy cooperation and coordination issues taking a back seat to more pressing 'trade' problems. In 1979, the US Secretary of State, upset over Japanese energy policies, publicly referred to Japanese behaviour in the Middle East as 'insensitive' (by which he meant irresponsible). Today American officials are concerned with a new form of Japanese 'insensitivity', primarily in bilateral trade relations, especially Japan's resistance to absorbing foreign imports. While energy issues sometimes are included in these new 'trade problems', more often this is not the case.

As Yasuo Imai suggests in his chapter, there are still fundamental differences between the United States and Japan regarding energy co-operation. In large part these differences stem from the same fundamental expectations about global responsibilities that created bilateral tensions in the 1970s. Despite the fact that the United States and Japan are global partners in many areas and that both nations today share quite similar values (democracy, peace, capitalism), there are very different forces driving their separate security and economic foreign policy considerations. These longer term forces cannot be ignored in the consideration of the two nations' prospects for co-operation in the future.

Despite the current mood to see energy issues as secondary to other considerations, we should not forget that energy issues played an important role in fostering many of the earlier economic or strategic tensions between the two nations that still exist today. For example, in the 1970s, Japanese carmakers were first successful in establishing a market for cheap, energy-efficient cars in the United States because American energy regulations distorted the real price of fuel and the US auto industry continued to produce 'gas-guzzlers'. American pressures on Japan to be co-operative with Asian sealane security was based upon an assessment of protecting oil supplies coming over vulnerable tanker routes. The decline of the American nuclear power industry and Japan's increasing strength in this area is related to a complex set of financing and technology policies that Japan has implemented more successfully. Japan's ability to penetrate the US market in a wide range of commodities, to avoid purchasing US energy resources, and to keep its defence expenditures low have a great deal to do with the close working relationship between Japanese business and government interests, a relationship that functions much less effectively in the United States.

ENERGY AS AN ECONOMIC ISSUE

Despite the drop in oil prices and the fall-off of concern about the Middle East as an energy supplier at the time of writing, the 'geopolitics of oil' is still an important issue for politicians. When Secretary of the Interior Donald Hodel stated on 5 September, 1986 that 'we're in very grave danger as a nation of finding ourselves in a short time back in the grasp of OPEC', his remarks went virtually unnoticed. Even he was not concerned with Middle East issues and the Organization of Petroleum Exporting Countries (OPEC); what he was very worried about was the plight of the US oil industry. This concern with domestic oil interests highlights one very important difference between the United States and Japan in the energy area.

Where the United States imports between 4.6 and 5 million barrels of oil daily, these imports account for only one-third of total US petroleum needs. Because of America's wealth in energy resources, domestic politics play a more important role in their overall energy policies. A low price for oil means more imports and less domestic production – dollars flow to the Middle East and US oil industry producers go out of business. While this is a big issue in the United States, in Japan, which has the lowest self-sufficiency rate in energy of the top seven industrialized nations (a mere 0.2 per cent), there is little in the way of a domestic Japanese oil lobby like that in the United States. For Japan energy is almost exclusively a trade issue.

Looking back, we can see that the huge oil price increases of the 1970s were the result of a complex set of factors that may no longer exist today: the fear that OPEC would act as a powerful cartel; that military conflicts and other disruptions would occur in the oil producing states; and that public policies could create a crisis in oil consuming nations. Oil became a weapon in international politics. As a result of the high oil prices of the 1970s, economic growth slowed and world oil consumption has been stagnant; conservation and alternative energy policies of the major oil consuming nations have reduced oil imports; and nations were given the incentive to explore new oil fields. OPEC created an environment that stimulated others to produce oil. In 1953 OPEC supplied 55 per cent of world oil production, today the figure is 28 per cent. As many analysts point out, the international oil market is significantly different as we enter the 1990s from what it was a decade ago and the earlier logic about the forces of supply and demand no longer seems to apply.

In the discussion of these issues one distinction to be made is the differences between import *dependence* on petroleum products and *vulnerability* to outside supply disruptions. A nation like Japan is 'dependent' on oil imports (as is the US to a lesser degree) because it does not possess the capacity to produce most of its own needs. 'Vulnerability', on the other hand, is a measure of the liability – both economic and political – to change in the availability or price of a commodity (oil) on which a nation depends. In this context the United States and Japan are equally vulnerable. In policy terms, however, the Japanese tend to emphasize their dependence, while Americans emphasize vulnerability. Japanese resource strategies that emphasize dependence are designed to disperse supply sources so that no one supplier has significant supply leverage. Imai makes this clear in Chapter 5. Americans, with a strategic approach to reducing vulnerability, are more concerned with securing the stability of the supply source.

But what do these differences mean for US–Japan relations? If, as many experts suggest, a major political disruption in Saudi Arabia or elsewhere in a major oil producing nation could again usher in a global oil crisis, what would the United States and Japan do? Would they again find themselves differing over policies? Would they be in any better position to co-operate today than they were in 1973 or 1979? Are, as I would maintain, trade, strategic issues and energy concerns linked in ways that point up the very different US and Japanese foreign policies on energy matters?

ENERGY AND SECURITY

Implicit in much of what I have suggested is the complex interaction of two key concepts – energy and security. Energy and security are linked in policy terms because economics and politics are linked in reality. For years the Japanese tried to decouple economics and politics (what they called *seikei bunri*), but dealing in the Middle East taught them the unreality of this distinction. By attempting to separate politics and economics, the Japanese hoped to deal with oil in economic terms and thereby not have to deal with it in security related ways that forced hard political choices. This led to their being accused of the 'insensitivity' mentioned earlier.

'Energy', as I use the term, refers to the supply and demand for electricity, power and so on from various energy sources – primarily petroleum, coal, natural gas, nuclear, and wind. Oil, because of its availability, energy qualities, easy transport, and, for most of the postwar era, cheap cost, has assumed the premier position as the major energy source in the industrialized nations of the globe. The fact that over half of the world's petroleum reserves are in the Middle East was not a strategic concern before 1973 and has become less of a concern since 1983.

'Security' is less easy to define because of its many uses and connotations. Americans, it is fair to say, are more concerned with the security than the economic dimensions of the problem. 'Energy security' as a concept refers to the reliability of critical energy supplies and a strategy to prevent the interruption of those supplies. The interruption of supply, some American strategists would argue, is prevented by sealane security or the ability to intervene militarily in a crisis situation. A nation like Japan can stockpile oil, participate in multi-lateral energy schemes (like that of the International Energy Agency), or strike government-to-government bilateral oil purchase deals to reduce vulnerability to supply cutoff. To minimize the domestic economic damage from supply shortfalls, countries have developed emergency oil supply allocation schemes, conservation strategies and long term energy diversification policies. Japan and the United States have pursued differing combinations of these policies.

Within this context, the fundamental issue for US–European and Asian alliance politics has been how to allow allies to maintain an independent foreign policy position and yet still have them pursue policies that are in co-ordination with US global interests. This is the context within which Americans evaluate Japan's performance. The record shows that energy has been a persistent irritant in US–Japan ties. In the 1973 Arab–Israeli war the Japanese disassociated themselves from the US pro-Israel position and have done so ever since. Japan allowed the Palestine Liberation Organization (PLO) to open an office in Tokyo in 1977 and Prime Minister Suzuki met 'unofficially' with Yassir Arafat. In 1979 Japan did not endorse America's military philosophy designating the Persian Gulf as a 'third strategic zone' after Europe and northeast Asia. The United States invested heavily to equip military facilities in Oman and Diego Garcia and develop a Rapid Deployment Force for regional stability.

Japan, on the other hand, had its petrochemical complex in Iran excluded from sanctions during the hostage crisis and only reluctantly supported US policies following the Soviet invasion of Afghanistan. Japan also tried to avoid being caught in US–Soviet rivalry – it made significant profits when US producers were excluded from construction projects by the US government in the Soviet–European gas pipeline deals. If one takes the long view, it is fair to say that Japan has been distancing itself from US positions on energy related foreign policy issues since the early 1970s. Tokyo did not take US energy supplies when they were secure and competitive in the 1960s and, as Imai points out in this volume, doesn't want them now when they are too expensive.

In the debate over petroleum as a 'security' issue as opposed to an 'economic' commodity, Japan and the United States have opted for quite different priorities. If one were to list the complex mix of Japanese and American security priorities in the 1970s as they relate to energy issues (in descending order of importance), the two lists might look something like this:

US Priorities	Japanese Priorities
Contain Soviet expansion	Diversify oil supply sources
	Stockpile crude oil
Protect US regional interests	
	Supply economic and technical
Foster international co-operation on energy security	aid to supplier nations
	Promote conservation and alternate energy
Build strategic oil reserves	
	Stimulate energy production
Promote conservation and alternate energy supplies	
	Foster international co-operation
	Protect national interests

A WANING SENSE OF SECURITY

Since 1981 the Japanese and American positions on these energy security issues have not changed dramatically, though a case could be made that their thinking has moved closer together: the Americans are now more market (price) oriented and the Japanese are more security 'conscious'. United States energy policy is now predicated on the belief that free market forces should be allowed to be unfettered by government regulation and intervention. There is also a sense in the United States that the energy crisis is over and that the future energy needs of the world are secure. As a result, high cost oil production and exploration should cease, oil demand should rise and high cost schemes for energy conservation policies and alternate energy investments will be delayed. This is exactly what is happening in response to market forces.

US policy makers doubt that the nation should spend more money on its Strategic Petroleum Reserve (SPR), which at the time of writing contains nearly four months' worth of net oil imports at their recent level of about 4.4 million barrels of oil. The United States has spent nearly $16 billion to create this half-billion barrel reserve to reduce American vulnerability to an interruption of oil imports. Total US oil imports have also been reduced but the figure is again rising. The quasi-governmental agency that was to lead the United States to energy independence, the Synthetic Fuels Corporation, disappeared in April 1986 after six years of intermittent action. Some alternate energy projects in the United States involved Japan but once they were closed down in the United States, the Japanese government continued to support the experiments at home or in new joint ventures in other countries. Inconsistencies in US policy have left investments and new technologies to be developed by countries with a more long term view, like Japan.

For the Japanese the immediate sense of crisis is also gone, but the national psychology of feeling totally dependent on energy imports has led to far greater consistency in all areas of energy policy. While they do not want to over-invest in oil replacement schemes or risky new technologies, they are not yet ready to abandon such projects the way the United States has. The motivation is, however, still not defined in strategic terms, but in economic terms – the drive for economic survival and competitiveness as a nation still dominates the Japanese concern.

The International Energy Agency, in its 1985 country review of Japan, praised Japanese energy security measures, primarily for the 'substitution of coal, gas and nuclear power for significant volumes of oil in power generation' and the 'maintenance of budgetary commitments to all major aspects of the energy programme, including oil stockpiling, nuclear development work and fiscal encouragement to conservation investments.' Tokyo is also restructuring its oil industry and increasing its investments in overseas oil exploration. The one energy issue that potentially would have created a bilateral problem, Japanese restrictions on oil product imports, has been defused by the 'Provisional Measures Act' (December 1985) liberalizing the import of specified petroleum products. Imai analyzes these domestic issues in his chapter.

The focus on competition and co-operation in US–Japan issues is shifting from the resource to the energy technologies development area. Japan, unlike the United States, has not lessened its search and support for technical improvements in the development of alternative energies. With the creation of the New Energy Development Organization (NEDO) in 1980, it has doubled its efforts in the areas of solar and other energies. Japan's co-operative research and development activities with the US Department of Energy (some $25 million annually) are mostly in the areas of fusion, breeder reactors and nuclear physics – all areas in which Japan can be expected to assume more of a leadership role. Information and research exchanges were once a one-way flow (from the United States to Japan), but Americans are increasingly aware that Japanese advances and research contributions are ahead of the American efforts.

ENERGY IN THE FUTURE OF US–JAPAN RELATIONS

Japan has never been overly supportive of the domestic or international energy policies of the United States. In foreign policy, in particular, as I have argued, there have been major differences. In terms of imports of US energy resources, Japan has been taking less and less. And in terms of new energy technologies, Japan has made maximum use of US innovations and will soon replace the United States in key markets for commercialized energy products. While this has been 'good policy' for Japan, it may be bad 'politics' as trade deficits and more direct competition in high-tech areas stretch the patience of policy makers on both sides. Energy issues are one important component of the total relationship.

The high cost of US energy sources, when combined with Japan's policies of diversification of supply, has led to US exports of coal, gas and oil being replaced by exports of competitive producers. Australia, China, South Africa and the USSR have gradually replaced the United States as coal exporters to Japan. The hopes for Alaskan and West Coast US oil exports to Japan have slowly been eroded by Japan's own exploration developments: with the help of the Japanese government, analysts figure that by 1995, 30 per cent (1.2 million barrels a day) of Japan's total crude oil imports will be from projects developed from independent Japanese sources. (This development is demonstrated by the chart in the appendix.) While Japan's first natural gas project was in the United States (North Cook Inlet, Alaska, 1969), Japanese utilities and other investors have since turned to Brunei, Abu Dhabi, Indonesia, Malaysia and Australia for new supplies.

Japan as an energy consumer dominates Asian energy markets. Since it accounts for nearly 70 per cent of the energy consumed in Asia, Tokyo has used its energy import investment strategy to balance its export needs with major Asian trading nations. It has, one could argue, even fostered Asian coal and gas trade with an eye to 'over production' and cheap prices. By encouraging 'over supply' it has kept prices low and placed itself in a good position as a major energy consumer.

While the cultivation of new energy supplies and the diversification of supply sources to areas outside of the Persian Gulf can be viewed as enhancing global energy security, there is still the broader issue of US–Japan trade friction. As with American experiences in other areas of US competitiveness, the United States has lost Japanese markets for its energy exports and has seen many of the initiatives of energy research and development being commercialized by Japan.

As long as these energy related trends are perceived as consistent with other trade and security concerns, they are not likely to be identified as unique or special to the energy security area. As such they will draw less attention than they would have in the 1970s. This does not, however, imply that these will not be serious areas for US attention or analysis in the year ahead. Quite the opposite, the growing disparities in energy cooperation have helped fuel the bilateral trade deficit and raise serious questions about the trend lines for other areas of US–Japan ties.

References

Ronald A. Morse ed. (1986) *Japan and the Middle East in Alliance Politics* (University Press of America).

Ronald A. Morse (1982), 'Japanese Energy Policy', in *After the Second Oil Crisis* ed. Wilfrid L. Kohl (Lexington Books), pp. 255–69.

Ronald A. Morse (1984), 'Japan's Search for an Independent Foreign Policy: An American Perspective', *Journal of Northeast Asian Studies*, Vol. 3, No.2 (Summer). *The Washington Post*, 4 May 1986, p. F4.

Appendix: Overseas Oil and Natural Gas Exploration and Development Projects by Japanese Oil Development Companies (As of November, 1985)

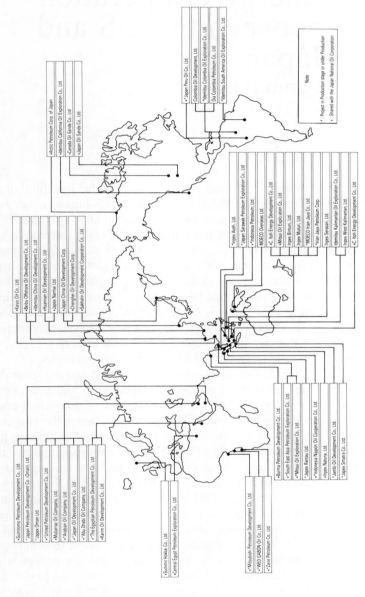

5 Energy Cooperation between the US and Japan
Yasuo Imai

INTRODUCTION

In this chapter, I would like to address the question of energy cooperation between the US and Japan. US–Japan energy relations are often a point of focus in the discussion of US–Japan trade friction, or are seen as an immediate remedy to the trade imbalance between the two countries. Typically, as in the US demand to expand coal trade with Japan and in the field of energy as well, there are many different voices, saying such things as, 'Japan should increase imports', or 'the issues must be solved in a short period of time'. I am not denying that there is trade friction associated with US–Japan energy issues, and I would strongly like to see US–Japan energy trade enlarged, thereby strengthening US–Japan energy security, as well as contributing to improved US–Japan trade relations.

The United States and Japan are the largest and the second largest energy consumers in the free world respectively, and at the same time they are the largest and the second largest oil importing countries. With this in mind I am sure there are many things the two countries can deal with in a concerted manner in terms of energy policies. While Japan is the world's largest energy importing country that has virtually no energy resources, the US, quite to the contrary, is an enormous resource producer and has a considerable energy export potential. In this regard, these two countries stand in a mutually complementary relationship. Thus, the US and Japan have a relationship with both common and contrasting elements and that necessitates an enlargement of close co-operative ties in the energy field in a long term perspective. I would like to give an overview on this cooperative relationship, before I go on to the specific details.

First, let us examine the concerted actions of the two governments on energy policies. Although some may not be aware of the existence of such co-operation, since there is little public attention given to it, collaborative policies have constantly been adopted between the two governments through the IEA (International Energy Agency) forums, as well as through bilateral consultations. The relaxed situation in energy demand and supply as I write can be said to be the result of the cooperative policies of the advanced countries, including the United States and Japan. Another example can be found in the cooperative policies on petroleum stockpiling and the fact that Japan, in January 1986, began importing gasoline and kerosene.

Second, as to the complementary aspects of US–Japan energy relations, we must take into consideration a characteristic which is inherent to energy. That is that the energy supply situation can change drastically overnight from a tight condition to a relaxed one and vice versa, but energy development cannot be immediately adjusted to such sudden changes, since it takes considerable time as well as enormous investment. Although since the mid-1980s Japan has been asked to purchase more energy from the US, in the late 1970s when the energy situation was tight, Japan faced difficulties in securing not only oil, but coal and LNG (liquified natural gas) and other energy resources. Distressed by the uncertainty of a stable energy supply, high energy costs, and many strikes, Japan decided to take steps to stabilize the energy supply through increased direct investment and long term contracts, and to diversify energy supply sources. As the effects of these policies become manifest, Japanese importers have, ironically, been hit by the recent decline in energy demand and over-supply. While Japan is facing over-commitments, the United States is asking Japan to increase energy imports. The unfavourable timing of this request has resulted in more energy trade friction.

Third, although there are these complementary and co-operative aspects of the US–Japan energy relationship, there is a limitation on interdependence in the energy field, because energy is deeply connected with national security both from the point of view of economic and military considerations. Therefore, some aspects of US–Japan energy relations cannot be dealt with within the framework of a more co-operative relationship. The ban on the export of the Alaskan North Slope crude oil is an example. There is also the question of how co-operative energy relations will be sustained in the event of another energy crisis.

Within the preceding framework, I would like to further explain US–Japan energy cooperation, and I would hope that my analysis may relate to future energy cooperation in the Pacific Rim region as it is hoped for by many who deal with these issues.

THE POSSIBILITY OF COOPERATION IN ENERGY POLICIES

Both the US and Japanese governments, which represent large importers of oil and larger consumers of energy, have propelled collaborative energy policies through the IEA forum and through continuous consultations among policy makers repsonsible for energy. Here, I would like to give examples of these: Japan's recent stockpile policy, its gasoline import policy, and joint oil exploration efforts between the US and Japan.

Stockpile

When the Iran–Iraq war intensified in the spring of 1985, the necessity to increase petroleum stockpiling was reaffirmed by the IEA, and it was agreed that in the event of a crisis, a disturbance should be avoided through a collaborative stockpile drawdown at an early stage in the crisis. Accordingly, Japan sped up the fill rate of the stockpile from 2.5 million kl/year to 3.0 million kl/year. As recently as 1986, Japan further increased the rate to 3.5 million/year in keeping pace with the strengthened stockpile policy of the US under the current energy situation. As of July 1986, Japan had a national stockpile of 37 days' supply (based on its consumption level, which is the equivalent of its import level), with a stockpile in the private sector of 105 days' supply, or 142 days' supply in total. At the end of FY1988 Japan planned to raise its national stockpile to 30 million kl, which is 54 days' supply based on the consumption level of 1985. (In addition to this, the private sector is required by law to have a stockpile of a minimum 90 days.) This figure of 30 million may, possibly, be reviewed depending on the rate of consumption in light of the current oil situation or the possible change of US stockpile policy.

Gasoline Imports to Japan

In the past, Japan had maintained a policy which is known as 'onshore refining policy': that is, importing crude to be refined only at Japanese refineries. Securing a stable supply has been imperative to Japan, a country which is more than 80 per cent dependent on oil imports for its total energy supply. It was later thought that a policy of importing crude which is easily obtained from various sources,

ould make the greatest contribution to a stable supply, rather than
nporting petroleum products which have not yet developed an
1ternational market, and which come from limited sources. Japan
radually started importing residual fuel and naphtha for which an
1ternational market was developed and which could be reliably
upplied, becoming the world's third largest petroleum products
nporting country after the US and West Germany. Given these
onditions, imports of gasoline or kerosene were not allowed.
Iowever, under pressure for more product exports from the Middle
:ast countries, where refineries have been successively completed in
ccordance with the request of the United States, Japan started
asoline and kerosene imports in January of 1986. Recently, the
nportation of these products amounted to between six and seven per
ent of domestic consumption. Japan, along with Europe and the
Jnited States, will have to share the burden of increasing supply
ressure of petroleum product from oil producing countries.

JS–Japan Joint Efforts in Oil Exploration in the US

$ecause of the sharp decline of world oil prices and the financial
ressures associated with large-scale mergers among US oil firms,
1vestment in oil exploraiton and development by US oil companies
as been dramatically decreased. Consequently, many fear a decline
1 domestic production in the medium term and a resultant increase
1 oil imports. On the other hand, Japan, with no resources, is
/orking to encourage Japanese involvement in oil exploration and
·roduction through the Japan National Oil Corporation by providing
apanese oil development firms with risk money, with the hope of
1creasing Japanese flag oil to one-third of total oil imports. (The
urrent ratio is a little over ten per cent). This year Nippon Oil, a
apanese oil company and an affiliate of Texaco, concluded an
greement for joint exploration in the US with Texaco, together with
 $100 million investment from Nippon Oil. Other joint ventures of
his kind include one between Conoco and Nippon Mining, with an
1vestment from Nippon Mining of $50 million; and a joint venture
·etween Idemitsu and Arco. If these joint ventures succeed, the
apanese side will obtain its share oil from a third country through a
wap arrangement, since federal law prohibits the export of US crude
·il. At the time of writing other US oil companies, including majors
nd many independents have also proposed such joint exploration
·entures with Japan. Although these projects are not the results of

collaborative policies between the two governments, they are highly valued by the US government and members of Congress as promoting exploration activities in the US.

Technology Development of Oil Conservation, and Alternative Energy

Although no project is under way as I write, I believe there are many areas where co-operation is possible between the two countries. I hope to see co-operative energy policies in this field in the future, as both countries are grappling with decreased incentives under low oil prices and budgetary limitations.

COOPERATION IN ENERGY TRADE

A stable supply of energy, in particular diversification of sources, has been the highest priority of the energy policy of Japan. At present, Japan still depends on foreign sources for 85 per cent of its total energy consumption, 60 per cent of which is imported oil. It would be in the interests of Japan to secure a long term stable energy supply from the United States, which is a giant producer of oil, coal and natural gas, and which has a large potential for export. However, due to the problems which I will refer to later, we cannot say energy trade between the US and Japan has been expanding. In 1983, the US–Japan energy working group was established between the two governments, and the possibility of energy cooperation was examined. Great effort is being made to encourage related industries in both countries. It is of the greatest importance to cope with this issue of energy from a long term viewpoint. Here I will introduce examples of possible cooperation in the energy field, such as oil, coal and LNG.

Oil

In June 1986, the US government lifted the ban on the export of Alaskan Cook Inlet crude oil. The state government of Alaska has since begun bidding procedures. Although the crude available for bid is as little as 3600 b/d, I strongly feel this is the first step toward the crude oil trade between the US and Japan. On the other hand, the administration sent a report to Congress in June 1986 dealing with the export of North Slope crude from Alaska, placing much importance on it. The report's executive summary stated that '[t]he administration believes that reliance on market forces is the most effective means to promote US energy security,' and that 'lifting the ban on Alaskan North Slope crude oil exports would be in line with this objective'. It concludes, however, that 'the appropriate Federal agencies continue to review the prospects for Alaskan North Slope exports, in light of changing market conditions' since it involves many interested parties. The report also pointed out that in the event of the removal of the ban on the export, 870 000 b/d will be exported at the peak, and more than 30 tankers of four million tons will become unnecessary, displacing militarily useful tankers. In the US Congress there has been strong opposition to the removal of the ban on Alaskan crude exports for several reasons: energy security, the spirit of the construction of the Trans-Alaskan pipeline, and in the interests of the domestic maritime industry. It is quite natural for an energy producing country to have its own security measures as a producer, just as Japan, as an energy consuming nation, had adopted its policy of domestic refining for reasons of energy security. When it becomes a matter of energy security or national security, it is extremely difficult to convince another country that there is no cause for alarm. The advantages of the removal of the ban on the export to Japan cannot be argued within the same dimension as considerations of national security, such as the possible shortage of tankers that are militarily useful, although the removal would be very beneficial to Japan's diversification of oil sources, economic efficiency, and as a solution to the trade imbalance issue. Earlier in this chapter, I described the relationship between the US and Japan as being a complementary one. However if considered from the standpoint of national security, the situation becomes more complicated. In the bidding for the Alaskan Cook Inlet crude, there is included a clause stipulating that when the regulations of the Commerce Department are revised due to changes in supply and demand in the United States, and if the export becomes unavailable, the contract will be cancelled unilaterally. The insertion of this clause is understandable, but when viewed by the energy importer, it appears to mean that in times of a glut situation one can count on being provided with the energy, or perhaps even being requested to purchase more energy, while in the case of a tight supply and demand situation the export will be banned, as in past instances with other US commodities. It might follow that a mono-cultural country is more reliable as a supplier that is totally dependent on exports to sustain its national economy. This point should be further studied when considering expansion of the energy trade between the two countries, not only for the case of oil.

Coal

There are two issues associated with coal trade. First, the US has been requesting that Japan increase its import of coking coal. The second issue is projects to export coal to Japan to be realized in the mid- to long term. The first issue creates a friction problem associated with the decrease of coking coal imports from the US to Japan from its peak of 23.7 million tons (which correspond to 36 per cent of Japan's import of coking coal) in 1981 to 12.9 million tons in 1985. There are other background problems to be considered. First is the matter of cost. Since US coal's inland freight cost is higher, it is less competitive than coal from other sources. The average CIF (Cost of Insured Freight) price of imported coking coal to Japan is $58.7 per ton, while the price of US coal is $67.3 per ton. US coal is more costly by as much as $10 per ton. Second, following the first and second oil crises in the 1970s, the coal market became tight, and Japanese firms decided to develop coal mines in Australia and Canada by means of increased direct investment and the provision of loans. Now is the time of harvest for these efforts. Many of these mines are starting their production stage, and delivery to Japan has begun. However, given the current decline in steel production, Japanese are now putting forth requests and negotiating with these producers to cut back the amount of delivery. These situations have much impact on spot market contracts.

With respect to coal trade between Japan and the US, Japan purchases only ten to twenty million tons from the US, which is a giant producer of coal with an annual production of 800 million tons. The coal trade with Japanese importers amounts to between 2 and 3 per cent of the total US coal export, and accordingly, these have been usually covered by a one-year contract. At the time of writing Japanese steel producers are under heavy pressure due to expanding production in newly industrialized countries, the recent decline in steel production, and the strong yen: consequently, they have been obliged to reduce costs. Given this, it would be an extreme burden for Japanese steel producers of the private sector to continue to take coal delivery at a rate as much as ten dollars over its competitors. The most crucial point, I believe, is that US coal should recover its price competitiveness. At the time of this writing, the Japanese government is reviewing its medium term domestic coal policy, and the revised policy, announced in 1986 would cut the present production goal of twenty million ton a year in half. As a result of such a drastic cut in the Japanese coal industry, chances are likely to favour the import of US coal, provided that an effort is made to reduce cost.

I turn my attention now to the Beluga coal project of Alaska, a US–Japanese joint project, which is to develop the Beluga coal mine in southern Alaska with a view to starting production around 1990 to export steam coal at twelve million tons per year to Japan and other nations. The total development cost of this project is estimated to be $600 million. Currently, a pre-feasibility study is being conducted in the private sectors of both countries. After the study was started, a number of discouraging factors have emerged, such as the great decline in energy costs and the appreciation of the dollar against the currencies of the main coal producing countries. Nevertheless, it is to be hoped that great effort will be made for the adjustment of the total magnitude of the project to meet the starting date of production, and for cost reduction in order to make this project feasible and to promote this project as one of the long term co-operative projects between the two countries.

Liquefied Natural Gas

There are two LNG projects which have hitherto been discussed between the US and Japan, both in Alaska. They are the North Slope LNG Project and the Second Cook Inlet LNG Project. The former is a project to transport the gas from North Slope to the Pacific coast through a pipeline, then to liquefy it for export to Japan and other importers at the rate of ten million tons a year. It is targeted to begin at the start of the twenty-first century. A pre-feasibility study is currently being carried out in the private sectors of both countries. The latter of the two projects is to export the gas to be produced from the fields existing in the vicinity of Cook Inlet gas field, which now provides annually 960 000 tons of LNG, to Japan at the rate of some one million tons per year. This project is in the preliminary stages prior to the pre-feasibility study.

Currently, Japan imports LNG at a rate of 28 million tons per annum. Demand for LNG is estimated to grow to 36.5 million tons in 1990, and 40 million tons in 1995. Arrangements have already been made to meet this demand. Due to the inflexibility in price and supply, namely the 'oil-slide' clause in price and the 'take-or-pay' clause in supply, LNG has become less attractive to its users such as electricity and city gas companies. Given these conditions, it is very difficult to have a clear picture of the future of LNG. However, as I mentioned earlier, it is vitally important to look at energy issues or energy projects over a very long time span. I see the discussion and examination of the possibility of such projects, to be realized over the long term, as being very encouraging.

COOPERATION IN THE PACIFIC RIM

Lastly, I would like to comment on cooperation in the Pacific Rim region. At present, the Pacific Rim region is an area where dynamic economic growth is taking place. The decade between 1973 and 1983 recorded these high rates of economic growth: 5.7 per cent in Japan, 7.4 – 8.0 per cent in Korea, Taiwan and Hong Kong, and 5.1 – 7.8 per cent in ASEAN countries. While securing a stable supply of energy is an obvious prerequisite for sustainable economic development in the countries around the Pacific, Asian–Pacific countries, including Japan, depended 67.4 per cent on oil as their primary energy source in 1983. On the other hand, the Pacific Rim region abounds in various energy resources, such as coal, natural gas, oil and uranium. Among these, 50 per cent of the world reserve of coal exists in the Pacific Rim countries like the US, Canada, Australia, and China. The Asian–Pacific countries, including Japan, have adopted energy policies with more emphasis on coal, after experiencing two oil crises. Based on the energy plans of these countries, MITI, Japan's Ministry of International Trade and Industry, estimates that demand for steam coal in the Asian–Pacific Rim region will increase from the level of 53.5 million tons in 1984, to 89.1 million tons in 1990 and 140.4 million tons in 1995. Supposing the increase in steam coal demand would be met by coal from the US, Canada and Australia, the coal export from these countries to the Asian–Pacific Rim region is estimated to expand five times, from eighteen million tons in 1983 to 93 million tons in 1995.

The implementation of energy plans, particularly electricity development plans, in these countries will certainly contribute the following: (1) enhancement of energy security of resource-poor countries in the region; (2) an increase of export and investment in the resource-abundant countries in the region; (3) an increase in the welfare and political stability in the region; (4) an increase in demand and investment in less developed areas through a greater electrification rate. These long term visions formed the basis of my work when I was at MITI. My original idea was to promote the development of power generation by means of coal and LNG in the Pacific Rim region by utilizing coal and natural gas technologies which developed countries in this area possess as well as utilizing their development aid. Energy co-operation in the Pacific Rim is still at an embryonic stage, and there is no concrete plan of action as I write. The scope is too wide in time and in space. It is my sincere hope, and to be expected, that this will be pursued as one of the long term cooperation programmes between the US and Japan.

6 The Impact of Trade Problems on US–Japan Security Cooperation
Martin E. Weinstein

From the vantage point of the summer of 1986, it is clear that trade problems have not yet caused substantial damage to US–Japan security cooperation. The US–Japan Security Treaty is intact. Japan is still under the American nuclear umbrella. The US Seventh Fleet and Fifth Air Force continue to operate from bases in Japan, and together with US Army divisions in South Korea, provide Japan with a conventional defensive shield. The Japanese Self-Defence Forces are still not powerful enough to defend Japan. Their main functions are to raise the threshold of a Soviet attack, thus reinforcing the credibility of the Security Treaty, and also to help persuade Americans that Japan is making some effort to defend itself. The US–Japan Security Treaty continues to be what the Japanese government have always officially called it, an *anzen hosho*, a security guarantee, a guarantee extended by the US to Japan.

It is also abundantly clear as I write in the summer of 1986, that the justification for this security guarantee, which is the basis of US–Japan security cooperation, is not Japan's economic weakness. The Japanese economy has been sufficiently strong and productive to support large conventional forces since the 1960s, and Americans have repeatedly called for greater Japanese defence efforts and more burden sharing, with very little effect. The US–Japan security relationship is embedded in political–strategic perceptions and goals, in both Japan and in the United States. The resistance of these political–strategic perceptions and goals to the economic shocks and quarrels of the past two decades has shown us how deeply held and persistent they are. It would, however, be unrealistic to conclude that political and strategic considerations will remain forever impervious to economic forces. If the American voters and the Congress decide that trade deficits, declining industries and unemployment should be cured by protectionism, it is not likely that our security relations will escape the ensuing trade war without serious damage.

It may be worthwhile to remind ourselves what the political–strategic factors are that have shaped our security relationship with Japan. Since the creation of the present global system in the late 1940s and early 1950s, the United States and the Soviet Union have in fact been the principal adversaries in what is essentially a loosely bipolar world. In the 1970s, the Nixon, Ford and Carter administrations attempted to redefine and restructure the world in multi-polar terms, but the world did not respond. The American vision of a multi-polar, economically interdependent world, pursing detente and economic cooperation, did not materialize. The Soviets continued to act as though they were engaged in a global political–strategic contest with the US, in which arms build ups and political interventions were the major instruments of foreign policy. They demonstrated this in the Middle East, in Africa and in Central America as well as in Europe and in the Asian–Pacific region. OPEC did not respond to calls for economic interdependence and co-operation. It pushed oil prices up to $40 a barrel when it could, and then fell into disarray when the Saudis refused to continue cutting their production and sales in order to hold prices up for the Iranians and Libyans, who were trying to overthrow the Saudi government. The Chinese continued to purse a policy of pitting the barbarian super-powers against each other while trying to come to grips with their own fundamental problems of industrialization. Western Europe and Japan did not become autonomous centres of power. On the contrary, the extended oil crisis in the 1970s demonstrated that they were strategically dependent on the US.

By the time the Reagan administration took office in 1981, it was obvious that the United States had little choice but to resume its role as a super-power in a bipolar world. If a reasonably stable and secure global balance of power is to be maintained, the US must be militarily strong enough to counter the Soviet Union and must possess the will to use its power for this purpose. In essence, this means that the United States is the protector of the non-communist world against Soviet attacks and threats. The United States' allies, who are in reality their military wards, have not chosen this world any more than the Americans have. In general, they simply do not have the capability to defend themselves against the Soviets – only the US has that capability – and ultimately, their own military efforts do not count for much in providing for their security. If the US will guarantee their defence, they are reasonably safe. If not, what will become of them, and of the US? That is the basic political–strategic (reality) conception that underlies the US–Japan security relationship.

The problem is that while the political–strategic environment virtually dictates a super-power role for the United States, the US economy has not been performing up to super-power standards. The non-communist world which the US must protect is a world of competing industrial powers, and the US has not been holding its own in this economic competition – especially in relation to Japan.

A wide range of Japanese manufacturing industries have become world leaders in high quality, low cost production. Not only have the Japanese outsold American products in the international market place, they have also pushed vigorously into the American market itself, at the expense of the US automotive, electronics, television, steel and computer industries, to mention only the most prominent. In a number of industries, American producers have been able to make a good case that they are cost and quality competitive and ought to be able to sell more in Japan, which would reduce the US trade deficit and help American industry. Unfortunately, however, the overall picture of US and Japanese industrial performance from the late 1960s to the present indicates that in general American manufactured products have been getting less competitive. The following indices of output per man-hour in manufacturing and unit labour costs in manufacturing show why American industry has been losing ground at home and in the world, and why the struggle to open the Japanese market to American goods is not likely to solve US trade problems.

Table 6.1   Index of output per man-hour in manufacturing

	Japan	*United States*
1970	61	79
1976	93	98
1970	117	102
1981	126	105
1982	128	105

Note   1977 = 100
Source   US Commerce Department,
International Economic Indicators,
September 1983.

Table 6.2 Index of unit labour costs in
manufacturing in national currencies

	Japan	United States
1970	55	73
1976	98	95
1970	96	117
1981	102	140
1982	104	153

Note 1977 = 100
Source US Commerce Department,
International Economic Indicators,
September 1983.

The Japanese have more than doubled their per man-hour productivity while not quite doubling their industrial wages. Wages in US manufacturing industries have more than doubled, while productivity has increased by only 25 per cent. Americans have earned more than they have produced, and the quality and price of Japanese manufactured goods have been irresistible to American consumers. That is the basic cause of the trade deficit, and of the declining condition of many American industries.

This analysis suggests that while the US cannot escape its role as a strategic super-power, it could fail in that role if it is unable to compete successfully in the world market place, and most especially in its own market. However, restricting imports in an effort to protect American industries and jobs is not a way of competing at all. It is a way to escape the competition and to undermine the relatively free, open international market place which the United States created after the Second World War, to be the economic foundation for the stable, peaceful world order which Americans have been trying to build. Nevertheless, protectionism has been steadily growing in strength and legitimacy in the United States since 1970. It has become one of the main planks of the Democratic party platform, and it attracts an increasing number of Republicans as a solution for the US trade deficit, business losses and failures and unemployment. It was a major issue in the 1986 congressional election, and in the 1988 presidential election.

Speaker Thomas T. O'Neill, Jr. sounded the protectionist theme in what has become a typical fashion in a speech to a rally of textile workers in Washington, DC, when he said: 'With some hard work, we can send President Reagan a message on trade. We can say loud and clear that is time, Mr President, for you to take off your little "Stay the Course" button and start wearing a "Made in the USA button.""[1] On the same day, in Washington, Secretary of State George P. Shultz, addressing the President's Export Council, explained why the administration continued to oppose the dozens of protectionist bills in the Congress, which the Speaker was supporting. Secretary Shultz said: 'People should think of the strategic implications of a world of protectionism. Our trading partners will certainly retaliate, world trade will shrink, and we will all be worse off.' After going over the economic case against protectionism – higher prices, reduced quality and choice of goods, and the damage to all those US firms engaged directly and indirectly in foreign trade – Secretary Shultz pointed out that the protectionism, trade wars and recession of the 1930s had set the stage for the Second World War. Referring to the dangers of the protectionist legislation pending in Congress, he said: 'That's exactly where this virulent protectionism would take us. Enacting laws restricting American import of foreign goods sends a very undesirable message about our political objectives.'[2]

WHY JAPAN DOES NOT REARM

Although trade and economic problems between Japan and the United States have dominated the headlines in recent years and their security co-operation has appeared relatively untroubled, the Japanese government's tiny defence budget and small, lightly-armed Self-Defence Forces continue to puzzle and frustrate Americans. If trade problems and American economic conditions worsen, Japan's defence efforts and defence burden sharing will very likely become a source of tension again.

Given the strength of Japanese industry and its demonstrated technological sophistication, why does not Japan shoulder the burden of its own defence – if not entirely, then at least on the conventional level? Why does Japan spend only 1 per cent of its GNP on defence, while the US spends 7 per cent? After all, would not the Japanese have less manufactured goods to sell in America and in the world, if they were building and paying for all or most of the warships, tanks and aircraft necessary to offset Soviet conventional forces in Asia and the Western Pacific? In Congress, a Japanese military buildup has repeatedly been suggested as a fair way to strengthen security cooperation, which would also ease the growing strain in US–Japan economic ties. In the early years of the Reagan administration, an energetic effort was made to induce the Japanese government to assume a larger strategic responsibility. That effort seemed to wane after Yasuhiro Nakasone became Prime Minister in 1983. Yet Prime Minister Nakasone was known in Japan as a hawk, a former Director-General of the Japan Defence Agency (JDA), and a known advocate throughout his political career of a defence buildup. Why as Prime Minister did Nakasone not do any better than his predecessors on the defence question?

The causes of Japan's continued low posture defence policy are numerous, complex and intrinsic to Japanese history since 1945. They can, however, be understood quite clearly in the context of recent Japanese politics. Within a few months of taking office in 1983, Prime Minister Nakasone met with President Reagan and clearly reaffirmed Japan's support of the Security Treaty and his intention to enlarge Japan's role in mutual defence arrangements. Moreover, in numerous public appearances in Japan, Prime Minister Nakasone expressed this same forthright, outspoken approach on defence policy. In December 1983, he called a General Election. In that election, the Liberal Democratic Party (LDP) lost 32 seats or 28 seats, depending on whether the Liberal Club was considered an independent party or an LDP faction. In either case, this was the party's worst election setback since it was established in 1955. Most political analysts in Japan, both in the LDP and in the media, ascribed a significant part of this loss to the Prime Minister's outspokenly hawkish behaviour. In effect, Prime Minister Nakasone had to choose between his outspoken hawkishness and the Prime Ministership. He chose to remain as Prime Minister, and his public position on defence became as low posture and inoffensive to the Japanese voters as the mildest of his predecessors. After two and a half years of playing down defence issues and concentrating on economic policy, Prime Minister Nakasone called the July 1986 General Election. The LDP gained 50 seats in the National Diet, its biggest gain and its greatest majority to date. The political message in Japan is too clear and strong to be ignored.

More than 40 years after Japan's traumatic defeat in the Second World War, the Japanese voters remain attached to their No War constitution and opposed to the maintenance of anything more than token armed forces. Although the Japanese who lived through and remember the war, the surrender and its immediate aftermath are now less than half the voting population, they are extremely influential in shaping both policy and opinion in Japan. Japan and the Japanese people were devastated by the Second World War. In addition to the millions of men killed in combat and the loss of a sizeable empire, the Japanese home islands and the Japanese civilian population suffered from air raids that left tens of millions of people homeless and from a sea blockade and food shortages that left virtually all Japanese hungry and most of the population suffering from malnutrition and its accompanying infections and diseases. In a study I am doing of conservative Japanese leaders in their 40s and 50s, I have found that the war and occupation was perhaps the most formative experience of their lives and that, despite more than three decades of security and growing affluence, almost all of them are still reluctant to consider any military or strategic role for Japan.

Those younger Japanese voters under 40, who can have no memory of the war and its immediate aftermath, have been deeply influenced by a very effective system of public education and by a generation of Japanese teachers who have made Article 9 of the constitution for postwar Japan what the Emperor was to pre-war Japan – a sacred principle. Since the aversion of the younger voters to defence questions is based on principle rather than personal experience, it may not be as deep as their parents' aversion. Nevertheless, as Prime Minister Nakasone discovered, despite their affluence and self-confidence, and despite ample evidence during the last ten years of Soviet military power and aggressiveness, an overwhelming majority of these younger voters oppose a defence buildup.

The Japanese voter's negative attitude toward the defence question plays directly into the factional struggles in the LDP. The Prime Minister of Japan is the head of a coalition of LDP factions, the leaders of which are all hoping to become Prime Ministers themselves. They are, as a general rule, waiting for the incumbent to be pushed out of office and are manoeuvring for the succession. If a Japanese Prime Minister gets into political trouble on a defence issue, he cannot count on the support of his LDP colleagues.

In addition to these political factors, there is also a powerful set of strategic considerations which inhibit a defence buildup in Japan. Ever since the late 1950s, there has been a quiet, behind-the-scenes debate going on at the upper levels of the bureaucracy on the need for a defence buildup. Generally speaking, officials from the Foreign Ministry and the National Defence Agency have favoured a bigger defence budget. Foreign Ministry officials have usually argued that a bigger defence budget was necessary to keep the goodwill of the American people and Congress, which are the basis of the American security guarantee. Defence Ministry officials have frequently argued that the reduction of American forces in Asia and/or the Soviet military buildup necessitated an increase of Japanese forces to maintain a stable military balance in the region.

The economic bureaucrats, from the Finance Ministry, the Ministry of International Trade and Industry (MITI) and the Economic Planning Agency (EPA), have consistently and successfully resisted these arguments. Of course, their primary concern has been to hold down the government budget, and to allocate resources to productive industries. However, the economic bureaucracy has also addressed the strategic question with care and intelligence. Their basic arguments have been that the Seventh Fleet, the Fifth Air Force and US Army divisions in South Korea are adequate to deter Soviet attacks and threats against Japanese vital interests. They have been most reluctant to enlarge Japan's responsibility for its own defence because they believe that in this nuclear age a resource dependent Japan cannot defend itself, and that it would be dangerous to start a defence buildup that implied that it could.

Although Japan has the second most powerful industrial economy in the world, its military position is extremely vulnerable. Firstly, the bulk of Japan's population and industries are concentrated along a small coastal plane stretching from Tokyo to Osaka. They could be destroyed by 24 nuclear missiles. Secondly, Japan is heavily dependent, much more so than either the United States or the Soviet Union, upon food and industrial raw materials imported from all over the world. (see Table 6.3) To even make a pretence of protecting its vital shipping, Japan would require a navy and air force second to none – a navy and an air force that is beyond its capacity to build. Finally, it is argued that a Japanese military buildup would be more likely to destabilize than stabilize the Asian–Pacific region, especially if it took place in the context of a reduced American military role. As much as they complain about American imperialism, the Soviets, the Chinese and the North Koreans all operate on the assumption that the Americans are not aggressive and dangerous. Would that be the case if Japan tried to fill some of America's military missions in the region? As reasonable and fair as the arguments for more defence burden sharing appear to be, they do not come to grips with this central question. Is it realistic and prudent to talk about US and

Table 6.3 International comparison of overseas dependence on key resources, 1979

	Japan (%)	United Statets (%)	West Germany (%)
All energy sources	87.0	20.6	57.7
coal	79.2	−9.6	−8.7
oil	99.8	42.3	95.8
natural gas	88.7	5.8	65.8
Iron Ore	98.6	29.7	96.9
Copper	95.6	33.5	99.9
Lead	82.4	59.9	90.9
Zinc	68.7	70.6	71.9
Tin	97.7	100.0	100.0
Aluminium	100.0	63.6	100.0
Nickel	100.0	93.0	100.0
Lumber	62.9	3.8	20.7
Wool	100.0	23.2	92.3
Cotton	100.0	−84.4	100.0
Soybeans	95.4	−51.2	100.0
Corn	100.0	−42.9	79.1
Wheat	93.0	−147.1	−0.8

Note Negative numbers mean that not only is domestic demand met from domestic supplies but that exports occur as well. Minus 100 per cent implies exports are as large as domestic demand.

Source MITI data, as reproduced in Japan Economic Institute, 'Japan's Dependence on Overseas Raw Materials' (Washington DC: Japan Economic Institute, July 1982, p. 9.

Japanese military forces and missions in the Western Pacific and Asia as though they are interchangeable parts in a machine?

NEGOTIATING TRADE PROBLEMS – SYMBOLS AND SUBSTANCE

The main reason that trade problems have not done any substantial damage to US–Japan security cooperation is that both governments have consciously and carefully done their best to compartmentalize these two issues. Moreover, an overview of the US–Japan trade negotiations since the 1960s also suggests that in addition to avoiding security issues, the negotiators have understandably concentrated on very specific, relatively short term trade questions and, in most cases, they have concluded satisfactory agreements on these questions. Nevertheless, despite numerous trade agreements on textiles, steel, television sets, and cars, amongst others, the imbalance in US bilateral trade has continued to worsen, American industries have continued to decline, and the political pressures for a protectionist response have grown.[3] In 1969, the Nixon administration was upset by a $1.4 billion bilateral trade deficit. In 1986, the Reagan administration was forced to cope with a deficit that approached $60 billion.

The current US approach is to focus on devaluing the dollar to the point of making American goods competitive with Japanese. Although currency exchange rates certainly affect the terms of trade, they do not deal with the problems of industrial productivity and quality which appear to be the basic cause of American economic difficulties. These problems appear to be the result of a pattern of extremely high consumption and very low rates of savings and productive investment. A cheaper dollar can buy time for American industry and create a more favourable environment for productive investments, but as the British have shown us, currency devaluations do not automatically produce industrial reforms and revitalization.

Why have the negotiators evaded the basic questions? It was probably due to their suspicion that virtually the entire US and Japanese economic systems lie at the heart of the problem. As the complainant in these negotiations, and as the senior partner in the relationship, the US has generally defined the issues to be dealt with. In the late 1960s and early 1970s it was not clear that increases in Japanese productivity would continue to dramatically outstrip those in the US. On the contrary, the prevalent thinking in those days was that the Japanese economic miracle was in large measure a result of Japan's recovery from its devastation in the Second World War, and that as Japan completed the recovery process its rate of productivity increases would level off and become comparable to those in the US.

When it became clear by the late 1970s and early 1980s that this was not happening, American policy makers were put in a most unenviable position. They realized that US industry needed revitalization, but the problem was how to accomplish this while still getting elected. People who have to run for office are reluctant to tell their constituents bluntly that they are not 'cutting the mustard'. President Carter, after having made a number of political blunders in public himself, did suggest that the American economy was lagging because the nation was suffering from a 'spiritual malaise', and his criticism was not well received. The Reagan administration's approach to fundamental economic difficulties was supply-side economics – shrink the government, reduce taxes, put more money in the hands of private investors and consumers, and the result should be more productive investment, greater consumer demand, and revitalized American industries – without hurting anyone's feelings. Unfortunately, while taxes have been reduced, government expenditures, especially defence expenditures, have soared. The result has been an unprecedented public debt, and a surge in demand by both the government and private consumers that has not been met by American industry, but by foreign industries, especially Japan's.

The basic reason that negotiators have not solved the trade problem is that responsible, elected American policy makers have realized that it goes far deeper than the current bilateral trade imbalance and have correctly perceived the trade negotiations as a way to buy time and contain protectionist pressures while finding ways to revitalize US industry. In recent years, Japan has been exhorted to stimulate its domestic demand and shift away from its aggressive export policies. Some shifts in this direction would help, but so long as Japanese industry continues in its present path of high quality and low cost, Japanese goods will become more competitive in the world market and in the US market, as well as in Japan.

The Japanese government has been quite willing to cooperate in this negotiating process, realizing that it has been a device for gaining time and containing protectionist pressures. It has had to deal with interest groups in Japan, in the bureaucracy and in the business world, which have on occasion vociferously opposed its compromises and concessions to the US. The most spectacular instance was the US–Japan textile dispute of the early 1970s. In that case, the Japanese textile industry which was itself in a state of decline, refused to cooperate with the government of Prime Minister Eisaku Sato in restricting in exports to the United States. President Richard Nixon believed that he had a promise from Prime Minister Sato that such restrictions would be forthcoming as a *quid pro quo* for the reversion of Okinawa to Japanese administrative control. President Nixon produced on the Okinawa side of the deal, but Prime Minister Sato was not able to produce on the textile export restrictions. The result was an acrimonious dispute that contributed to one of the most tense and dangerous periods in postwar US–Japanese reliations. That period included the secret visits to Peking by Henry Kissinger in July 1971, the forced revaluation of the yen a month later, and then an ultimatum to the Japanese government to accept American terms on textiles or have restrictions imposed unilaterally by the US.[4] The textile dispute is a good example of how quickly a trade problem can spill over into political relations.

Following the textile dispute, the Japanese government and business world seems to have concluded that a major part of their problem in 1970 and 1971 was not being sufficiently well informed about what the White House, Congress and numerous American pressure groups were thinking and doing on trade policy. Consequently, the Japanese have since invested in a huge lobby in Washington, composed of lawyers, business consultants and former US officials. The main function of this lobby seems to be to keep the Japanese informed of what is going on in Washington, and to protect them from the kinds of shocks and surprises that hit them in 1971.

On a micro level, the US–Japan trade negotiations have been relatively successful. They have concluded dozens of orderly marketing agreements. The Japanese government has also responded to American arguments for liberalization of the Japanese market by frequently removing restrictions to the point that Japan is now among the most liberal trading countries in the world. On a macro level, however, the trade negotiations have not alleviated the problem. They may even have unintentionally contributed to its aggravation. Firstly, they have helped to divert the American public's attention from the weakness of US manufacturing industries by raising the hope that Japanese voluntary export restraints and trade liberalization measures would solve the trade problem. Secondly, by having implied that they were a solution and then having failed, the trade negotiations have unwittingly strengthened the protectionist movement. The protectionists point to the long list of partial, compromise restrictions on trade that have been reached, and conclude that the medicine has not been strong enough. Many of them can argue quite logically albeit unrealistically, that the US has been practising protectionism for years, but has not been practising it thoroughly and energetically enough for it to be effective. This is the danger of using orderly marketing agreements to ward off protectionist legislation. When they do not work, they tend to pave the way for protectionism.

IS INDUSTRIAL POLICY THE SOLUTION?

Having acknowledged that the quality and efficiency of American manufacturing industries is at the heart of their economic and trade problems, the obvious next step is to find ways to improve that quality and efficiency. And what could be more counter-productive than to give too much importance to Japan's industrial policy and to the role of the Ministry of International Trade and Industry (MITI) in the Japanese economic miracle?

First of all, the heyday of industrial policy and of MITI's authority and influence were in the 1950s and early 1960s, when Japan was in the process of rebuilding its war-shattered economy and was extremely short on investment capital. In that situation, given the traditional role of the higher level civil servants in Japan, it was quite natural for MITI and Finance Ministry officials to consult with bankers and industrialists to decide where the scarce investment funds would go. In those days, MITI officials made a persuasive case for giving preference to heavy and chemical industries over light industries and consumer goods, for exports over domestic consumption, for steel, shipbuilding, chemicals and later petrochemicals. There is no doubt that the MITI plan worked and set Japan on the road to its present affluence and international competitiveness. However, it is hard to see how American economy at the end of the 1980s can be compared to Japan's in the early 1950s.

Industrial policy in Japan in the 1950s and the early 1960s also included protectionist measures – restrictions on imports, restrictions on technology transfers and on both the inward and outward flow of currency and investments. In the 1950s, Japanese protectionism was tolerable. Japan was economically so weak, its prospects so dim, and its economic impact on the United States and the world so negligible, that its protectionism could be temporarily condoned. Obviously, in all these respects the position of the United States in the world economy in the closing years of this century is diametrically opposite to that of Japan in the 1950s. American protectionism would have enormous effect not only on Japan, but on the entire world economy, and it would almost certainly lead to retaliation and mutually destructive trade wars.

It should be kept in mind that what is usually referred to as industrial policy was substantially weakened, perhaps even eclipsed, in Japan by the end of the 1960s when international and American pressures forced Japan to commit itself to liberalization of its trade and foreign exchange practices. Once Japan had set out on the path of liberalization, it ultimately had to dismantle the import quotas, foreign exchange controls and the controls on the import of technology which had been the basis of MITI's power in the early postwar years.

MITI's initial reaction was to draft temporary measures of law that would have enabled it to organize business, labour, and government into consultative councils to decide the future of each industry that was deemed crucial to the economy's future. The law would also have given MITI some power to direct bank lending to crucial industries. Had this law been passed, it would have perpetuated and even strengthened MITI's earlier position. However, the bankers and industrialists of Japan were alarmed by the part of the law that would have given MITI control over the flow of investments to industry. For that reason they pressured LDP politicians not to introduce the legislation. Opposition parties joined in opposing the law, which they believed emasculated the anti-monopoly law of the occupation period.[5]

In the end, this law, which really would have embodied industrial policy, never made it through the Diet. Instead, MITI was reduced to using lesser means, the most important of which was 'administrative guidance'. When MITI really had control over the allocation of bank loans, this guidance was authoritative. With the passing of the capital shortage and the lifting of government economic controls, however, administrative guidance came to rely much more heavily on the persuasiveness and potential profitability of MITI's proposals.

The early 1970s also brought even more restraints on the Japanese industrial policy maker. These included the budget, especially in the late 1970s and early 1980s. Japan has been faced with high government deficits and a relative decrease in the amount of money available to fund projects. MITI has been cutting back on special tax incentives for particular industries. Therefore, today MITI has far fewer instruments with which it can induce businesses to go along with its plans for industry. Moreover, MITI's position has also been offset to some extent by the growing authority of the Japan Fair Trade Commission, which was established in 1947 by the anti-monopoly law, but which languished through the 1950s and 1960s. In the mid-1970s, Japanese consumers discovered that they were paying far more for a Japanese produced television set than the American consumer was paying. As a result, many questions were raised about the pricing practices of major corporations, and a movement began to strengthen the anti-monopoly law and the Fair Trade Commission. Since 1977 when the law was amended, there has been one well-known court case involving administrative guidance in which the Tokyo High Court held that oil refiners were guilty of price fixing even though they had been guided to do it by MITI. Again, since price fixing and cartels were instruments of MITI's earlier industrial policy, its powers were further cut by this decision.[6]

Finally, in view of the differences between American and Japanese cultures and political traditions, it is highly doubtful that any departments or agencies in Washington could successfully assume roles comparable to those of MITI and the Finance Ministry in Tokyo. As Chalmers Johnson put it:

> The development of MITI was a harrowing process, but its special characteristics and the environment in which it works arise from the special interaction of the Japanese state and society. The Japanese built on known strengths: their bureaucracy, their *zaibatsu*, their banking system, their homogeneous society, and the markets available to them.

> This suggests that other nations seeking to emulate Japan's achievements might be better advised to fabricate the institutions of their developmental states from local materials. It might suggest, for example, that what a country like the United States needs is not what Japan has but, rather, less regulation and more incentives by the government for people to save, invest, work and compete internationally.[7]

REFLECTIONS ON THE FUTURE

This analysis of US–Japan trade problems and security cooperation suggests that it is not in the American interest nor is it realistic to expect that US trade and economic problems will be solved by protectionist measures, by Japanese rearmament, by bilateral trade negotiations, or by emulating Japan's industrial policy of the 1950s. Moreover, although the Japanese government will continue to co-operate in trying to ward off protectionism and trade wars, since it is painfully aware of how damaging these would be, it cannot be expected to stifle the efficiency, energy and competitiveness of its manufacturing sector. The most constructive and realistic path out of present American trade and economic problems is for Americans to own up to their lacklustre performance in manufacturing industries and to use their enormous natural advantages – the free institutions, natural resources and space – to rebuild a competitive position.

Probably the first and most crucial step which is now being taken is a widespread realization that high quality, competitively priced products are the indispensable prerequisite to manufacturing and business success. Imaginative financing and marketing can certainly contribute to profitability, but they cannot substitute for competitive products. The American automotive industry has been absorbing this lesson, and it will hopefully spread to other industries.

When, in the spring of 1983, the National Commission on Excellence in Education warned that '. . .our very future as a nation and people is threatened by a decline in the quality of our education system', it was thinking of the effect that American schools have on economic performance as well as the entire social and political fabric of the United States. It is neither necessary nor useful to try to import educational ideas or systems *in toto* from Japan or any other country. What is needed, however, is a responsible understanding of the fact that people's work habits and attitudes are shaped in the most basic sense by what they experience in school. If students learn that they will get by with shoddy, late, incompetent work they will develop the habit of shoddy, late, incompetent work. If they learn that dropping out of tough courses and having papers written for them are useful ways to appear to excel, they will develop habits of cheating and making their performance look better than it is. The work habits and attitudes absorbed in schools are at least as important as the subjects listed on the curriculum. The American industrial and business worlds might be able to revitalize themselves despite the educational system, but their task will be greatly assisted if American schools act on the principle that their main task is to educate children to competence, not to teach them how to get away with incompetence.

Perhaps the most promising areas in which government and legislative action could be taken are savings and investment. The real danger to United States–Japan security cooperation and to the entire international political economy is not trade problems, but the decline of American industry. If the vast array of taxes, fiscal and monetary policies are directed toward creating incentives for greater savings and more productive investments, we will have taken a most crucial and indispensable step toward industrial revitalization.

Notes

1. *The New York Times*, 31 July 1986, p. 1.
2. Ibid, p. 31.
3. A good detailed description of the negotiations can be found in Stephen D. Cohen (1985), *Uneasy Partnership: Competition and Conflict in US–Japanese Trade Relations* (Cambridge Mass: Ballinger Publishing Co.), especially chapters 1 and 6.

4. I. M. Destler, Hideo Sato, Priscilla Clapp and Haruhiro Fukui (1976), *Managing an Alliance: Politics of US–Japanese Relations* (Washington, DC: The Brookings Institutio), pps. 35–43.
5. Robert L. Innes (1986) 'Japan's Industrial Policy', *Toward a Better Understanding: US–Japan Relations* (Washington, DC: Foreign Service Institute) pp. 85–8.
6. Ibid, p. 88.
7. Chalmers Johnson (1984), *MITI and the Japanese Miracle* (Stanford: Stanford University Press), pp. 332–3.

7 Defence Burden Sharing between the US and Japan in the 1980s
James E. Auer

There are some who advocate closing US markets to Japanese goods. Other critics suggest linking US–Japan trade and defence issues, some even advocating the pullout of US forces from Japan if necessary as a way to lever Japan to decrease its trade surplus with the United States. They argue that if Japan spent more on defence, Japanese industry would not be as competitive. Still others call for Japan to buy more US defence equipment to counterbalance purchases of Toyotas, Sonys, and other high quality Japanese manufactured goods by Americans.

Talking about and threatening linkage is much easier than doing it. Closing US markets would certainly get Japan's attention, but it would be a dangerous policy. What about the effects in the US? Americans who purchase Japanese goods are not doing so under duress. Japanese products are not cheap. It is never wise to threaten what one is not prepared to do.

Yet some of these threats are more serious than others. Trade concerns are important, but even if many choose to suppress the dangers free nations face, steps which would affect important security concerns need to be more carefully thought through than some of these critics have done. For example, the majority of US forces which support Japan's defence are not stationed in Japanese territory. They are in the Western Pacific and Indian Ocean areas because it is in the interest of the United States to promote the stability which enables the Pacific Basin to be the economic centre of the globe. It is also in the US interest to defend its shores as far from them as possible – nearer to potential threats. Moreover, unless the US is prepared to compromise Pacific tranquillity in general, a reduction in US defence efforts in the region will have to be very carefully considered, given the nature of the threats in that region.

In reponse to those who want Japan to buy more military equipment from the US, Tokyo is already buying over one billion dollars' worth per year – virtually all of its front-line air and naval weapons systems and many other items which are less visible. Since Japan proscribes itself from selling military equipment to any foreign country, the trade balance in military hardware is 100 per cent in favour of the US.

There are critics in Japan, on the other hand, who claim that the US is not really interested in Japan increasing its defence efforts to contribute to a greater deterrent to Soviet military adventurism. They argue that such increases only make Japan a greater Soviet target and that what the Americans are really promoting is the purchase of American weapons rather than deterrence and stability. Critics on both sides of the Pacific must understand that defence of Japan is vital to America as well as Japan. The US must not ask Japan to do more simply because the US happens to be running a large trade deficit with Japan. To do so concedes logically that a lesser defence effort would be satisfactory if the US were to someday be the surplus country owing to large sales of Alaskan oil, Japan's needs for superior US high technology goods, even more Japanese tourists going to Hawaii, or whatever. The real and growing military threat facing both the United States and Japan is the reason the Reagan administration did not favour such linkage of the trade and defence issues.

American proponents of linkage are not always convinced of US needs for national defence. In fact, some of them claim that 'excessive' US defence spending, along with unfair Japanese trade practices, have damaged the American economy. Some feel qualified to speak on Japan's defence efforts, however, and criticize Tokyo on this score as well. For proof, they cite the well-known fact that Japan is spending about one per cent of its Gross National Product for defence while the United States spends more than six per cent. These spokesmen for linkage do not mention that Japan's GNP is sufficiently large that the defence budget is the third largest in the world and first among non-nuclear powers.

Exactly what Japan should do if it spent far greater sums on defence is unclear in statements of these critics. Presumably, they do not desire Tokyo to acquire nuclear weapons or to procure offensive forces to an extent which could worry Asian neighbours or which could be used to intimidate countries who threaten to put up trade barriers against Japanese exports. The question one must ask is, how much does each country, given its position in the world, and hazards to its existence, need to spend?

In 1986 the Soviet Union published a book entitled *Japan's Military Power*. Far from belittling Japan's defence efforts, Moscow's publication talked of the potential for rapid expansion, claiming that the Japanese Ground Self-Defence Force could quickly grow from its present 155 000-man size to more than 900 000. Aside from the typical rhetorical embellishments, the Soviet book represents a serious concern over Tokyo's contribution to the US–Japan defence partnership. Those who favour linkage of trade and defence issues should take note of the Soviet concern. Short of a meaningful arms control agreement, making Moscow believe that the price of armed conflict with the US and Japan would be too high is what deterrence in the Pacific is all about.

Is the Soviet Union concerned about a paper tiger whose percentage of defence spending in relation to GNP is less than that of any NATO country? A line drawn west from the northernmost tip of Hokkaido intersects the east coast of the Soviet Union at a point 300 miles north of the key Soviet naval port of Vladivostok. A similar line drawn west from the southernmost point of Okinawa Prefecture touches Taiwan. If Japan were to gain effective air and anti-submarine defence capability in the seas and skies surrounding its territory as called for in Tokyo's national defence policy, not only would Soviet ships and aircraft exiting from the Vladivostok area face surveillance for 300 miles to the frigid north, but they could not avoid Japanese shadowing to the south for more than 1000 miles. Thus, as the Japanese Self-Defence Forces continue their steady buildup as called for in the 1986–1990 Japanese defence programme, most of Soviet naval and air access to the Pacific theatre is becoming subject to close Japanese monitoring.

Yet is it reasonable to expect even these enhanced Japanese defence efforts of the 1990s to contain the nuclear-capable Soviet forces? In the 1980s the Soviets had more than 162 nuclear-tipped, mobile SS-20 missile sites based east of the Ural Mountains, all of which were capable of reaching Japanese territory. These were removed under the INF treaty, but the Soviets have ICBMs and other nuclear systems capable of reaching Japan. The Soviet naval and air forces in the Vladivostok area number more than 900 ships and 2000 combat aircraft, and the buildup continues. Despite an advantageous position, Japan might seem seriously under-armed, even for self-defence. Some Americans worry that Japan might fearfully opt for 'neutrality'.

The United States–Japan Treaty of Mutual Co-operation and Security provides the framework for a complementary defence partnership, and Japan does not stand alone against the Soviets in northeast Asia. US nuclear capability in the Pacific checks a Soviet blackmail threat to Japan as well as to the US. American air and naval capability deployed throughout the western Pacific and Indian Oceans complements Japanese anti-invasion forces and the Japanese sea and air defence forces which monitor Soviet Pacific access. 'Going neutral' is not a realistic Japanese option. Even the Japan Socialist Party which called for such a policy has been forced to re-examine it due to lack of public support. Japan is not a military super-power. However, because of geological realities and socio-political processes, Japan stands, like bars on a bear's cage, blocking free Soviet access to the Pacific. Japan can thus pursue a defence relationship with the US or play by Soviet rules.

Acting together, the US and Japan have the potential to provide Japan with a very secure self-defence and to render the entire Pacific a benign area in which to conduct free trade to each country's advantage. The Soviet rules would be far different, and the Japanese know so from experience. Japan's choice to cast its lot with the US makes eminent sense.

This does not suggest that Japan is without fault in the trade frictions which presently exist between Washington and Tokyo. Despite the fact that Japan has started to remove tariff and non-tariff barriers as the government's new 'Action Programme' is carried out, even greater efforts are needed lest Japan, in light of its economic super-power status, be seen as reaping the benefits of the free trade system without fully reciprocating in a responsible manner. Nor is it certain that the United States and Japan, by co-operating together in defence, have checkmated Soviet capabilities to threaten strategic destruction or otherwise to interfere with the free economies in the Pacific. Japan needs to accelerate its defence efforts even more. Japan should, in a reasonable period of time, meet its limited defence goals as befits its status as a member of the advanced free nations. A good start has been made. This point is clearly understood if one examines what has been achieved in our mutual defence efforts since 1981, and where the US and Japan are going together.

A relentless Soviet worldwide military buildup since the mid-1960s has continued, and intensified in the 1970s and 1980s, as the political and economic models of communism have lost all credibility in the non-Soviet influenced parts of the world. This is unlike the 1950s and 1960s, when some intellectuals in Western Europe, Japan, and in the United States thought that Marx, Lenin, and Mao Zedong provided models worthy of emulation. Faced with rejection everywhere, the Soviets have found it difficult to demonstrate anything their system can do well other than to build more, and, unfortunately, increasingly higher quality tanks, ships, guns, missiles, and aircraft. And much of the higher quality comes from technology purchased or stolen from the West rather than developed in the Soviet Union. Even under Mr Gorbachev's *glasnost* and *perestroika* Soviet Far East levels continued to increase through the end of the 1980s.

Worried about what Tokyo saw as a US drawdown in the Pacific following the war in Vietnam and the ill-advised and later reversed decision to remove US ground forces from the Republic of Korea in the late 1970s, Japan increased its defence spending by almost eight per cent per year in real terms throughout the 1970s. During this same 'detente' era, the United States and its NATO Allies moved much more slowly – even reduced expenditures – yet Japan was criticized by the Carter administration for not increasing its defence spending though Tokyo's increase was percentage-wise higher than that of the US and almost all other US allies.

But monetary figures are not the only important indicator. Japan's Self-Defence Forces have thirteen active army divisions – the US, by way of comparison, has seventeen. US divisions are much larger, but the Japanese number is impressive, since the direct threat of invasion is not immediate, and Japan's territory is smaller than the state of Montana. The Japanese naval arm has more than 50 modern destroyers, more than twice the number in the US Seventh Fleet which has responsibility for the entire Western Pacific and Indian Oceans. The Japanese naval air force has on hand or on order 100 P3C ORIONs, America's most modern anti-submarine aircraft, which is more than three times as many as are in the US Seventh Fleet. The Japanese Air Self-Defence Force already has as many interceptors as the US Air Force has guarding the continental United States. By 1990 the Japanese force will be spearheaded by 200 F-15 Eagles, the US Air Force's most advanced fighter.

Rather than pursue negotiations with key allies in an adversarial manner by arguing over what percentage of GNP is being spent on defence or what percentage of defence spending increase is contained in each year's national budget, the Reagan administration chose instead to pursue defence relations with its allies on the basis of roles and missions. Secretary Weinberger met with then Japanese Foreign Minister Ito in March 1981 and outlined what the United States was willing to do on Japan's behalf: namely, to provide a credible nuclear umbrella and to provide offensive striking power if necessary in the northwest Pacific – two types of capability Japan denies itself legally; to maintain US forces in the Republic of Korea; and to maintain security in the sealanes of the southwest Pacific and Indian Oceans, important oil lifelines necessary to Japan's economic vitality.

In May 1981, Prime Minister Suzuki visited Washington as the guest of President Reagan, and the two leaders agreed in a joint communique that a division of defence roles was appropriate. The significance of the communique, and of the Prime Minister's statement of national policy that Japan could, within the limits of its constitution, defend its territory, air and sealanes to a distance of 1000 miles, was initially overlooked by the media which concentrated on a Japanese domestic political squabble over the use of the word 'alliance' by the Prime Minister.

Nine years later, the use of the word 'alliance' is routine. The strategic significance of the meshing of the US and Japanese roles in severely complicating Soviet military operations in the Pacific is also becoming clear. Complaints have been heard from Moscow, but, more importantly, an atmosphere of respect and the reopening of US–Soviet arms control and Japan–Soviet diplomatic negotiations have come about.

Prior to 1985, Soviet conduct *vis-à-vis* Japan could hardly have been less heavy-handed, short of actual conflict. Japanese who surrendered in the Asian mainland at the close of the war were forced into slave labour, starved and brainwashed. Having expelled native citizens from Japan's Northern Territories illegally seized at the same time the Kurile Islands were retaken, the Soviets have refused to discuss the mere existence of a territorial question with Tokyo since the early 1970s. Instead, later in the 1970s, they began to fortify the Northern Territories with 10 000 troops and to add numerous MIG-23 aircraft. Although senior Japanese government officials have visited the Soviet Union, Moscow refused to send its Foreign Minister to Tokyo for more than ten years. This practice ended with Foreign Minister Eduard Shevardnadze's visit to Tokyo in 1986. When Prime Minister Suzuki attended the Brezhnev funeral in 1983, Andropov refused even a courtesy meeting. In 1984, Soviet officials in Tokyo held several press conferences to denounce US–Japan defence co-operation, a move the Soviets previously made only in underdeveloped countries. Allowing the US within its treaty rights to station two squadrons of F-16 aircraft at Misawa Air Base in northern Japan and to have Tomahawk-cruise-missile-capable US ships call at Japanese ports came in for Soviet censure.

Japan's decision to protect its sealanes to 1000 miles was particularly criticized. The significance of defence of the sealanes to 1000 miles has been sometimes misunderstood. Japan's Defence Agency does not propose, and the Pentagon has never suggested, that Japan station destroyers, anti-submarine patrol aircraft, or air-to-air interceptors every so many miles between Tokyo and Guam and between Osaka and the Bashi Channel. Although these two approximately 1000-mile routes represent major arteries of Japanese commerce, the best manner of defending Japan's strategic interests cannot and should not be reduced to a mechanical, tactical formula.

Japan, its Asian friends and trading partners, and the United States have all agreed that Japan should not become a regional defence power 'standing-in' for the United States in northeast Asia. The United States removes the very real threat of nuclear blackmail to Japan. Even within 1000 miles, the United States assumes any offensive mission requirements such as striking back at the Asian land mass if Japan comes under an attack launched from the Soviet Far East. As to how Japan provides for conventional, anti-invasion, air and sealane defence within 1000 miles, there is more than one way, and Japan is best served if it can provide a credible and flexible self-defence. For example, Japan is increasing its capability to blockade the straits leading from the Sea of Japan. This will significantly improve Japan's control of its sealanes southeast and southwest of mainland Japan because, if access to the open sea can be monitored and potentially denied to Soviet submarines, these submarines cannot credibly interfere with Japanese commerce in the Pacific.

To cite another example, Japan's Defence Agency is now studying-whether an Over-The-Horizon-Radar (OTHR) will aid its air defence. Some critics have maintained that such a radar system which provides a long range, large area, air-surveillance, early warning capability for a very low cost is useful only for defending aircraft carriers. Although the Defence Agency will make its own decision, the Pentagon's evaluation is that OTHR is a completely defensive system and the early warning intelligence it provides is useful to ships, aircraft, or to land bases which face a potential air threat. If Japan decides that such an OTHR system is cost effective and can be smoothly integrated into its own air defence posture, Japan may be able to reapply defence resources and have an effective self-defence tool which can be defensively deployed well within 1000 miles.

An earlier point cannot be over-emphasized. Defence to 1000 miles makes no sense for Japan if the United States is not working with Japan inside 1000 miles and is not defending Japan outside 1000 miles. If it had to stand up to Soviet intimidation single-handedly, Japan would be subject to blackmail in various forms (including nuclear) as well as threats of invasion or the interruption of shipping east of Cam Ranh Bay, off Okinawa, or in the Indian Ocean. Japan's complementary defence efforts with the United States inside 1000 miles, however, constitute a meaningful, legitimate self-defence role for Japan and, through the US–Japan division of defence responsibilities, provide critical defence to Japan, both near to, and far from Tokyo in areas vital to Japan's livelihood.

It is unclear how successful the US or the Japanese government will be in future negotiations with Moscow, but the Reagan administration sincerely believed Washington and Tokyo were on the right track. The US and Japan are engaged in co-operation which has worked and is being continued. Neither the United States nor Japan desires to fight the Soviet Union, and both countries hope the Soviets also want to continue to avoid armed conflict. The US–Japan defence partnership makes war in the Pacific difficult for the Soviets and, thus, not only acts as a deterrent, but also as a positive force arguing for arms negotiations with the potential of lowering both the danger of war and the terrific financial burdens. Some trade friction between the United States and Japan will continue. Hopefully this will decrease; however, it should not be surprising that the world's two most dynamic democracies and the largest financial powers in the world find themselves in competition in certain areas. The positive aspects of US–Japan cooperation and friendship far overshadow these problems. While he was US Ambassador to Japan Mike Mansfield would tell everyone who would listen of the importance of this partnership. While he was President, Ronald Reagan said that the US–Japan relationship is USA's most important bilateral tie, bar none.

Military-to-military the US–Japan defence relationship is thriving. Cooperation is at an all time high and Japan significantly supports the costs of keeping US forces based in Japan. With strong public support, the US–Japan alliance is truly unshakable and is the most significant influence for continuing peace in the Pacific community.

8 Trade Friction, Security Cooperation, and the Soviet Presence in Asia
Tsuneo Akaha

INTRODUCTION

The visible decline of the US hegemony in the liberal capitalist world since the 1970s has had profound consequences for American allies. First, the development has undercut the credibility of the United States as a reliable deterrent against the growing Soviet military might. Second, it has raised serious doubts about the ability of the United States to provide a credible leadership in the management of the international economic system. For Japan, this means Tokyo now has to seek ways to supplement, if not supplant, its security ties with Washington in the face of the growing Soviet presence in Asia on the one hand, and, on the other, search for an expanded role for itself in the management of the capitalist world economy. The ongoing debate in the country about the future of the Trans-Pacific alliance reflects Japan's effort in the first instance and the discussion about how to deal with the burgeoning US–Japanese trade gap represents Japan's effort in the second instance. The present chapter is an assessment of these processes.

The present study analyzes the impact of the US–Japanese trade friction on the security co-operation between the two countries with respect to the Soviet military expansion and political manoeuvring in Asia. The main argument of the study is that in the face of relentless Soviet military expansion in the Asian–Pacific region and in spite of the partial loss of American deterrence credibility in the region as well as the unwarranted politicization in the United States of the trade dispute across the Pacific, the security co-operation between Washington and Tokyo will continue in the foreseeable future. This analyst believes that short of a major, unlikely regional power realignment in the immediate future, Japan and the United States will continue to need each other because of their largely compatible

113

security interests in the region and that they will jointly overcome potentially damaging effects of the economic issue upon their political and security relations. Over the long haul, however, the author postulates that a deepening political conflict may cause serious strain in the Trans-Pacific alliance as Japan's burgeoning economic power and the declining US hegemony will move the two countries closer to a parity in regional influence.

This author believes, on the one hand, that the decline of US hegemony is caused primarily by the weakening of the US position in the capitalist world economy and by the deterioration of the US domestic economy and, on the other hand, that neither Japan nor any other American ally would be able or willing to replace the United States as the leader in the Western security alliance. The writer questions, however, whether the United States will be able to reverse its hegemonic decline by both maintaining military vigilance and reinvigorating its civilian industry. While Japan cannot and should not be expected to shoulder more than a modest security burden in Asia–Pacific, Tokyo is willing to expand its political role in the region. If a mature and stable relationship between the United States and Japan is to develop and if that relationship is to contribute to the peace and stability of the region, the United States must reprioritize its domestic and foreign policy programmes, with less emphasis on the military dimension of its relations with Japan and more on the political–economic aspects of the bilateral relations. Furthermore, the two governments should promote an open dialogue between the two countries if their policies are to be supported by broadly-based political coalitions within and between the United States and Japan. Should the two countries fail to move in this direction, either the two government's policies would lose their legitimacy, or incompatibilities in future US–Japanese security perspectives and interests would cause serious conflicts which might be more effectively exploited by the Soviet Union than has so far been the case.

The study is divided into two parts. The first part examines the mainstream US and Japanese perspectives on the military threat and political objectives of the Soviet Union, an acknowledged adversary of Washington and Tokyo. If close US–Japanese security co-operation is to continue, it is imperative that the two countries' assessment of their adversary's military capabilities and political objectives be sufficiently close. Indeed the study finds this to be the case. This despite the dynamic and fluid political situation in the region over the past few decades.

The second part discusses possible implications of the now perennial trade friction between the United States and Japan for their
future security co-operation. It posits several possible ways the trade
dispute can adversely affect the two countries' efforts to broaden
their security co-operation but notes that so far the potential economic–security linkage has not been exploited in either Washington or
Tokyo. The author points out that Washington's bilateral approach
to the US–Japan trade problems does not sit well with Tokyo's
emphasis on a multi-lateral approach to the management of international political economy. It warns that Washington's excessive and
'unfair' demand on Tokyo on the trade issue has the potential of
alienating the increasingly nationalistic Japanese including those
mainstream elements whose support for the bilateral security
co-operation is essential for stable relations across the Pacific. Should
the United States demand a correction of the trade gap in a manner
that threatens sustained Japanese economic growth the study argues,
this may result in the weakening of public support for Tokyo's
defence buildup plan and its security co-operation with Washington.
This would be a 'worst case scenario' which is unlikely to develop in
the foreseeable future, however. Assuming that both Washington
and Tokyo will continue to see each other as the closest and the most
important allies in the Asian–Pacific region, the study concludes that
a more realistic prognosis points to careful, if painful efforts in
Washington and in Tokyo to manage the trade friction and to
maintain stable but potentially costly security co-operation between
the two countries.

The study concludes with a brief speculation as to the longer term
prospects of US–Japanese relations. It takes the view that the now
perennial trade friction between the United States and Japan is a
manifestation of a more profound and more permanent, structural
feature of the bilateral relations. It also argues that the ongoing
debate in Japan about a comprehensive approach to national security
represents not a temporary Japanese preoccupation with the subject
but a genuine, long term search for a foreign policy that meets
Japan's security concerns and priorities which are defined in broader
than military terms. No longer can trade and other economic issues
dividing the United States and Japan be defined in purely economic
terms or on a bilateral basis alone; nor should warnings about the
growing nationalism in Japan be dismissed simply as pacifists' exagge-
rated fear of a resurgence of Japanese militarism. The short term
political wisdom of Washington and Tokyo notwithstanding, the

author expects development over the long haul of a more serious political conflict between the two countries. Should the United States fail to recognize this and respond effectively and appropriately by reinvigorating and expanding its industrial base and by reorienting its foreign policy toward a more politically sophisticated one which is based less on the nation's military might and more on its economic energies, the United States will contribute to its own demise, just as did the United Kingdom after its imperialist days of the nineteenth century.

US AND JAPANESE VIEWS ON THE SOVIET PRESENCE IN ASIA

US–Japanese Assessment of the Soviet Military Buildup in Asia

The postwar international environment surrounding Asia–Pacific has been dynamic and fluid. The certainty of a bipolar regional power balance in the 1940s and 1950s gave way to the uncertainty of a multi-polar power configuration in the subsequent decades, with the Sino–Soviet conflict, the Sino–US and Sino–Japanese reconciliations, the US defeat in Indochina, and Japanese rise to the status of global economic power. Fluidity in the political environment of Asia–Pacific in the last three decades notwithstanding, there has been one persistent pattern in the region since the 1970s, and that is the continued Soviet buildup of its Far Eastern and Pacific forces. The Soviet military buildup in Asia is viewed as alarming in both Washington and Tokyo.

A major Soviet military buildup in the region began in the middle of the 1970s, about the time of the US defeat in the Vietnam war, and according to Admiral William J. Crowe, Jr (Crowe, 1984: 54), Commander-in-Chief Pacific (CINCPAC), it shows no sign of slowing down. By 1982, the Soviets had deployed in the region almost one-third of its entire strategic missiles, including ICBMs and SLBMs; between one-quarter and one-third of their intermediate range nuclear missiles; almost a quarter of their air force's entire operational aircraft, including the much-feared Backfire bombers; about a quarter of their total naval strength assigned to what is now the largest of their naval fleets, that is, the Pacific Fleet; and about 360 000 ground troops in 49 divisions, including a division on the Japanese-claimed 'Northern Territories' just off the eastern coast of Hokkaido (*Defence of Japan*, 1982: 31–3).

Soviet nuclear deployments in the region have been viewed as particularly alarming in Washington and Tokyo alike. One US military analyst (Collins, 1985: 141) has written, 'The Sea of Okhotsk. . .is becoming a fortress for Soviet ballistic missile submarines with long range SLBMs that could strike point targets in the United States, if launched from semi-stationary positions.' Soviet long range theatre nuclear systems include 40 naval and 40 other Backfires east of Lake Baikal and obsolescing Badger bombers (Collins, 1985: 141). Three-warhead mobile SS-20 intermediate range ballistic missiles (IRBMs) have awesome destructive power. Each warhead has almost four times the yield of those of the US Poseidon SLBMs (150 kilotons vs. 40), and they are far more accurate. At the time of the INF treaty's ratification the Soviets had 135 launchers in central Siberia and east of Lake Baikal. Capable of reloading, they threatened targets in Alaska, the Aleutians, and along the US Pacific coast and US and allied bases throughout East Asia. Before INF mandated their destruction, the number of launchers was eventually expected to surpass 200 (Collins, 1985: 141), and Japan was certainly within their reach, a fact that was particularly alarming to Japan (*Defence of Japan*, 1984: 31).

Conventional deployments have also continued. Mostly deployed along the Sino–Soviet border, they are considered insufficient to directly influence the US–Soviet military balance (Collins, 1985: 141). Japanese defence authorities (*Defence of Japan*, 1984: 31) note that about 470 000 troops, formed into 52 divisions out of the entire Soviet ground force strength of about 1.91 million troops in 194 divisions, are now deployed along the Sino–Soviet border. Of these, 370 000 troops in 40 divisions are assigned east of Baikal. They are armed with qualitatively improved equipment such as T-72 tanks, armoured infantry fighting vehicles, surface-to-air missiles, and multi-rocket launchers.

The buildup of Soviet naval air power in recent years is also regarded in the United States and in Japan as one of the most alarming developments in the region's military balance. The Soviet Pacific Fleet is the largest single unit of the Soviet Navy. Composed of 87 major surface combatants and 122 submarines, these forces are considered an increasing threat to the US Seventh Fleet (*Defence of Japan*, 1984: 33). Most recent acquisitions include two VSTOL aircraft carriers, Victor III and Kilo class attack submarines, an Ivan Rogov amphibious ship, and air cushioned landing vehicles (Collins, 1985: 141). Most of the 40 navy Backfires in Maritime Province and on Kamchatka have arrived since 1980, together with 40 other

Backfires east of Lake Baikal and interceptors and fighter/attack aircraft. Soviet naval aircraft in the region outnumber all US in-theatre rivals (air force, navy, and marine) by more than two to one (Collins, 1985: 141). The primary naval aviation mission of the Backfires is believed to be interdiction of the West's vital sea lines of communication (SLOCs) and attack on the US Seventh Fleet in the event of war, rather than homeland defence (*Defence of Japan*, 1984: 30). The naval Backfires, for example, can cover sealanes as far as Midway, Guam, and the Philippines, then return home without refuelling (Collins: 141; O'Neill 1977). The Soviet base at Petropavlovsk on Kamchatka is said to offer the supersonic bombers almost unrestricted access to the open sea and with in-flight refuelling, there is virtually no point in the north Pacific which the bombers cannot reach (O'Neil, 1977: 34). The Japanese Defence Agency (*Defence of Japan*, 1982: 32) is alarmed: 'With the deployment of the Backfire bombers, the Soviet Far Eastern forces have now obtained a far more superior capability to conduct anti-ground and anti-ship operations than before. It seems that Japan's air defence and protection of the seaborne traffic around Japan would be gravely affected.'

Increasing Soviet warship and aircraft movements in the areas around Japan constitute a major irritant to the Japanese as well. Such manoeuvres include yearly flights of TU-22M Backfires over the Sea of Japan and frequent flights of TU-95 Bears and TU-16 Badgers over the Tsushima Straits. In April 1984, the *Minsk* was spotted passing through the Tsushima Straits on its way to a landing drill, the first of its kind, in the Gulf of Tonkin. In March of the same year, the US aircraft carrier *Kitty Hawk*, engaged in the joint 'Team Spirit 84' exercise with South Korea, collided with a Soviet Victor I class nuclear powered attack submarine off the coast of Japan. Naturally this caused consternation in the country (*Defence of Japan*, 1984: 36).

Another source of Japanese apprehension are the Soviet forward deployments in East Asia which now comprise five divisions in Mongolia, 8000–10 000 troops in the Kuriles, and a growing agglomeration in Vietnam. The Kurile occupation forces are mostly on the Japanese-claimed islands of Shikotan, Kunashiri, and Etorofu immediately off the coast of Hokkaido. Between December 1982 and August 1983 MiG-17s on Etorofu were replaced in quick succession by MiG-21s and then Mig-23s which now number more than twenty. A pair of air strips on Kunashiri are believed to be unoccupied but serviceable. Early warning radars and anti-submarine warfare (ASW) sensors along the Kurile chain help shield the Okhotsk sanctuary and Maritime Province (Collins, 1985: 141; *Defence of Japan*, 1984: 35). The Japanese Defence Agency (*Defence of Japan*, 1984: 35) states; 'It seems that the redeployment of ground troops on the Northern Territories has been done because the military importance of [islands]. . .has become greater with the increase in the strategic value of the Sea of Okhotsk as the waters for Soviet SSBN activities, and politically, for instance, the Soviet Union has aimed at forcing upon Japan the [*fait accompli*]' in the area.[1]

An additional concern to the Japanese and American defence authorities is the growing Soviet naval presence in the South China Sea and the Indian Ocean (Akaha, 1986). Regular deployment of a Soviet naval presence in the South China Sea in recent years has been facilitated by the 1978 Soviet–Vietnamese treaty of friendship and co-operation. The pact has provided the Soviets with permanent access to the naval facilities at Cam Ranh Bay and Da Nang, enabling them to maintain patrol operations over the South China Sea (*Defence of Japan*, 1982: 28). The increasing Soviet use of the air base at Da Nang, the expansion of port facilities at Kompong Som and at Ream in Kampuchea on the Gulf of Thailand, and the establishment of an electronic intelligence post at Cam Ranh Bay are seen by Japanese defence authorities (*Defence of Japan*, 1984: 27) as increasing the Soviet capability to influence the safety of SLOCs in the area. Admiral James D. Watkins of the US navy agrees. Watkins (1986: 7) writes: 'From [the naval base at Cam Ranh Bay] Soviet forces can strike key United States and friendly forces and installations as far north as Hong Kong,' and '[The Soviets] steadily improve their ability to sever vital sea lines of communication, while improving their ability to counter US crisis reaction moves.'

These alarming observations must be balanced, however, with more cautious assessments of the Soviet presence in and around southeast Asian waters. A Western naval analyst (Leifer, 1983: 21–22) observes, for example, that the Soviet Union is equally concerned about maintaining naval and commercial navigation through the strategic waters in the region and that Soviet competition with China for influence among ASEAN nations can also be best served by a friendly, non-threatening presence in the area. He concludes: 'Soviet sealane or maritime interdiction would entail both military–political and economic costs that the Soviet Union would be unlikely to take short of global conflagration in which normal economic considerations could well be discarded.' Moreover, as an

American analyst (Collins, 1985: 142) points out, the current Soviet lodgement in Vietnam has severe limitations, including the inability to sustain large naval forces for extended periods or repair extensive battle damage to ships. Moreover, one should remember repeated assurances of US commitment to the safety of the Pacific–Indian Ocean sea.[2] US forward deployments to the western Pacific are considered an essential part of American naval strategy in peacetime, in crisis, for deterrence in low-level warfighting, and for war termination. 'The probable centrepiece of Soviet strategy in global war would be a combined-arms assault against Europe, where they would seek a quick and decisive victory,' writes Admiral Watkins in describing the current US naval strategy. '[T]he Soviets would, of course, prefer to be able to concentrate on a single theatre;' Watkins declares, 'a central premise of US strategy is to deny [the Soviets] such an option' (Watkins, 1986: 7).

Soviet Political Gains in Asia: A Negative Account

There is general agreement among mainstream Japanese and American analysts of the Soviet behaviour in Asia–Pacific about Moscow's political objectives behind its incessant military buildup in the region. Soviet objectives are generally believed to include the following: (1) to counter the coalition of the United States and its allies and to develop a counter-coalition of pro-Moscow governments; (2) to isolate and to encircle China in order to keep it weak; (3) to discourage Japan from becoming a strong military ally of the United States or from establishing a closer relation with China; (4) to consolidate the ties among Indochinese communist states, that is, Vietnam, Laos, and Kampuchea, to weaken American and Chinese influence in southeast Asia and to prevent the formation of an anti-Soviet coalition in the area; (5) to increase Soviet naval and maritime power in the strategic waters of the western Pacific, South China Sea, and the Indian Ocean; and (6) to further strengthen friendly relations with the major non-aligned power in south Asia, India.[3]

Moscow has feared a possible Washington–Tokyo–Beijing (one might also add Seoul) coalition against the Soviet Union. The fear has so far not materialized. What we have instead are Washington's bilateral security alliance with Tokyo and with Seoul and limited Sino–American cooperation in the modernization of the latter's defence hardware. After Tokyo and Beijing signed a peace treaty in

1978 and the Chinese refused to extend its 1950 treaty of friendship and alliance with the Soviets beyond its expiration at the end of 1979, Moscow intensified its propaganda campaign against the possible tripartite (or quadripartite) coalition.

There are formidable obstacles to a tripartite or quadripartite coalition against the Soviets. Firstly, as was pointed out earlier, China is determined to maintain its independent posture toward the Soviet Union. While it will utilize the US military weight to counter the Soviet threat and use American and Japanese help in modernizing its economy, industry, and military capabilities, China will not be brought into an anti-Soviet coalition, much less alliance. Such a coalition would only cause the Soviets to increase their military investment against China. Beijing also continues to harbour apprehensions about political ambitions of a future military power in Japan, and China is generally satisfied with Washington's dominance in the US–Japanese alliance. Secondly, the United States, while hoping the present friendly relations between Tokyo and Beijing will continue as a political weight against Moscow, would not want Japan's technological assets to contribute too much to China's military development without some American control. Thirdly, China's direct contact with South Korea has only just begun, and Seoul's interest in expanded ties with China is based more on its fear of Soviet-backed provocation by Pyongyang than on a desire to establish any political coalition, much less a military alliance with Beijing. Finally, Japan is quite reluctant to expand its security ties with the United States beyond the existing bilateral framework. Japan's security policy is based on the interpretation of the country's constitution that prohibits Tokyo's participation in any collective security system. While a tripartite alliance among Washington, Tokyo, and Seoul has been proposed by some and feared by others, it only remains a theoretical possibility and a practical impossibility. The most that Washington can realistically hope and the most that Moscow should justifiably fear are a stepped-up political dialogue between Tokyo and Seoul about Soviet intentions in northeast Asia on the one hand and on the other, Japan's support for sustained economic growth in South Korea through economic aid and expanded ties, which some hope will help reduce Seoul's defence burden and maintain political stability in South Korea.

Moscow's attempt to block further strengthening of US–Japanese security cooperation against the Soviet Union has all but failed. Tokyo's attitude toward Moscow has become increasingly pointed since the end of the 1970s. The Soviet invasion of Afghanistan in 1979 prompted Japan to join in an international condemnation of that action and in the US-led boycott of the Moscow Olympics. Japan has not openly criticized the US decision to postpone indefinitely ratification of the 1979 SALT II agreement, but simply pleaded that the two super-powers make utmost efforts to reduce their strategic weapons. Since the super-power talks on strategic arms were resumed in June 1982, Japan has repeatedly reaffirmed its support for the US position. On the European INF talks that began in November 1979, Japan has stressed the importance of close consultation among the US allies, fearing adverse consequences of a European-focused agreement on the INF for Soviet deployments in Asia. Specifically, Tokyo has insisted that Washington would not accept a reduction of Soviet SS-20s in Europe that would result in an increase in the mobile theatre nuclear weapons in Asia and the final version of the treaty in fact mandated the destruction of Asian SS-20s, much to Tokyo's pleasure.

The more critical Japan became of Soviet foreign and strategic policies and the more public support Tokyo showed for Washington's approach, the more pointed became the Soviet accusation of Japan's participation in the US-led coalition against the Soviet Union. Prior to 1986 the Soviets charged that the Japanese were allowing the Americans to turn Japan into the 'Pentagon's forward base', a 'nuclear weapons carrying vessel' and an 'unsinkable aircraft carrier' and warned Japan that it would become a target of Soviet retaliation should Japan become a US nuclear base (*Yomiuri Shimbun*, 3 April, 1983: *Asahi Shimbun*, 3 April, 1983: 1 and 9 April, 1983: 2).[4]

Instead of having the intended effect, Moscow's attempt to intimidate Tokyo into a more submissive posture further cooled Japan's attitude toward the Soviet Union and pushed Tokyo into closer security co-operation with Washington (Kamiya, 1982; Kimura, 1985; Stockwin, 1985). The Soviets continue to be the most disliked people in Japan; the Japanese today are more fearful than ever before of the possible outbreak of war involving Japan and of the growing Soviet threat; and the influence of opposition forces in Japan, which has hitherto limited the speed of Japanese defence buildup and the scope of US–Japanese security cooperation, is gradually waning, in part because of the increasing apprehension among leftist supporters about Soviet intentions.[5] Moscow's continuing claim that it has no territorial dispute with Japan has also had a sobering effect on those in Japan who hoped for significantly improved relations between Tokyo and Moscow (cf. Kamiya, 1982).[6]

Contrary to Soviet wishes, the US–Japanese security cooperation has become stronger, not weaker, and broader, not narrower. After coming to power, Nakasone took specific steps to intensify his government's security arrangements with the United States. His predecessors, Masayoshi Ohira and Zenko Suzuki had paved the way for this by Ohira pledging that Japan would undertake sacrifices for the 'Western Community' and Suzuki publicly acknowledging that 'the US–Japanese alliance' was built on the two countries' 'shared values of democracy and liberty'. Suzuki had even committed Japan to take steps to build up its defence capabilities sufficient to protect sea lines of communication out to the distance of 1000 nautical miles from Japanese shores. Nakasone defined promotion of 'solidarity with Western countries, particularly with the United States', as 'the fundamental principle of Japanese diplomacy' and called the bilateral relations between Tokyo and Washington *unmei kyodotai*, or a community bound together by a common destiny (Kimura, 1986: 109–110).

Japan's response to the Soviet attempt to drive a wedge between Tokyo and Washington is also influenced by its own and American assessments of Moscow's successes and failures in achieving its other political objectives cited above. In northeast Asia, Soviet–Chinese competition for influence over North Korea has shown some changes since the late 1970s. Pyongyang's visible tilt toward Beijing in much of the 1970s was held back around 1978–80, as Kim Il-sung took cautious but significant steps to improve relations with the Soviets. However, the strains in North Korean–Soviet relations, based most importantly on the two countries' conflicting appraisals of the possibility of Korean reunification, have not disappeared and will most likely continue. So will Kim's balancing act between Moscow and Beijing, barring any major, unlikely breakthrough between either of the communist giants and Seoul (Clough, 1986). The US inability to effectuate any significant change in the relations between the two Koreas, Seoul's strong apprehension about any outsiders' attempt to impose a change in its relations with Pyongyang, the intensified super-power military rivalry in northeast Asia have contributed to the continuation of the stalemate between North and South Korea (Ha, 1986).

Under Brezhnev the Soviet attempt to encircle its communist rival, China, produced some gains, but for a substantial price. Through its strengthened ties with its newly gained Indochinese allies, Moscow created a major irritant for the Chinese (Zagoria and Simon, 1982; Simon, 1986; Jackson, 1986). Moscow's support for Vietnamese control of Kampuchea succeeded in frustrating the effort by the pro-Beijing opposition forces in that war-torn country to forge a viable alternative to the regime in power. Until recently the continued fighting made any serious effort to reduce the level of Sino–Soviet conflict virtually impossible. Recently both Moscow and Beijing have stepped up their efforts to put their relations on a more tolerable, if not satisfactory basis. The withdrawal in 1989 of all Vietnamese troops in Kampuchea represents the resolution of one of Beijing's three conditions for normalized relations with Moscow.[7]

The Soviet support for Vietnam also won them continued access to naval and air bases in Vietnam, but again at a substantial cost both economic and political. In 1982, Moscow supplied 200 000 tons of grain, all of Vietnam's oil needs, and 90 per cent of Hanoi's other imports (Simon, 1986: 93). Soviet aid to its southeast Asian ally amounts to about $1 billion annually (Scalapino, 1986: 35). Moreover, Soviet–Vietnamese ties have alerted the members of the Association of Southeast Asian Nations (ASEAN) to possible Vietnamese expansion in its neighbouring countries in Indochina and ironically prompted the ASEAN members to strengthen regional co-operation. Equally, the refugee problem resulting from the continuing war in Kampuchea has caused severe economic strains on its neighbouring countries, particularly Thailand, and this has led to sustained Japanese humanitarian and economic assistance to Thailand. Japan thus finds it difficult to restore normal relations with Vietnam, the source of the problem. Tokyo's diplomatic initiatives to serve as a possible intermediary between Vietnam and ASEAN countries are also strained because ASEAN countries are apprehensive about political settlement of the Kampuchean problem engineered by outsiders.

The Soviets have so far been unable to make any significant inroad into the mainstream politics of the Philippines, the country whose domestic political difficulties have caused some anxieties in both Washington and Tokyo (Akaha, 1986). Despite the political deterioration in that archipelagic state since the assassination of opposition leader Benigno Aquino, the United States has succeeded, with some luck, in holding the new government, headed by Mrs Aquino, to its standing commitment to allow US use of the Subic Bay naval base and the Clark airfield, at least until 1991 when the base agreements expire. The communist insurgents in the country have been badly split between pro-Moscow and pro-Beijing forces. Nor have they been able to score major political gains in the newly constituted Aquino government. There is much uncertainty about the future of the government, however, due to a possible takeover bid by the pro-Marcos elements, difficulties in developing a viable power sharing scheme involving the leftist groups and massive economic problems that Mrs Aquino must solve before she can consolidate her power on a long term basis.

In south Asia, the Soviets can pride themselves on their rather careful and sophisticated approach to maintaining close ties with India. The friendly Indo–Soviet relations have survived the Soviet invasion of Afghanistan, and the transition from Mrs Gandhi to Rajiv Gandhi is not expected to bring about any abrupt change in these relations, although apparently there have been some concerns in Moscow about India's future intentions (Scalapino, 1986: 35). Moscow's political success in south Asia notwithstanding, its attempt to bolster the Soviet maritime presence in the Indian Ocean has been countered by Washington's equally determined move to maintain its naval superiority in the area. The US presence in the Persian Gulf and its stepped-up campaign of intimidation against Libya have added to the US naval strength in the area (Akaha, 1986).

Finally, Soviet efforts to penetrate the South Pacific have produced only a token result in the form of a new fisheries agreement with Kiribati. The Soviets see some opportunities for expanding their influence in the *de facto* breakup of the ANZUS alliance, caused by the dispute between Washinton and Wellington over the latter's non-nuclear policy, and in the growing anti-nuclear sentiments throughout the South Pacific island countries. Conversely, however, the harder Moscow pushes for an increased presence in the region, the more potential Soviet threat the South Pacific nations are likely to see. At any rate, the Soviets do not have much to offer in the way of inducement (Millar, 1986). Even in New Zealand, where the anti-nuclear sentiment is very strong among its public, pro-Moscow elements are virtually non-existent. Nor is the Labour government led by Geoffrey Palmer assured a long term rule, and its replacement by the Conservatives may result in a reversal of the current policy of not allowing nuclear-armed ships into New Zealand ports. Furthermore, so far the US fear of the 'New Zealand syndrome' (Millar, 1986) spreading to other Pacific allies has not materialized.[8]

In summary, according to the mainstream American and Japanese assessments, the Soviet record of political achievements *vis-à-vis* its neighbours Japan, China, and North and South Korea has been largely negative and Moscow's gains in Indochina have been accompanied by substantial costs in its strained relations with ASEAN countries. Given the shared assessments of the Soviet military–political presence in Asia, security cooperation between Washington and Tokyo has proceeded fairly smoothly in the past decade. It is beyond the scope of this chapter to provide a detailed analysis of the evolution of US–Japan security cooperation. Suffice it to point out that Tokyo's efforts to meet the US expectations regarding Japan's role in the bilateral security relations and in the peace and security of Asia–Pacific include: the bolstering of Japan's naval and air power to defend its sea lines of communication to the distance of 1000 nautical miles; the Maritime Self-Defence Force's increased participation in joint naval exercises RIMPAC; increased Japanese cost sharing in support of the US forces in Japan; the working out of arrangements for the transfer of military–civilian dual-purpose technology to the United States; the deployment of US F-16's at the Misawa air base in Aomori Prefecture; continuing permission for US naval ships, suspected of carrying nuclear weapons, to make port calls in Japan; annual increases in defence spending at rates far outpacing most other government spending programmes; and closer and regularized consultation between the two governments on a broad range of international political, military, and economic issues.[9]

The importance of the bilateral security co-operation has ensured that the matter is given ample attention at the highest level of governments in Tokyo and in Washington. Close security ties between Washington and Tokyo are periodically affirmed at the summit meetings between the Japanese Prime Minister and the US President. Recent summits have also addressed the other pillar of US–Japanese relations, the economic dimension. It is this aspect that the second part will address.

TRADE FRICTION AND ITS EFFECT ON US–JAPAN SECURITY COOPERATION

Japan's Global Perspective on International Political Economy

Mainstream Japanese obervers (Sogo Anzenhosho Kenkyu Gurupu, 1980; Heiwamondai Kenkyukai, 1985, Tsushosangyosho and Sangyo-kozo Shingikai, 1982) see the growing trade friction between Japan and the United States not as a temporary problem that will soon disappear but as a lasting, structural problem that requires highest level attention in Tokyo and in Washington. They also see the problem in a broader context of major structural changes in the world economy. They point to the declining US hegemony in the liberal capitalist world. They note the emergence of Japan and the European Economic Community (EEC) as powerful economies, challenging the hitherto dominant position of the United States in the capitalist world economy. They also see the emergence of a highly nationalistic and increasingly sophisticated coalition of Third World countries, exemplified most remarkably by OPEC. These analysts see the importance of Japan's international economic position both in terms of how the world economic system affects Japan's economic security and from the perspective of how Japan's performance impacts upon the international system. They therefore call for an expanded role for Japan in the management of the international economic system and for necessary policy adjustments between Tokyo and Washington.

The increasingly global perspective of the mainstream Japanese is both a product of the growing Japanese self-confidence based on their economic successes of the postwar period and a result of their continuing sense of vulnerability to the vagaries of world political economy. The growing Japanese self-confidence and their chronic sense of vulnerability are clearly reflected in the ongoing debate in Japan on what has come to be known as comprehensive security. A study group originally established as a personal advisory group for Prime Minister Masayoshi Ohira on security issues declared that the clear US dominance in the international economic system has ended. In 1980 the group published its report (Sogo Anzenhosho Kenkyu Gurupu, 1980) (hereafter cited as the Inoki–Kosaka Report, taking the name of the chairman of the study group, Masamichi Inoki and the name of the rapporteur, Masataka Kosaka). The advisory group observed 'the US position has relatively declined because of the economic recovery and growth in the Western European countries and Japan.' 'Moreover', it pointed out:

the American economy itself has shown sluggishness since the latter half of the 1970s. Its productivity has grown at a very slow rate and the price of its goods has continued to climb. This seems to be more deeply rooted than a result of the failure of the [US] government's economic policy. . .There is no denying that the international competitiveness of the United States had declined, and, along with the massive increase in the US import of oil, this has caused the deterioration of its balance of payments and the depreciation of the US dollar. As a result, the international currency system based on the US dollar has been shaken.

'No longer is it possible for Japan,' declared the report, 'to depend on the international economic system and pursue its own economic interests without making a special contribution' to the stability of the IMF–GATT system (Sogo Anzenhosho Kenkyu Gurupu, 1980: 36–37).

Another major report on Japan's national security (Tsusho-sangyosho Sangyo, kozo, 1982) was released in 1982. It emphasizes Japan's economic vulnerabilities. Accepting the Inoki–Kosaka Report's assessment that the world has left the period of *Pax Americana*, the economic security report presents the recognition that Japan can no longer depend on the US ability to maintain stability in the global political economy. In the area of international trade, the report maintains that the liberalization of the trading system among the advanced industrial countries and between them and the developing countries is essential to the stability of the international economic system and warns against the dangers of growing protectionist sentiments in the advanced capitalist countries. The report then calls for Japan's active role in promoting free trade.

Some even compare the decline of the US economy to that of British economy from 1919 to 1931. One observer (Hayashi, 1985) warns that the decline of the US economy has undermined the very logic of free trade, and the world economy is at a divide that, once crossed, could well lead to a slide into protectionism.

As the Japanese look to participate actively in the construction of an alternative economic system to the one dominated by the United States, US–Japanese trade friction has important implications for the political and security relations between Washington and Tokyo. The following discussion offers several possibilities. First, from the dominant Japanese perspective just stated, a bilateral approach to the issues of trade is not expected to bring about desirable results; indeed it is assumed that exclusive focus on the bilateral trade imbalance is harmful in that it ignores the structural causes of the imbalance and the consequences of US–Japanese bilateral policy adjustments for the two countries' relations with other countries, particularly those in the Third World. Therefore, the Japanese prefer a multi-lateral approach to trade and other economic problems.

Second, there is the possibility that the essentially economic problem of trade imbalance between the United States and Japan may become linked, in a politically charged atmosphere in Washington and in Tokyo, to the primarily political and military considerations of US–Japan security cooperation. Such an issue linkage has been hinted at or feared in both the United States and Japan. So far, however, there is no public evidence that the linkage has been exploited by Washington or Tokyo. Third, the continuing trade dispute between Japan and the United States may result in major erosions in public confidence in the government in Tokyo. This also is yet to materialize but lingering concerns exist. Fourth, a solution to the trade conflict that may have an adverse effect on Japan's economic growth may cause political difficulties for the party in power in Tokyo. In view of the importance of Japan's economic growth for the country's political stability, a visible slowdown in economic expansion may reduce the ruling Liberal Democratic Party's credibility as the party in power. This, too, is offered as a possibility rather than as a statement of fact at this point. Fifth and finally, regardless of the outcome of the trade dispute, prolonged disputes in the trade issue area will likely promote a further rise in Japanese nationalism that may have a lasting effect on US–Japan political–security relations.

Bilateralism vs. Multilateralism: Japan's Comprehensive Security

Most mainstream Japanese (Hayashi, 1985; Ito and Kamiya, 1985; Hiraiwa and Okawara, 1985; Uraga, 1985; Shimomura, 1985) define the current period as one of multi-party management, which calls for multi-lateral coordination of international economic policies of the advanced industrialized countries. They no longer believe the United States can single-handedly support the international trade and currency regimes. They see an increasing role for Japan, if not to replace the declining US leadership, to become a key, co-equal participant in the multilateral management of the international economic system (Sato, 1985).

This is the conceptual framework within which the mainstream Japanese look at the current trade friction. From this perspective, the Japanese believe whatever policy adjustments may be made for solving the bilateral problem ought to be mutual, not one-sided and, equally important, Japan and the United States should recognize the definite limits to the effectiveness of a bilateral approach to the solution of their trade friction.

The Japanese are aware of the growing importance of their economy to Third World economies. According to a simulation study by the Industrial Structure Council of the Ministry of International Trade and Industry (MITI) a 30 per cent reduction in Japan's Gross Domestic Product (GDP) from 1982 to 1984 would have reduced the GDP growth in ASEAN countries in 1983 from the then projected 6.6 per cent to 4.7 per cent and in East Asian countries from the projected seven per cent to 4.3 per cent, as compared with reductions from 3.2 per cent to 3.1 per cent for the United States and no change, at 2.8 per cent, for the EC countries. The same decline in Japan's GDP would have cause the trade balance of ASEAN countries with Japan to jump from the projected deficit of $2.2 billion to $17.4 billion and in East Asian countries, from the expected deficit of $7.2 billion to $14.1 billion, as compared with increases in the US deficit from the anticipated $25 billion to $38.9 billion and the projected surplus for EC countries of $180 million to a deficit of $4.1 billion (Tsushosangyosho, 1982: 12).

To the extent that Japan's economic growth is dependent on its trade activities, bilateral corrective measures between Japan and the United States that would have an adverse effect on the former's economic growth would be resisted on the ground, at least in part, that such measures would be detrimental to Japan's role as a catalyst of political stability and economic growth in other Asian–Pacific nations. In fact, a report by Prime Minister Nakasone's private advisory group, published in 1985 argues that just as the British current account surplus before the Great Depression made possible its investment abroad and as the US chronic current account surplus enabled the US government and American multi-national corporations to provide the necessary economic assistance and capital investment for the postwar recovery efforts in Europe and Japan, so Japan's current account surplus is not in and of itself bad and that it should assist Japan in becoming a major exporter of capital, thus contributing to the stabilization of the world economy (Heiwamondai Kenkyukai, 1985: 46). Mainstream Japanese define Japan's economic aid to the Third World, particularly to the developing countries in Asia, as part of the nation's comprehensive security. The advisory group for Ohira had pointed out that Japan's military capabilities were strictly for the purpose of self-defence and Japan should not be expected to either influence or win friends in other countries by contributing such capabilities to their military security. The group's report had declared: '*Economic co-operation is the only active means Japan has in its international relations* (emphasis added)' (Sogo Anzenhosho Kenkyu Gurupu, 1980: 40).

These views are supported by the public as well. A Tokyo Broadcasting Systems' opinion poll in April 1986 shows 62 per cent of the Japanese interviewed believed Japan had become a world power with responsibilities to other nations. When asked how Japan should discharge its international responsibilities, 56 per cent answered that Tokyo should increase its economic aid to developing countries, 31 per cent said Japan should make more effort to reduce its trade imbalance with other countries, 22 per cent proposed Japan should accept more refugees from southeast Asia, and only 12 per cent said Japan should spend more on defence (*New York Times*, 3 May, 1985, p. 6).

Ironically, at the same time that the mainstream Japanese have cultivated an increasingly global, as opposed to bilateral, perspective on international political economy, the importance of the United States as Japan's bilateral trading partner has grown in recent years. As Table 8.1 indicates, Japan's exports to the United States in 1980 accounted for 24.2 per cent of Japan's total exports in value that year, and they have since grown annually and reached 35.2 per cent in 1984. Japan's imports from the United States have also grown during the same period: from 17.4 per cent of Japan's total imports in 1980

Table 8.1   Japan's leading trading partners, 1980–4 (percentage of world total)

	Japan's exports to					Japan's imports from				
	1980	1981	1982	1983	1984	1980	1981	1982	1983	1984
USA	24.2	25.4	26.2	29.1	35.2	17.4	17.7	18.3	19.5	19.7
EC	12.8	12.4	12.3	12.6	11.4	5.6	6.0	5.7	6.4	6.8
Saudi Arabia	3.7	3.9	4.8	4.6	3.3	13.9	15.0	15.6	12.3	10.8
Indonesia	2.7	2.7	3.1	2.4	1.8	9.4	9.3	9.1	8.3	8.2
PRC	3.9	3.4	2.5	3.3	4.2	3.1	3.7	4.1	4.0	4.4
Australia	2.6	3.1	3.3	2.9	4.2	5.0	5.2	5.3	5.3	5.3
ROK	4.1	3.7	3.5	4.1	4.2	2.1	2.4	2.5	2.7	3.1
West Germany	4.4	3.9	3.6	4.0	3.9	1.8	1.7	1.8	1.9	2.0
Canada	1.9	2.2	2.1	2.5	2.5	3.4	3.1	3.4	3.5	3.6
Taiwan	4.0	3.6	3.1	3.5	3.5	1.6	1.8	1.9	2.1	2.3

Sources   Keizai Koho Centre (Japan Institute for Social and Economic Affairs), *Japan, An International Comparison, 1983*, Tokyo: Keizai Koho Centre, 1983, p. 32; *Japan, An International Comparison, 1985*, Tokyo: Keizai Koho Centre, 1985, p. 40.

to 19.7 per cent in 1984. Ironically, as well, during the same period while the US global merchandise trade deficit increased fourfold, from $27 978 million in 1981 to $108 282 million in 1984, its deficit with Japan grew by about 115 per cent, from $15 801 million to $34 022 million (Keizai Koho Centre, 1985: 38).

In the end, however, Japan's approach to international economics will not be determined so much by these statistics as by the Japanese perception and expectation regarding their role in promoting political stability and economic development in the world. Particularly important in this context is the Japanese view that they have a special role to play in the developing countries in the Asian–Pacific region.

So far, Tokyo and Washington have managed to contain the potentially adverse effect of the gap in the two countries' frames of reference in their trade negotiations, but the gap has the potential to grow.

Trade-Security Linkage: The 'Free Ride' Criticism

Even if the United States and Japan agreed to confine their discussion on their trade friction to the bilateral framework, they might offer competing explanations for the widening trade imbalance across the Pacific and, therefore, look for incompatible solutions. The chronic trade imbalance may be seen as a failure of one side to appreciate the problems of the other and the latter may increasingly see the former as insensitive, selfish, and unfair. If bilateral corrective measures prove totally ineffective at worst or immediately ineffective at best, and if the trade gap grows, then efforts at policy co-ordination themselves may lose credibility. As domestic problems in the United States, such as unemployment and sluggish economic growth, are seen as insoluble through 'rational' policy adjustments, some may demand a political solution to the trade gap. Indeed this has occurred. As Japan's merchandise trade and current account surpluses have continued to grow despite the series of pledges and decisions in Tokyo to open Japan's market and to control export pressures, Japan bashing has increased and protectionist sentiment has mounted in the US Congress. This has prompted many Japanese (Shimomura, 1985; Komine, 1985; Shinpo, 1985) to criticize the US Congress as attempting to shift the blame from the United States to Japan.

Criticisms of scapegoating by the United States abound in Japan because many Japanese are not convinced at all that the bilateral trade problem is either significant or that Japan is to blame for it (Galenson and Galenson, 1986: 155).[10] First of all, many Japanese believe it is not the bilateral trade balance that is economically significant but the multi-lateral trade balance. They also believe that the current account balance is more important than the trade balance and that the large US services surpluses in the 1970s and early 1980s were sufficiently large to offset or exceed the US multi-lateral merchandise trade deficit. Second, many Japanese reject the notion that Japan's trade surplus is caused by the closed nature of the Japanese market. Third, given Japan's dependence on resource and food imports, they do not see anything wrong with the high proportion of manufactured goods in the total Japanese exports and relatively low percentage of imports accounted for by manufactured goods. Fourth, they deny that Japanese exports are an important source of unemployment in the United States. Fifth, they blame the dramatic increase in the trade imbalance in the early 1980s on the overvaluation of the dollar. Most of them in turn attribute the overvalued dollar to Washington's failure to control its budget deficit. Sixth, they point to the failure of US industry to plan ahead and invest in additional productive capacity. Seventh, they observe there is no coherent national economic policy in the United States. Eighth, many Japanese see efforts to export almost totally lacking among much of the US industry. Finally, they note that some pressures for Japanese imports into the United States have come from US industry itself (Cohen, 1985: 131–150).

Temptation to link the trade issue to the US–Japanese security relations has been mounting. The possible linkage, particularly with respect to Japan's defence spending and its trade surplus, has been hinted at or feared by many observers in Japan. For example, Professor Fuji Kamiya (Ito and Kamiya, 1985) of Keio University is concerned that the US–Japanese economic issues and Japan's defence spending have already been linked in the 'free rider' criticisms in the United States and warns that if the US Congress continues to make a public issue of Japan's defence efforts, the Japanese people's attitude toward the United States will turn sour. Professor Chalmers Johnson (Johnson, 1986) also cautions against the 'free ride' argument. He asserts that in the first half of the 1980s the large US budget outlays for national defence and the equally large federal budget deficits have forced Americans to borrow from foreigners and that one of the major lenders was Japan. Johnson (1986: 561–562) writes:

Japan could plausibly argue that it was itself paying for about a quarter of the American defence burden and that this was no free ride inasmuch as the Japanese loans to the United States were denominated in dollars, with each percentage point of decline of the dollar against the yen being also a percentage point of pure loss for Japanese investors.

The 'free ride' argument does not lose its appeal, however, and some in the United States see the possibility that under pressure from pro-protectionist forces, Washington may tie the trade dispute to the issue of Japanese defence spending and impose a *quid pro quo* demand on Japan. American observers (Galenson and Galenson, 1985: 157) note:

> It is important. . .that the United States realize that there is a conflict between its two objectives *vis-à-vis* Japan. Curbing imports from Japan will make it more difficult to persuade the Japanese to raise their defense expenditures. On the other hand, the importance of the American market to Japan gives the United States considerable leverage in defence discussions with Japan, and it might not be unreasonable to require a *quid pro quo* from Japan in return for the maintenance of relatively free trade between the two countries.

To date there has been no visible attempt in Washington to link the two sets of issues. As the US trade deficit continues its seemingly endless climb, however, and as Washington's painful effort to cut its budget deficit continues, as mandated by the Gramm–Rudman Amendment, the rising protectionist temperature in Congress may boil over into the issue of Japanese defence spending. As it was reported in July 1986 that Japan's trade surplus with the United States might exceed $60 billion in fiscal 1986, US Secretary of Commerce Malcolm Baldrige exclaimed that the United States was coming close to the point of 'unilaterally stopping imports of Japanese goods' (*Christian Science Monitor*, 30 July, 1986, pp. 7, 9). The Democratic Speaker of the House, Thomas P. O'Neill, Jr., called on President Reagan to change his lapel button from 'Stay the Course' to 'Made in the USA' (*New York Times*, 26 August, 1986, p. 26).

The protectionist fervour in Congress and the Reagan administration's anti-protectionist policy came to a showdown on 6 August,

1986. Congress almost overrode the Presidential veto on a bill earlier passed by Congress, designed to place strict limits on imports of textiles from twelve countries, mostly in Asia. The narrow margin of Congressional defeat, 276 to 149, or only eight votes short of the requisite two-thirds, indicated the growing popularity of protectionism in the United States. Amid reports that the US economy was growing significantly more slowly than had been hoped, Democrats vowed to use the issue in the Autumn election campaign (*New York Times*, 8 August, 1986, pp. 1, 13).

Under these circumstances, the Japanese fear the US administration may be forced to succumb to the temptation to link the trade and defence issues. After all, it was only a few months before the almost successful Congressional vote just cited that the Senate had passed by a vote of 88 to 7 an amendment strongly urging Japan to complete its 1000 mile sealane defence buildup by the end of the 1980s, to review its National Defence Programme Outline, discussed below, to substantially increase its defence spending by 1990, and to increase its share of the cost of the US forces maintenance in Japan (*Asahi Shimbun*, 12 June, 1986, evening, p. 1).

Concerns and apprehensions about the possible defence-trade linkage have produced several different reactions in Japan. First, pro-defence elements (for example, Kinko Sato, 1985; Takeuchi, 1986) advocate substantially strengthened Japanese defence capabilities commensurate with the nation's economic power and call for the abandonment of the post-1976 government policy to limit Japan's defence spending to less than one per cent of GNP.

Second, among those who endorse the existing policy of limiting defence spending under one per cent of GNP and of emphasizing Japan's economic contribution to international peace and security, there are those (for example, Hiraiwa and Okawara, 1985) who believe it is politically wise to make some sacrifices on the economic front even though such compromises are not altogether called for on purely economic grounds. This is a dangerous approach, however. Some will believe Tokyo is giving in to Washington when such a move is either unjustified on economic grounds or harmful to their interests. They look to their government with increasing frustration and dismay. In Japan's increasingly nationalistic political climate seeming weakness of the government will be harmful for its credibility. As a Western observer put it: 'It is. . .important that the United States should not push either defence or trade issues to the point of producing a popular reaction in Japan which could lose all that has been gained and once again polarize Japanese opinion' (Langdon, 1985: 406).

Third, among the status quo supporters on the security front there are some who advocate more systematic and ambitious co-operation between Japan and the United States on the economic front, rejecting both the defence–trade policy linkage and Japan's increased defence spending. One such analyst (Igarashi, 1985: 32) maintains that Japan should stop making piecemeal concessions on the trade issues but boldly promote the formulation of some form of international industrial policy that, among other things, facilitates economic development in both Japan and the United States, as well as in developing countries. He suggests, for example, the creation of an international co-operation fund contributed to by those in Japan and elsewhere whose interests are closely tied to exports.

Fourth, there are others (for example, Seizaburo Sato, 1985) who support both some concessions on the trade issues and moderate increases in defence spending but would hold in contempt Washington's attempt to link the two sets of issues. The two Prime Ministers' advisory groups cited above, for example, advocate significant defence spending increase. The spending they propose is substantially higher than the current level of slightly more than 1 per cent of GNP but no higher than two per cent of GNP. They maintain that such a spending increase would not turn Japan into a major military power; they counter the fear, expressed by many (for example, Sakamoto, 1986) in Japan, that the abandonment of the current defence ceiling would kill the political symbolism of the limit, namely, that Japan has nothing but peaceful intentions.

Yet others (for example, Miyazaki, 1985), particularly those who advocate comprehensive security policy, emphasize Japan's economic security more than military security. To them, Japan's continuing emphasis on economic contribution to international peace and security should not be viewed as Tokyo's attempt to hedge its international responsibility.

Recognizing the negligible effect that lengthy negotiations on product- and sector-specific market opening measures and trade practices in Japan have had on the bilateral trade imbalance, the Reagan administration decided to press for more fundamental changes in Japan's economic policies. In particular, Washington was reported to be pressing for increased domestic consumption and reduction of incentives for saving in Japan. Reduction of domestic taxes and boosting of domestic wages are hoped to expand Japanese appetite for foreign consumer goods (*Asian Wall Street Journal Weekly*, 31 March, 1986, p. 10). Tokyo's recent moves also point in the direction of structurally altering Japan's economy to one whose growth depends less on export expansion and more on increased consumer spending and imports. In April 1986 Japan's economic cabinet ministers adopted measures to spur economic growth and assist industry in fighting the negative effects of the yen's sharp rise. The package called for flexible implementation of monetary policy, stepped-up public works projects, urban development, housing construction, private investment, and the recycling of gains from the stronger yen. The package was received by Reagan administration officials as a potentially important political document that could lead to the most sweeping changes in Japan's economic behaviour since the Second World War. It was also hoped that the measures would help Japan achieve a 4 per cent GNP growth projected by the government for fiscal 1986 (*Asian Wall Street Journal Weekly*, 14 April, 1986, pp. 1, 10). The package will require major changes in the way things have been done in Japan and its implementation will be difficult, if not impossible. There was even speculation that the measures were designed as window dressing for the Tokyo summit scheduled for May of 1986 (*New York Times*, 29 April, 1989, pp. 27, 31).

The Fear of Export Contraction and Slowing Economic Growth

Correction of the bilateral trade imbalance in ways that would cause a substantial reduction in Japan's exports or a slowdown in its economic growth would likely have three important consequences for Japan's defence policy. Firstly, a reduction in exports would cause a slowdown in the nation's economic growth and, as a result, government revenue would grow at a slower rate than would be required to meet domestic spending needs. This would make sustained defence spending increases unachievable (cf. Galenson and Galenson, 1986). Secondly, a significantly slower economic growth would cause some erosion of the popularity of Japan's ruling party, the Liberal Democratic Party (LDP) (cf. Inoguchi, 1986: 49). Third, if these two effects take place, Japan's specific efforts to improve its defence capabilities in co-operation with the United States will face difficulties. This section will discuss these possibilities.

Table 8.2 shows that Japan's defence spending has steadily increased but remains below one per cent of GNP. Without the

Table 8.2   Trends in level and share of Japan's defence expenditures, fiscal years 1955–86

	Defence expenditures[a] (billion yen)	Change in amount over previous year	Ratio to GNP	Ratio to general account budget
1955	134.9	−3.3%	1.78%	13.61%
1960	156.9	0.6	1.23	9.99
1965	301.4	9.6	1.07	8.24
1970	569.5	17.7	0.79	7.16
1975	1 371.3	21.4	0.84	6.23
1978	1 901.0	12.4	0.90	5.54
1979	2 094.5	10.2	0.90	5.43
1980	2 230.2	6.5	0.90	5.24
1981	2 400.0	7.6	0.91	5.13
1982	2 586.1	7.8	0.93	5.21
1983	2 754.2	6.5	0.98	5.47
1984	2 934.6	6.5	0.99	5.80
1985	3 137.1	6.9	0.99	5.98
1986	3 343.5	6.6	0.99	6.18

[a] Initial budget.

Source   Keizai Koho Centre (Japan Institute for Social and Economic Affairs), *Japan 1985: An International Comparison*, Tokyo: Keizai Koho Centre, 1985, p. 86; *Japan 1986: An International Comparison,* Tokyo: Keizai Koho Centre, 1986: p. 86.

remarkable economic growth of the past decades, it is doubtful that Japan would have been able to increase its defence spending as much as it has.

The record of Japan's economic growth is shown in Table 8.3. Only in 1974 as a result of the oil crisis, did Japan's economy record a negative growth. Throughout the 1970s and the first half of the 1980s Japan outpaced other advanced capitalist countries in economic expansion. The decline in foreign demand caused by the second oil shock of 1979 and the global recession in the early 1980s again had a dampening effect on Japan's economic growth, although not nearly as severely as in the other industrialized countries.

The importance of Japan's foreign trade to its economic growth is more directly and clearly indicated by the statistics in Table 8.4, which shows the exports of goods and services as a proportion of GNP, the balance of trade surplus as a percent of goods exports, and the trade balance with the United States. Foreign trade is an important variable in assessing the future potential of Japan's

Table 8.3   Japan's nominal GDP and real growth rate,1973–86

	Nominal GDP (billion yen)	Nominal annual growth rate	Real annual growth rate	Real annual growth rate in USA	FRG	UK
1973	113 498	21.8	7.9	4.9	4.7	7.7
1974	134 244	19.3	−1.2	−0.6	0.3	−1.0
1975	148 327	10.5	2.6	−1.0	−1.6	−0.7
1976	166 573	12.3	4.8	4.8	5.4	3.8
1977	185 622	11.4	5.3	4.6	3.0	1.0
1978	204 404	10.1	5.1	5.2	2.9	3.6
1979	221 547	8.4	5.2	2.1	4.1	2.2
1980	240 176	8.4	4.4	−0.2	1.4	−2.3
1981	257 363	7.2	3.9	2.0	0.2	−1.4
1982	269 629	4.8	2.8	−2.5	−0.6	1.5
1983	260 257	3.9	3.2	3.7	1.2	3.4
1984	298 084	6.4	5.0	6.8	2.6	1.8
1985	317 305	6.3	4.2	2.5	2.6	—

Source   Keizai Koho Centre (Japan Institute for Social and Economic Affairs), *Japan 1985: An International Comparison*, Tokyo: Keizai Koho Centre, 1985: p. 12; *Japan 1986: An International Comparison*, Tokyo: Keizai Koho Centre, 1985, p. 12.

economy. The nation's economic growth has been export-led; its exports have increased even faster than its national product (Galenson and Galenson, 1986: 157).

A slowdown in Japan's economic performance, regardless of its causes, will intensify competition among government spending programmes. Table 8.5 shows Japan's general account outlays for fiscal 1985. The defence sector has done comparatively well in gaining a steadily increasing budget allocation in recent years. It increased by 6.9 per cent from fiscal 1984 to 1985 and by 6.58 per cent from 1985 to 1986, while most other spending items remained virtually unchanged or were reduced as they had during several previous years, with the exception of official development assistance, which has been increasing by an annual rate of about seven per cent.

In comparison with government expenditures in the United States and West Germany, Japanese government spending is relatively small, but Tokyo's revenue has been insufficient to cover even this relatively low level of government expenditure (Galenson and Galenson, 1986: 155). Since the 1970s, mounting public demands for improved standards of living and the increasing number of social

Table 8.4   Japanese foreign trade, 1972–83
(current prices)

	Trade with USA		
	Exports of goods and services as per cent of GNP	*Balance of trade surplus as per cent of goods exports*	*Percent by which exports exceeded imports*
1972	11.2%	32.0%	51.2%
1973	10.8	10.2	1.9
1974	14.5	2.6	1.0
1975	13.7	9.2	−0.4
1976	14.4	15.0	32.9
1977	13.9	21.8	59.1
1978	11.9	25.7	68.5
1979	12.7	1.8	29.2
1980	15.1	1.7	28.5
1981	16.6	13.4	52.6
1982	16.9	13.1	50.3
1983	15.8	21.6	52.2

Source   Walter Galenson and David W. Galenson, 'Japan and South Korea', in David B. H. Denoon, ed., *Constraints on Strategy: The Economics of Western Security,* Washington: Pergamon-Brassey's International Defence Publishers, 1986, p. 157.

welfare recipients have caused substantial increases in government spending on social welfare programmes. The government financed the growing needs with public bonds. As a result, the amount of outstanding public debt grew rapidly, from Y31 902 billion, or 16.8 per cent of GNP in 1977 to Y143 200 billion, or 42.5 per cent of GNP, in 1986 (Keizai Koho Centre, 1986: 83). Demands for social capital investment, particularly in such big spending items as housing, parks, sewerage and water supply, are expected to grow as the Japanese press their demands for improved quality of life. Pension and social security outlays are expected to grow so as to meet the needs of an ageing Japanese population (Galenson and Galenson, 1986: 158).

Under these circumstances, drastic increases in defence budget cannot be expected for the foreseeable future. Particularly if Japan's economy grows at significantly lower rates than it did in the 1970s, the 'bread or guns' debate will be high on the political agenda in the country. Indeed, due to the dramatic appreciation of the Japanese

Table 8.5   Japan's general account outlays, FY 1986

	Amount[a] (billion yen)	Change in amount over previous year	Change in amound over 1975[b]
Social Welfare	9 834.6	2.7%	2.5
Education, R&D	4 844.5	0.1	1.9
Public Bond Interest	11 319.5	10.7	10.8
Pensions	1 850.1	− 0.7	2.5
Grants to Local Government	10 185.0	5.1	2.3
Defence	3 343.5	6.6	2.6
Public Works	6 233.3	− 2.3	2.2
Aid for LDCs	623.2	6.3	3.2
Small Enterprise Assistance	205.2	− 5.1	1.6
Energy Measures	629.7	0.1	7.1
Food Management	596.2	−14.3	0.7
Other Items	4 083.7	− 5.6	1.5
Reserves	350.0	0.0	1.2
General Account, total	54 088.6	3.0	2.6

a.   Initial budget
b.   1975 = 1.0
Source   Keizai Koho Centre (Japan Institute for Social and Economic Affairs), *Japan 1986: An International Comparison*, Tokyo: Keizai Koho Centre, 1986, p. 80.

yen since September 1985, Japan's economic growth has slowed. During the first three months of 1986, Japan's economy shrank by 2.1 per cent (*New York Times*, 21 July, 1986, p. 20). Major research institutes and private-sector economists saw the government estimate of a 4 per cent inflation-adjusted growth in fiscal 1986 as too optimistic; they projected growth between 1.7 and 3 per cent for 1986, and the actual growth ended up being only 2.1 per cent. In the meantime, Japan's trade surplus keeps soaring, due in large part to the J-curve effect of the rise in the value of the yen. Analysts predict a current account surplus for fiscal 1986 at $84–89 billion, larger than the record surplus of the previous year (*Asian Wall Street Journal Weekly*, 14 July, 1986, P. 9)

The second related effect of a reduction in Japan's exports and a resulting slowdown in its economic growth will be an erosion of the political support for the ruling Liberal Democratic Party. In the postwar period the pro-US Liberal Democratic Party has made economic growth one of its fundamental policies and the policy has paid off (Inoguchi, 1986). Despite the difficult and sometimes unpopular decisions the LDP-dominated government has made on security matters, the government has been able to maintain its popular support in large measure because of its successful economic expansion policies. The Japanese and American obligations in their mutual security treaty are the costs that Tokyo and Washington have been willing to pay to maintain Japan's political loyalty to the western world. The US hegemonic protection over Japan has been a key feature of this arrangement. When the decline of the US power has begun to threaten the stability of the international environment, both militarily and economically, Tokyo has naturally begun to feel apprehensive. Now that the US hegemony has ended, can Japan sustain its economic growth and at the same time manage its trade friction with its ally across the Pacific? Particularly crucial will be the government's ability to bring about visible improvements in the quality of life among its people – an area where the government admits Japan is lagging far behind other advanced countries (Economic Planning Agency, 1983: 167).

Growing Japanese Nationalism and Obstacles to Full Security Cooperation

Growing self-confidence among the Japanese, as mentioned earlier may also pose a problem. Self-confidence, if challenged by what the Japanese perceive to be an American attempt at scapegoating Japan or excessive and unreasonable US demands on the trade issue, may likely turn into a nationalistic and recalcitrant attitude toward the US–Japan relations. Resulting strains in the bilateral relations would have important consequences for domestic politics.

After the disastrous results of the 1986 national elections, the opposition forces had good reason to overcome their differences and mount a comeback by forging a united front against the Liberal Democrats, and sensitive defence issues are likely to provide a focal point they may wish to exploit. Increasingly self-assured Japanese can be found across the political spectrum, from the conservatives on the right to the progressives on the left. Under strained US–Japanese economic relations, the anti-government forces would be able to make a larger inroad than in the past in appealing to Japanese nationalism. Alternatively, moderate opposition groups might find a common ground with some LDP members and form a coalition against the mainstream, pro-defence elements in the conservative party. This might intensify the continuing infighting among the major

LDP factions. Despite Nakasone's unprecedented popularity among the public, political foes within the ruling party raised serious issues with the Prime Minister during his tenure in office concerning defence and trade issues. And they are not likely to let up as they vie for the party presidency and the premiership, especially in light of the recent scandals and resulting rapid succession of three different Prime Ministers.

Growing nationalism in the country would make more palatable to the public an independent political and defence posture for Japan. This may or may not be accompanied by greater support for a major military buildup. If the perception of Soviet threat persisted, as it most likely would, and if the Japanese sense of insecurity should grow as a result of an irreversible deterioration in US–Japanese relations, support for political independence would likely grow in parallel with support for military buildup in Japan. A Gaullist Japan, with an independent political mind and major military muscle, would surely cast a dark cloud over the future of the peace and security in Asia–Pacific. Rather than a promoter of stability and peace in the region, Japan would be seen as a political–economic maverick with militaristic intentions in the future. Without the US sponsorship and guardianship, Japan's defence buildup would be seen by other Asian countries as a sure sign of the resurgence of Japanese militarism. A militarized comprehensive national security policy with an emphasis on Asia–Pacific would remind the other Asians of the disastrous history that Japan's concept of the Great East Asia Co-Prosperity Sphere once wrought upon them. Fortunately, in this author's view, this would be a likely development only under extreme circumstances of a major break in US–Japanese relations. Although one can never say 'never', at the time of writing we are far from such eventuality.

Less unrealistic would be a nationalistic Japan without accompanying military power. Such a scenario would be less frightening to other Asian peoples. It would, however, represent a course of conflict within Japan. On the other hand, such a development would frustrate those who might support an accelerated defence buildup now that Japan would no longer be confident with its security partnership with the United States. On economic grounds, as well, they would argue for expansion of domestic military production to take advantage of the economy of scale now that Japan would no longer be able to count on much assistance from the US arms suppliers. On the other hand, there would be those who would push for a neutralist Japan, either disarmed or no more armed than at the present time. They would argue either that a major break with the United States would leave Japan with no alternative but to revive its omnidirectional diplomacy of the 1960s and early 1970s within a new framework of political neutralism or that such a future would be desirable in a world without US hegemony. The appeal of a neutral and either disarmed or lightly armed Japan would depend to a large degree on the state of Japanese relations with the Soviet Union and with the People's Republic of China. Disarmament or freezing of armament at the current level would be an acceptable option to the majority of the Japanese public if and only if they no longer saw the Soviets as a potential threat to their security. Sino–Soviet normalization, US–Soviet detente, and the momentous changes underway in Eastern Europe make this coalition far more likely than anyone would have predicted just four years ago.

Short of these worst and next-to-worst case scenarios, deterioration of US–Japanese relations would have adverse effects in the immediate future on specific issues in the security co-operation between Washington and Tokyo. Among the most important items in security co-operation between Japan and the United States is Japan's development of defence capabilities to protect its sea lines of communication (SLOC) out to the distance of 1000 nautical miles from its shores. There are a number of questions being raised in the country about the military, legal, and political implications of Tokyo's pledge to bolster Japan's sealane defence capabilities (Akaha, 1986). Just to state a few here: what strategic role is Japan expected to play by expanding its defence perimeter seaward to 1000 nautical miles from its coast? Is Japan's commitment in this area an expression of its political endorsement of the US effort to establish an anti-Soviet alliance in the Asian–Pacific region? Is Japan's sealane defence buildup designed primarily for the protection of commercial vessels carrying oil and other important materials from the Middle East through the strategic straits in southeast Asia, where, arguably, there is no credible threat, or is it designed for more militarily-oriented operations in the northwest Pacific against the potential Soviet threat? Are Tokyo and Washington contemplating a 'division of labour' in the defence of the Pacific, with Japan charged with the task of enclosing the bulk of the Soviet Pacific Fleet in the Sea of Okhotsk and the Sea of Japan by blockading the strategic straits of Soya, Tsugaru, and Tsushima? Or will Japan jointly block the Soviet outlet into the Pacific with the US forward deployment forces? Will Japan be called upon to protect not only Japanese shipping but US

nd other commercial ships carrying strategic materials to Japan
vhen Japan is not yet under direct attack? Even if these are
ontingencies being planned for crisis or war situations, would not
apan's participation in peacetime military planning based on crisis or
vartime scenarios constitute a threat to Japan's neighbours, namely
he Soviets (Akaha, 1986)?

The government's response to these and other questions has
radually revealed the fuller implications of the buildup of Japan's
ealane defence capabilities. Initially the government stated that the
Maritime Self-Defence Force (MSDF) and the Air Self-Defence
'orce (ASDF) would be bolstered sufficiently to provide, in emer-
ency situations, escort and protection to vessels carrying food, oil,
nd other resources to Japan along two sealanes – the Tokyo–Guam
nd the Osaka–Bashi Channel (between Taiwan and the Philippines)
ealanes. Subsequently, however, the Defence Agency stated the
ealanes are not necessarily limited to specified widths, that the
lefence of SLOCs is based on the combined efforts of anti-submarine
atrol, sealane escort, and straits protection, and that the overall
bjective includes the protection of strategic materials in case of
ational emergency. Furthermore, the government has indicated the
ossibility that Japan may be engaged in the protection of foreign-
egistered vessels carrying shipments to Japan if they are under attack
rom Japan's adversary (*Asahi Shimbun*, 14 March, 1984, evening,
. 1).

Joint operations with the US navy under circumstances short of a
lirect threat against Japan are an extremely controversial issue
ecause of the widely-shared view that the JSDF's participation in
ollective defence operations in peacetime violates their strictly
rescribed self-defence role. The current position of the government
s that the closing, whether alone or in conjunction with the US
orces, of Japan's strategic staits is within the limits of Japan's right to
elf-defence. The controversy continues, however, regarding the role
f Japan's sealane defence *vis-à-vis* the US strategic objectives in
Asia–Pacific, and consensus is not in sight. Nor does the United
States appear prepared to provide an explicit statement about the
bjectives and the limits of US prodding of Japan in the area of
ealane defence.

Beyond the strategic, political, and legal questions about the
ealane defence issue, there are a number of formidable issues on
vhich there is neither national consensus or full public support
Akaha, 1986). First, budgetary constraints under which Japan's

military buildup, far sealane defence, or other programmes must be undertaken leave Japan's effort to meet the post-Suzuki pledge largely wanting. In an effort to overcome the shortcomings of the Defence Agency's five-year (1983–87) defence buildup programme, or 56 *Chugyo*, in meeting the goals of the 1976 National Defence Programme Outline and to elevate the *Chugyo*, which was an agency document, to a cabinet level document, the government decided on 19 September 1985 to reinstate the cabinet-level defence buildup plan approach that had been suspended after the Fourth Defence Buildup Plan of 1972 (for 1972–77). According to the new five-year plan (for 1986–90), the SDF is expected to meet the force structure and equipment goals of the 1976 Outline (*Asahi Shimbun*, 19 September 1985, p. 1). Even with these changes, however, Japanese force levels would be insufficient to meet the US expectations regarding sealane defence, for the goals outlined in the 1976 National Defence Programme Outline themselves are seen in the United States as wanting in this regard (Bouchard and Hess, 1984).

Yet another problem that threatens to create a tension between Tokyo and Washington relates to Japan's desire to enhance its own ability to develop and produce weapons deemed crucial to the modernization of its forces. So far Japan has been heavily dependent on the US weapons research and development, procurement, and sales policies, particularly for its navy. The new five-year defence buildup plan just cited, for example, calls for the procurement of major US-made or designed weapons, for example 50 additional P-3C anti-submarine aircraft, 63 F-15 fighter planes, nine new escort vessels, five E-2C patrol planes, and five units of land-to-air missiles, the Patriots (*Asahi Shimbun*, 19 September 1985, p. 1). Some defence officials not only recognize their increasing reliance on the United States, but they seem to prefer it, believing that this will ensure interoperability among its maritime, air, and ground Self-Defence Forces and also between them and the US forces operating in and around Japan (Karube, 1979; Yoshida and Katayama, 1983).

Recently, however, there appears to be increasing support within Japan's defence circles for improving Japan's self-sufficiency in weapons acquisition. A good case in point is the controversy that surrounds the pending decision regarding a new support fighter to replace outmoded F-1s and perhaps F-4s as well. Some in Japan prefer production of the proposed aircraft, commony known as FSX, entirely by Japanese industry, or at least as much as possible. Others, including many observers in the United States, either oppose or doubt Japan's domestic production of the new fighter plane, citing prohibitive cost, damage to the US–Japanese security relations, and incompatibilities that may develop between Japanese and US–made weapons systems (Chinworth, 1986). Japan's continuing desire to develop self-sufficiency in weapons development and procurement is an expression of growing nationalism among the increasingly self-confident Japanese, whether such confidence is warranted or not.

A further potential thorn in the US–Japan security relations concerns the transfer to the United States of Japanese technology that has dual, military–civilian uses. In response to US prodding, the Nakasone government decided in January 1983 to make an exception in its weapons export ban and to develop a framework for dual-purpose technology transfers to the United States. The framework had been completed and institutional mechanisms worked out by December 1985, when detailed notes were exchanged between Tokyo and Washington outlining the precise procedures for request-ing and implementing such transfers. During this period much concern was voiced in both Japanese and American industries about 'giving away' their respective technical edge to a potential compe-titor. Some in the United States were even worried about increased reliance on Japanese components in US weapons systems. Given Japan's increasing interest in developing its own weapons and weapon systems, it is questionable how far Tokyo will go toward meeting Washington's expectations in this area, where the Depart-ment of Defense is said to have high hopes. These concerns and sceptic views continue. If the overall US–Japanese relations become strained because of the economic disputes between Washington and Tokyo, it is doubtful that Tokyo will go out of its way to give up what it believes to be a high-tech edge.

Another potential irritant in US–Japan security cooperation is Japan's ambivalence regarding Reagan's Strategic Defense Initiative (SDI). In Japan, as in the United States and elsewhere, strategic, political, technological, and economic concerns and doubts persist about the value of SDI. It is beyond the scope of this paper to address all of them. Suffice it to note the major concerns in Japan. Many Japanese are concerned about the potentially destabilizing effect of SDI on the super-power strategic balance in general and on the strategic balance in general and on the strategic arms reduction talks between Washington and Moscow in particular. They are also concerned that Japan's participation in the programme will further strain Tokyo's relations with Moscow. Politically, former Foreign

Minister Shintaro Abe, is said to be cool to SDI. Serious doubts also exist that Japan can maintain its position against participation in collective security should Tokyo decide to take part in the SDI programme for which most believe technological inputs from American allies are essential.

Many Japanese are sceptical as well about the technological feasibility and the financial burden that the programme entails. Finally, and perhaps most importantly from the perspective of US–Japan security co-operation, Tokyo appears reluctant to make an extremely long term commitment to Western security policies, for such a commitment will be necessary if Japan is to participate meaningfully in even the research and development phase of the SDI programme. Nakasone decided in favour of Japanese participation. Prior to the announcement, Tokyo was reported to be considering participation in the SDI programme not so much on its technological, economic, or even strategic merit as on its political value, namely, that Japan's participation would promote Western solidarity against the Soviet Union.

Finally, there is the perennial question of whether US naval vessels violate one of Japan's non-nuclear principles, not to possess, not to produce, and not to introduce nuclear arms into the country. The non-introduction part of the now twenty-year old policy is suspected by many as having been abandoned *de facto*, when US nuclear-capable surface ships and submarines are assumed to be actually carrying nuclear weapons as they make rather routine port calls in Japan. Washington maintains its standing policy of neither confirming nor denying the presence of US nuclear weapons anywhere in the world. Tokyo and Washington have thus far succeeded in preventing this sensitive problem from boiling over into a major political issue that opposition parties can exploit. Anti-nuke movements are gathering momentum at the grass-roots level throughout the country, however, and given the developments in the South Pacific, particularly in New Zealand, the issue of nuclear-armed ships' port calls in Japan will continue to provide a potential focal point on which the opposition may capitalize for political gain.

A Thaw in Soviet–Japanese Relations

Deterioration of US–Japanese relations would provide expanded opportunities for the Soviet Union to exploit the worsening ties across the Pacific and to drive a wider wedge between Tokyo and Washington. In fact, Moscow under the new leadership of Mikhail

Gorbachev has already launched a major initiative to first improve its relations with Tokyo and then, if possible, to drive a wedge between Japan and the United States.

At the Twenty-seventh Congress of the Communist Party of the Soviet Union (CPSU) in February 1986 Gorbachev stated: 'Ensuring security in Asia is of vital importance to the Soviet Union, which is a major Asian power,' and called upon Japan and other Asian countries to consider seriously the Soviet programme for eliminating nuclear and chemical weapons by the end of this century. Stressing that the Soviet call is in harmony with the 'sentiments of the peoples of the Asian continent, for whom the problems of peace and security are no less urgent than for the peoples of Europe,' the Soviet leader reminded the world that 'Japan and its cities Hiroshima and Nagasaki became the victims of nuclear bombings and Vietnam a target hit by chemical weapons' (Gorbachev, 1986).

The Political Report of the CPSU Central Committee to the twenty-seventh CPSU Congress underscored Gorbachev's position that the Soviet Union is an Asian power and it is deeply interested in the peace and security of the region. The document pointed out 'the significance of the *Asian and Pacific direction* is growing' (Petrov, 1986: 61).

Commenting on the significance of the document and outlining Moscow's efforts to promote its concept of 'Asian security' with renewed energy and vigour, M. Petrov writes:

> An important place in improving the international situation in the Far East and Asia as a whole, belongs to Soviet–Japanese relations. Unfortunately, owing to Japan's increasingly active adherence to US and NATO military strategy, their present state fails to live up to what could be expected. Another factor that does nothing to make this [*sic*] relations better is the non-existent 'territorial issue' resurrected by the Japanese side.
>
> The USSR has always wished to maintain friendly, extensive and many-sided relations with Japan. Soviet proposals still stand to conclude a Soviet–Japanese agreement on good neighbourliness and mutually beneficial co-operation, which would help create a favourable atmosphere for continuing the talks on the peace treaty. The Soviet Union has also advanced other proposals, which pertain, specifically, to economic co-operation and cultural contacts. Helping facilitate the development of bilateral relations was Eduard Shevardnadze's visit to Japan in January of this year [1986]. . .(Petrov: 69).

During Soviet Foreign Minister Shevardnadze's visit to Tokyo in January 1986, the first such visit by a Soviet Foreign Minister in ten years, the Japanese government wanted the record to show that there indeed existed a territorial issue between Japan and the Soviet Union over the 'Northern Territories'. The most Tokyo could get out of Shevardnadze during his talks with Nakasone and Foreign Minister Abe was an acknowledgement, included in the joint communique announced at the conclusion of the Soviets' visit, that the Foreign Minister held 'negotiations on the conclusion of a peace treaty', encompassing 'problems' that would become the basis of the treaty, 'on the basis of the agreement established by the 1973 Japan–Soviet Communique' (*Asahi Shimbun*, 20 January 1986, p. 1). The 1973 communique in question, between Leonid Brezhnev and former Prime Minister Kakuei Tanaka, had stated there were 'unresolved issues' since the Second World War, the resolution of which would be necessary for a peace treaty between Tokyo and Moscow, and the Soviet leader had verbally acknowledged that 'unresolved issues' included the territorial dispute over the 'Northern Islands'. Since then, however, the Soviets had repeatedly denied the existence of a territorial dispute between the two countries. Following the announcement of the Shevardnadze–Abe communique on 19 January, the Soviet Foreign Minister reaffirmed Moscow's position that there was no territorial dispute between the two countries.

Despite the fundamental disagreement on the territorial issue, the two Foreign Ministers agreed regular Foreign Ministers' meetings would be held at least once a year and Moscow and Tokyo would continue constructive discussions for the smooth functioning of their bilateral fishery agreement. Shevardnadze assured the Soviet Union would consider from a 'humanitarian standpoint' Abe's request that Japanese citizens be allowed to visit their ancestral graves on what the Japanese claimed were their islands, the two concurred that Tokyo and Moscow would promote the expansion of bilateral trade and other economic relations, and the two Foreign Ministers highly appraised the joint Geneva communique between Gorbachev and Reagan in November 1985 (*Asahi Shimbun*, 20 January, 1986, p. 1). Specific results of the Foreign Ministers' talks included the signing of trade and taxation agreements, the upgrading of trade consultations scheduled to be held soon after the Tokyo meeting, the reopening of talks on scientific and technological co-operation which Japan had suspended in the early 1980s as a protest against the imposition of martial law in Poland and the completion of arrangements to allow Japanese to visit ancestral graves on the disputed northern islands.

If the Foreign Ministers' talks in Tokyo did not produce any breakthrough, it did send an unmistakable signal about the two countries' deep desire to arrest and reverse the deterioration of their relations which started in the late 1970s. The Soviet Union and Japan have largely complementary needs and assets in the economic and technological fields. The Soviets would like to gain access to the fast advancing Japanese technology and Japan's accumulating surplus capital. Japan in its continuing effort to diversify sources of its energy and other natural resources, would gain much by improved economic ties with the Soviet Union.

At no time in the foreseeable future, however, are the economic and technological relations between the Soviet Union and Japan likely to improve and expand so much as to overshadow their political disputes, particularly over the thorny territorial issue.

CONCLUSIONS

There is a new recognition in Japan and in the United States that economic vitality has replaced military might as the most important base of national power. Lester Brown and others at the Worldwatch Institute warn:

> Preoccupied with each other, the two military super-powers apparently have failed to notice that global geopolitcs is being reshaped in a way that defines security more in economic than traditional military terms. While the United States and Soviet Union have concentrated on military competition, Japan has been challenging both nations on the economic front (*The [Toledo] Blade*, 16 February, 1986, p. A–3).

Lester Brown, president of the Washington-based research institute and director of the study continued: 'If recent trends continue, before 1990 Japan will supplant the United States as the world's leading trade partner.'

Historian Richard Rosecrance observes:

> [After 1985,] large-scale territorial expansion began to evolve as too costly – too dangerous and too uncertain as a general strategy

of national advancement. As that lesson gradually dawned, a trading strategy and the development of the international trading system could begin to substitute peacefully for the military–political and territorial system. When such a time arrived, one would have reached the 'Japanese period' in world politics, a period in which nations thought not in terms of mastery of the three dimensions of height, width, and breadth of territory and space but of the fourth dimension: persistence over time (Rosecrance, 1986: 20).

He then points out that heavy military spending has weakened both the American and Soviet economies and Japan, with less than one per cent of its GNP devoted to armaments, has enhanced its trillion dollar economy through trade and productivity gains (Rosecrance, 1986: 20). Rosecrance declares that the days of what he calls the military–political and territorial system are over and the period of the trading system is here to stay. In his estimate, Japan is more suited to take advantage of the opportunities of the new era than is either the United States or the Soviet Union. Rosecrance issues a warning to the 'free ride' critics:

Many have misunderstood the differences between Japan and America, believing that Japan is simply a youthful, smaller edition of the United States, a still not fully developed major power with political and economic interests that have yet to be defined on a world stage. Sooner or later, many feel, Japan too will become a world power with commensurate political and military interests. This is a misconception of the Japanese role in world affairs and a mistaken assimilation of a trading state to the military–political realm. . .As a trading state it would not be in her interest to dominate the world, control the sealanes to the Persian Gulf; or guarantee military access to markets in Europe or the Western hemisphere. She depends upon open trading and commercial routes to produce entry for her goods. *It is not the American model that Japan will ultimately follow. Rather, it is the Japanese model that America may ultimately follow* (emphases added) (Rosecrance, 1986: xi).

To most Japanese these statements will be reassuring. The statements will not only reaffirm their conviction that Japan's postwar economic preoccupation has paid off. More importantly, the observations offered by the two Americans will relieve them of the pain it causes them when they are told time and time again by their 'senior', and supposedly more experienced and knowledgeable partners in Washington, that Japan will have to give up their continued emphasis on economic expansion and to devote more of its resources to military defence in order to fulfil its self-acknowledged international responsibilities. In the words quoted here, the Japanese will find encouragement rather than discouragement, assurance rather than intimidation, and affirmation rather than disaffirmation.

The Japanese are not the only ones who have realized that the costs of imperialist and military policies of the political–military and territorial system far outweigh their benefits, and that the opportunities for national advancement are found more readily in active participation in and support for the interdependent world of today. Should Washington either fail to recognize the lessons of history or succumb to the political temptation to link the trade and defence issues, the increasingly self-assured Japanese would further lose their confidence in American leadership in the liberal capitalist world.

Notes

The research on which this paper is based was partially supported by a Japan Foundation professional fellowship and a grant from the Bowling Green State University Faculty Research Committee. The author alone is responsible for the facts and interpretation of facts contained in the paper.

1. These developments generated such a widespread sense of insecurity among the Japanese that one fiction after another appeared and became bestsellers toward the end of the 1970s by suggesting that a Soviet attack on Japan was imminent. 'Soviet Forces land Japan', 'The Minsk on the Attack', 'A Japanese Naval Fleet Sunk', 'The Soviet Far East Forces Invade', 'Hokkaido Occupied', were the titles of works of fiction of which the publishers could not print enough to satisfy the insatiable appetite of Japanese readers. Popular magazines carried articles entitled 'The Soviet Forces in Massive Assault on Tokyo Bay and Hokkaido', 'A World War Starts in Asia, the Soviet Forces Launch an Attack on Tokyo from Sado', 'The Soviets Completely Surround Japan; Will Hokkaido Be Abandoned?' and 'The Inner Secret of Japan–US Joint Tactics; the Day the Soviet Forces Land Hokkaido'. Similar alarmist writings continued into the 1980s (*Asahi Shimbun*, 13 February, 1986, p. 4).

2. Admiral S.R. Foley, Jr., Commander-in-Chief, US Pacific Fleet, described the main aims of the force refurbishment and revised relations with Pacific friends and allies are 'to insure the free flow of oil from the [Persian] Gulf states, to protect US sources of raw materials, and guarantee access to markets, to maintain. . .freedom of the seas, to

assure allies that the United States is present in the event of an emergency and to keep vital sealanes of communication open' (Collins, 1985: 142).

3. The first five objectives are discussed by Zagoria (1982).

4. The reference to an 'Unsinkable Aircraft Carrier' was made by Konstantin Chernenko during his trip to Pyongyang in May 1984. The Soviet leader also charged that the United States was forging a 'Washington–Tokyo–Seoul bloc' in the Pacific (*Asahi Shimbun*, 25 May, 1984, p. 1).

5. The annual public opinion poll by the Prime Minister's office showed that in November 1985, 69.2 per cent of those asked said they believed Japan's security could be best maintained by the existing US–Japanese security arrangements and Japanese Self-Defence Forces. 54.1 per cent believed Japan's defence spending should remain at the current level of slightly less than 1 per cent of GNP. This represented an increase of 6.8 per cent since December 1981. Those supporting an increase in defence spending declined from 20.1 per cent in 1981 to 14.2 per cent, and those supporting a smaller defence budget increased from 15.0 to 17.7 per cent (*Asahi Shimbun*, 8 July, 1985, p.1.)

6. For recent developments surrounding Tokyo–Moscow relations, see the second part of this study.

7. The other conditions were that Moscow withdraw its troops from Afghanistan and substantially reduce its troop deployment in Mongolia.

8. Despite the continuing suspicion that US nuclear-capable vessels actually carry nuclear weapons when they transit Japanese territorial waters and call in Japanese ports, for example, US surface ships and submarines continue their visits to Japan virtually unhampered

9. Japan's ability and willingness to commit the necessary resources to these efforts will have an important bearing on Japan's action with respect to its trade problems with the United States. This aspect will be analyzed in part two below.

10. According to a Japanese–American public opinion poll in April 1985, 70 per cent of the Japanese interviewed said they felt Japan was being made a scapegoat, while 53 per cent of the American interviewees held the same belief. The Japanese opinion was shared by people of all ages, of all income levels, of all levels of education, and of all party affiliations, conservative and progressive alike. (Clymer, 1986).

References

Akaha, Tsuneo (1984), 'Japan's Non-nuclear policy', *Asian Survey* Vol. 24, No. 8 (August): 852–77.

——————(1986), 'The Threat of Shipping Disruptions and Japan's Response', *Pacific Affairs* 59 (Summer): 255–77.

Asahi Shimbun, 3 April, 1983; 9 April, 1983; 14 March 1984, evening, p. 1; 19 September, 1985, p. 1; 20 January 1986, p.1.

Asian Wall Street Journal Weekly, 31 March 1986, p. 10; 14 April 1986, pp. 1 and 10; 14 July 1986, p. 9.

Bouchard, Joseph F. and Douglas J. Hess (1984), 'The Japanese Navy and

Sea-Lanes Defense', *United States Naval Institute Proceedings* No. 110 (March): 90–97.

Chinworth, Michael W. (1986), 'Japanese Defence: Key Decisions Pending', *JEI (Japan Economic Institute) Report* No. 15A (18 April): 9–10.

Christian Science Monitor, 30 July, 1986, pp. 7, 9.

Clough, Ralph N. (1982), 'The Soviet Union and the Two Koreas', in Zagoria pp. 175–99.

Clymer, Adam (1986), 'The United States and Japan; Polling Two Unmatched Sets of Opinon on World War Two and on Today's Trade Conflicts', Paper prepared for delivery at the 1986 Annual Meeting of the American Political Science Association, the Washington Hilton, 29 August.

Cohen, Stephen (1985), *Uneasy Partnership: Competition and Confict in US–Japanese Trade Relations* (Cambridge, Mass: Ballinger Publishing Co.).

Collins, John M. (1985), US–Soviet Military Balance, 1980–1985 (Washington, Pergamon-Brassey's International Defence Publishers).

Crow, Jr., William (1984), 'Admiral William Crow, Jr', *Armed Forces Journal* (April).

Denoon, David B.H. (ed.) (1986), *Constraints on Strategy: the Economics of Western Security*, (Washington: Pergamon-Brassey's International Defence Publishers).

Defence Agency (1982), *Defence of Japan* 1982 (Tokyo, *The Japan Times*).

————(1984), *Defence of Japan* 1984. (Tokyo, *The Japan Times*).

Economic Planning Agency (1983), *Japan in the Year 2000* (Tokyo: Okurasho Insatsukyoku).

Galenson, Walter and David W. Galenson (1986), 'Japan and South Korea', in Denoon, pp. 152–94.

Gorbachev, Mikhail (1986), 'Statement by Mikhail Gorbachev', *International Affairs* (Moscow) (March): 9.

Ha, Young-Sun (1986), 'The Soviet Military Buildup in the Far East: Implications for the Security of South Korea', in Solomon and Kosaka (eds), pp. 141–4.

Hayashi, Kenjiro (1985), 'Nijuisseiki e no senko toshi ni chakushu seyo' [Embark on advanced investment for the 21st century], *Chuo Koron* (October): 199–209.

Heiwamondai Kenkyukai (1985), 'Kokusaikokka Nihon no Sogo Anzenhosho Seisaku' [Comprehensive security policy for the international state Japan] (Tokyo: O kurasho Insatsukyoku).

Hiraiwa, Gaishi and Yoshio Okawara (1985), 'Ima, doramachikku na Kodo no toki' [Time for dramatic action], Shukan Toyo Keizai (17 April): pp. 29–33.

Inoguchi, Takashi (1986), 'The Sources of Stability in the Japanese Political Process', in Morse and Yoshida, pp. 43–55.

Ito, Kenichi and Fuji Kamiya (1985) 'Laying the Ground Rules for Fair Trade', *Japan Echo*, Vol. 12, No. 4: 21–6.

————(1985) 'Mazakon kokka Nihon no katsuro' [The way out for the nation with a mother complex, Japan], *Shokun* (October): 44–59.

Jackson, Karl D. (1986), 'Indochina, 1982–1985: Peace Yields to War', in

Solomon and Kosaka (eds.), pp. 186–217.

Johnson, Chalmers (1986), 'Reflections on the Dilemma of Japanese Defence', *Asian Survey* Vol. 26, No. 5.

Kamiya, Fuji (1982), 'The Northern Territories: 130 Years of Japanese Talks with Czarist Russia and the Soviet Union', in Zagoria (ed.), pp. 121–51.

Karube, Tsutomu (1979), Beiso Kaijo Senryaku to Nihon no Kaijo Boei [US–Soviet maritime strategy and Japan's maritime defence], (Tokyo: Kyoikusha).

Keizai Koho Centre (Japan Institute for Social and Economic Affairs) *Japan, An International Comparison* (Tokyo: Keizai Koho Centre).

Kihl, Young W. and Lawrence E. Grinter (eds.) (1986), *Asian–Pacific Security: Emerging Challenges and Responses* (Boulder, Colo: Lynne Rienner).

Kimura, Hiroshi (1985), 'Soviet Policy toward Asia under Chernenko and Gorbachev: A Japanese Perspective', *Journal of Northeast Asian Studies* (Winter): 46–66.

Kimura, Hiroshi (1986), 'The Soviet Military Buildup: Its Impact on Japan and Its Aims', in Solomon and Kosaka (eds.), pp. 109–110.

Komine, Takao (1985), 'Keizai masatsu itsutsu no gokai' [Five misunderstandings about the economic friction], Keizai Seminar (June): 5–10.

Leifer, Michael (1983), 'The Security of Sealanes in South–East Asia', *Survival* (January–February): 21–22.

Maeda, Tetsuo (1983), 'Senshu boei kara shudan jiei e fumidasu nyu Nakasone ko so no kikendo' [The dangers of new Nakasone plans to move from strict defence to collective self-defence], *Asahi Janaru* (25 February): 20–21.

————(1985), "Taiko" o kankotsu dattai shita "shin boei keikaku"' [The new defence plan that scrapped the 'guideline'], *Ekonomisuto* (8 October): 20–23.

Millar, Tom (1986), 'ANZAC Perspectives on Soviet Power in the Pacific', in Solomon and Kosaka (eds.), pp. 155–170.

Miyazaki, Isamu (1985), '1985-nen Nihon keizai no kadai' [The agenda for Japanese economy in 1985], *Chuo Koron* (February): 90–101.

————(1985), 'Gunshuku no tame no keizai seisaku' [Economic policy for 'arms control' 17 *Chuo Koron* (March): 101–118.

Morse, Ronald A. and Shigenobu Yoshida (eds.) (1985), *Blind Partners: American and Japanese Responses to an Unknown Future* (New York: University Press of America).

New York Times, 3 May, 1985, p. 6; 29 April, 1986, pp. 27 and 31; 21 July, 1986 p. 20; 8 August, 1986, pp. 1 and 13; 20 August, 1986, p. 1; 26 August, 1986, p. 26.

O'Neil, William D. (1977), 'Backfire: Long Shadow on the Sealanes', *United States Naval Institute Proceedings,* (March): 27–35.

Ozaki, Robert S. and Walter Arnold (eds.), (1985), *Japan's Foreign Relations: A Global Search for Economic Security* (Boulder, Colo: Westview).

Petrov, M. (1986), 'The USSR for Peace and Security in Asia', *International Affairs* (Moscow) (5 May): 61.

Rosecrance, Richard (1986), *The Rise of the Trading State: Commerce and Conquest in the Modern World* (New York: Basic Books).

Sakamoto, Yoshikazu (1986), 'Gunshuku e no sentaku' [The choice for arms control], Sekai (January): 31–66.

Sato, Kinko (1985), 'Onna mo sunaru "boeihi 1% waku" rongi' [Even a woman participates in the debate on one per cent defense spending'] *Shokun* (March): 150–159.

Sato, Seizaburo (1985), 'Naze, soshite dono yona gunjiryoku ka' [Why and what kind of military power?], *Chuo Koron* (December): 88–98.

Scalapino, Robert (1986), 'Asia in a Global Context: Strategic Issues for the Soviet Union', in Solomon and Kosaka (eds.), pp. 21–39.

Shimomura, Osamu (1985) 'Ijo na Amerika keizai, rifujin na America' [Strange American economy, unconscionable America], *Next* (July): 90–5.

———————(1985), 'US Trade Demands Go Too Far', *Japan Echo* Vol. 12, No. 3: 25–30.

Simon, Sheldon W. (1986), 'The Great Powers' Security Role in Southeast Asia: Diplomacy and Force', in Kihl and Grinter (eds.), pp. 79–102.

Shinpo, Seiji (1985), 'Kokusaika no tettei koso masatsu taisaku no kihon' [Full internationalization is the key to countermeasure against the (trade) friction], *This Is* (September 1985): 48–53.

Sogo Anzenhosho Kenkyu Gurupu (1980), Sogo Anzenhosho Senryaku [Comprehensive security strategy]. (Tokyo: Okurasho Insatsukyoku).

Solomon, Richard and Masataka Kosaka, eds. (1986), *The Soviet Far East Military Buildup* (Dover, Mass: Auburn House).

Stockwin, J.A.A. (1985) 'Japan and the Soviet Union', in Robert S. Ozaki and Walter Arnold (eds.), pp. 67–84.

(*Toledo*) *Blade*, 16 February, 1986, p. A–3.

Tsushusangyosho and Sangyokozo Shingikai (eds.) (1982), Keizai Anzenhosho no Kakuritsu o mezashite [For the establishment of economic security] (Tokyo: Tsushosangyo Chosakai).

Uraga, Kohei (1985), 'No Magic Cure for the Trade Surplus', *Japan Echo* Vol. 12; No. 3: 11–15.

Watkins, James D. (1986), 'The Maritime Strategy', *The Maritime Strategy*, US Naval Institute Proceedings Supplement (January): 3–17.

Yomiuri Shimbun, 3 April 1983.

Yoshida, Manabu and Masahiko Katayama (1983), 'Kokubo Taidan, Part 1. Kaiyo kokka no Seimei o Mamoru. Fukugokyoika, C^3I Kyoka ga Kyumu' [A defence dialogue, Part 1. Defending the lifeline of the maritime nation under multiple threats, urgent task to strengthen C^3I], *Kokubo*, Vol. 32, No. 9 (September): 21–31.

Zagoria, Donald S. (1982), *Soviet Policy in East Asia* (New Haven, Conn: Yale University Press).

———————(1982), 'The Strategic Environment in East Asia', in Zagoria (ed.), pp. 1–27.

Zagoria, Donald S. and Sheldon W. Simon (1982), 'Soviet Policy in Southeast Asia', in Zagoria (ed.), pp. 153–73.

9 US–Japan Security Cooperation amid the shifting environment in Asia

T. David Mason

In recent years friction between Japan and the US over trade issues has threatened the stability of longstanding bilateral security arrangements that both nations have heretofore considered vital to their interests in the Pacific Basin. Between 1980 and 1986, the yearly US trade deficit with Japan rose from $9.9 billion to almost $60 billion, touching off a heated debate in the US Congress over where the blame for the deficit could be placed and how Congress might go about remedying this problem. Quite unexpectedly, this debate has become highly charged politically, with analyses of the origins of and remedies for US trade problems being more often geared to enhancing the short term political fortunes of individual Congressmen from states affected by trade problems than to devising realistic policies that might have some positive effect on the trade balance.

Not surprisingly, the arrangements governing US–Japan security cooperation have been drawn into the vortex of the political debate over trade issues. Because the politics of trade involve questions of jobs, industrial competitiveness, and the general health of the American economy, the issue of 'burden sharing' in US–Japan security relations inevitably is injected into the trade debate as a factor contributing to Japan's alleged unfair trade advantage with the US. The point is often raised that, if the Japanese were to assume their fair share of the mutual defence burden in the Pacific Basin, then their industries would not enjoy such a competitive advantage over American firms in such areas as electronics, automobiles, steel, and other manufactured goods. According to this line of argument, Japan has been able to invest so heavily in maintaining and enhancing the competitiveness of its industries (to the detriment of their American competitors) largely because the US has for decades relieved Japan's economy of the burden of providing for its own defence. In this sense, it is argued, American defence commitments to Japan amount to an indirect subsidy to the Japanese economy, and an indirect tax on the competitiveness of American industry. Therefore compelling Japan to shoulder its fair share of the defence burden would at least allow American industries to compete on a 'level playing field', and in time the trade deficit would begin to dissipate.[1]

Of course, the reality of the US–Japan trade problem is far more complex than this. However, this seems to be the central point by which trade friction enters the debate over bilateral security relations. The purpose of this chapter, however, is not to assess the validity of this or other contending positions in the debate over US–Japan trade relations. The origins of the trade imbalance and its impact on the US economy and on the politics of US–Japan relations have been the subject of numerous scholarly investigations and government reports in recent years, and are dealt with in considerable detail in other chapters of this volume.[2] The same can be said of the elements of US–Japan security arrangements and the specific issues of contention that define the politics of this relationship, both within and between the two partners.[3] What often seems missing in much of the recent debate on security cooperation – and what will serve as the focus for this chapter – is any explicit concern with the changing strategic environment in Asia and the new challenges that these transformations might pose for US–Japan security interests. Before the US and Japan allow their security relationship to become entangled in the politics of trade friction, we need to consider whether either nation can afford to risk the stability of this relationship at a time when unprecedented challenges to the alliance are evolving in the East Asian environment.

For at least the last two decades, the *raison d'être* of the US–Japan alliance has been defined in terms of the growing Soviet military presence in Asia. This has been the glue that held the US–Japan alliance together amid the often thinly veiled disputes over burden sharing and related issues, such as the '1 per cent' ceiling on Japanese defence spending, the size and capability of Japan's Self-Defence Forces (SDF), and interpretation of Article 9 of the Japanese constitution. At the same time, during most of this period, concern with the Soviet challenge was moderated somewhat by the fact that their buildup in Asia was directed at least as much as China as it was at the US and Japan. In this respect, the Sino–Soviet split served US and Japanese security interests by posing China as a mainland counterweight to the Soviet presence in Asia.

However, what seems to be absent in the current debate on US–Japan trade and security relations is any concern for the ways in which changes going on inside the both Soviet Union and China are altering the character of Sino–Soviet relations and, thus too, the fundamental parameters of the major strategic challenge facing the US and Japan. The transition to a new generation of leaders in both China and the Soviet Union has brought to power leaders whose concern with domestic economic problems and whose pragmatic approach to foreign policy questions have led them both to a cautious but significant interest in arranging some sort of Sino–Soviet detente. While the advent of new leadership in Moscow has yet to produce a significant reduction in the Soviet military presence in East Asia, there are clear signs that Gorbachev is pursuing a more subtle and sophisticated strategy in the region, one that is less exclusively reliant upon military power as an instrument of national security. This trend is especially evident in recent Soviet efforts to reduce tensions with China and, to a lesser extent, with Japan.

Any significant movement toward Sino–Soviet detente would represent a dramatic alteration in the strategic environment in Asia, an alteration that would have profound implications for the US–Japan security relationship. If the Soviet Union continues to pursue diplomatic efforts aimed at reducing tensions with its chief Asian rivals, what does this imply for the US–Japanese strategic relationship? If the security threat that defines the major *raison d'être* for the US–Japan alliance is significantly altered, will this catalyze fundamental realignment in that alliance itself? This chapter will explore the progress towards and prospects for a Sino–Soviet detente, the ways in which such movements would transform the nature of the strategic challenge facing the US–Japan alliance, and the ways in which the current trade frictions between the US and Japan might make the stability of the alliance vulnerable to the alterations in each nation's strategic calculus that might be catalyzed by a lessening of tensions between the Soviet Union and China.

CHANGING SINO–SOVIET RELATIONS: PROSPECTS AND IMPLICATIONS

With the emergence of a new generation of leaders throughout the government and party hierarchies in both China and the Soviet

Union, both nations have initiated substantial and (in the case of China) dramatic restructuring of their fundamental development strategies. Deng Xiaoping's 'Four Modernizations' and Mikhail Gorbachev's *perestroika* both signal a tacit admission by each that their nation's past strategy for socialist development was not without flaws and is, in a fundamental sense, inadequate for the developmental challenges with which they are now confronted. In China, the dismantling of the commune system and its replacement by the 'responsibility system' in agriculture, the substantial infusion of foreign industrial investments and technology, the decentralization of management authority in the industrial sector, the restructuring of admissions criteria and curriculum in education, and the streamlining of the People's Liberation Army all attest to the fundamental transformation of the Chinese system that has been carried out under the banner of the 'Four Modernizations'. In the Soviet Union, structural reform is still largely a matter of policy debate, with little in the way of real change having yet been introduced. However, as the generational transition in the Soviet leadership permeates throughout all levels of the Soviet party and administrative hierarchy, it appears that Mikhail Gorbachev is intent upon putting into place the personnel to effect a consensus on the adoption and implementation of economic and political reforms, especially in the areas of agriculture, industrial management and planning, and international trade. Gorbachev has already rendered obsolete much of the conventional wisdom in the West concerning the possibility of structural reform and policy change in a highly centralized command system such as the Soviet Union. Movements toward greater autonomy for enterprise managers, campaigns for workplace democracy and worker discipline, the institution of new joint venture laws, calls for structural reforms in Soviet agriculture and curriculum change in education, a willingness to criticize past leaders and their policies, and an overriding commitment to modernizing the technological foundations of Soviet society are among the domestic initiatives dominating the headlines concerning the Gorbachev reform agenda.[4]

These domestic reforms are not without their implications for foreign policy. China's pursuit of what its leaders refer to as its 'independent' foreign policy and the Soviet Union's 'new thinking' in foreign policy are both predicated on the assumption that a stable, less threatening international environment is necessary for the successful pursuit of domestic reforms and developmental initiatives. Indeed, there is clear evidence that the character of domestic reform in both nations has created incentives for a Sino–Soviet rapprochement and, simultaneously, has served to moderate if not remove certain of the longstanding obstacles to improved Sino–Soviet relations. To the extent that improvements of substantive import in Sino–Soviet relations continue to emerge, the delicate balance in the east Asian 'strategic triangle' cannot help but be altered, and in a manner that, arguably, will be to the detriment of the US and Japanese mutual security interests in the region, at least as they are now conceived. This section of this chapter explores the prospects for and progress toward a Sino–Soviet rapprochement. Following this, I will explore the implications of such a contingency for the stability of the US–Japan security relationship.

The origins and elements of the Sino–Soviet split have been the subject of numerous scholarly works and need not be restated in great detail here.[5] Suffice it to say that what began in the 1950s as a series of disputes between allies over points of ideology, foreign policy, and development strategy escalated in the 1960s into an open schism within the communist bloc. Mao Zedong's criticism of deStalinization and 'peaceful coexistence' with the West, his rejection of the Soviet model of economic development (made explicit in the initiation of the Great Leap Forward), and his irritation at the lukewarm Soviet support offered in the Qemoy–Matsu crises were eventually reciprocated by a Soviet withdrawal of economic aid and advisors, as well as a unilateral abrogation of their 1957 military aid agreement with China. With the accession to power of Brezhnev, Kosygin, and Podgorny in 1963, the Soviet Union began treating this schism within the socialist camp more as a conventional power politics rivalry, undertaking a doubling of their military forces in Asia during the last half of the 1960s. By 1969, the rift had erupted into open combat along the Ussuri River, and throughout the 1970s, the two nations dealt with each other as overt enemies, no longer pretending that the conflict was merely a matter of policy differences between socialist brethren. Sino–Soviet conflict has remained one of the most salient concerns shaping each nation's foreign policy for the last two decades. Thus, any fundamental changes in this relationship would signal alterations (or at least the potential for such) in each nation's dealings with other nations, including Japan and the US.

What, then, are the obstacles to Sino–Soviet rapprochement? Since 1969 a number of specific issues have come to define the parameters of Sino–Soviet conflict in that they represent the persistent obstacles to the diplomatic efforts by either nation to resolve the fundamental hostility that has characterized Sino–Soviet relations for the last twenty years. The major points of contention have by now been boiled down to the so-called 'three obstacles': (1) a series of boundary disputes, many of which date back to the nineteenth century 'unequal treaties' between the Russian Tsars and the last of the Qing dynasty emperors; (2) Soviet support of Vietnam's occupation of Kampuchea; and (3) the Soviet occupation of Afghanistan.[6]

Negotiations on border questions have been ongoing since 1982, and it appears that the legal issue of where the border lies, in and of itself, is no longer a major barrier to rapprochement (see Robinson 1987:242). Instead, the remaining element of this 'obstacle' that is most salient to China is the more pragmatic issue of the size, capability, and offensive configuration of the Soviet military forces deployed along the border with China. The Soviet buildup in Asia that was initiated by Brezhnev had as its end result the deployment of what amounts to an independent war-fighting capacity in Asia, with most of this capability arrayed along the Chinese border. The Soviets have some 45 combat divisions in Asia along with four tactical air armies and one long range aviation division. These troops are equipped with a full complement of the most advanced Soviet combat equipment, including some 6000 tanks, more than 1200 tactical nuclear rockets and (until recently) SS-20 IRBMS, and over 2500 combat aircraft. The Soviet Pacific fleet has grown to be the largest in the Soviet navy, with some 105 submarines (32 of which are nuclear capable), 352 surface ships, and approximately 400 naval aircraft. This offensive capability is supported by a sophisticated air defence system as well as advanced command, control, and intelligence capabilities.

China, for its part, can match or exceed the Soviets only in numbers of troops. But the People's Liberation Army (PLA) is seriously lacking in mobility, firepower, and modern weaponry. Chinese forces include some 3.2 million troops (down from 4.7 million earlier in this decade), 11 000 tanks, and 5300 combat aircraft. However, these systems are, for the most part, woefully obsolescent when matched up against comparable Soviet technology. And, to date, modernization of the PLA has remained fourth in priority among the Four Modernizations, with actual investments being limited largely to dual use technologies in the areas of communication and transportation, along with some efforts to upgrade the Chinese nuclear deterrent. Indeed, China announced in 1985 the demobilization of a million troops, justifying this unilateral cut on the grounds that more rapid and substantial progress could be made in modernizing a smaller PLA. The imbalance of military capabilities along their shared border (including the Chinese border with Mongolia, where the Soviets have some 65 000 troops stationed) remains the central issue preventing any meaningful rapprochement between the two nations.[7]

The second of the 'three obstacles' is Soviet support for Vietnam in its occupation of Kampuchea. In 1978, the Soviet Union signed a Treaty of Peace and Friendship with Vietnam, and within months Vietnam invaded Kampuchea and replaced the Khmer Rouge government of Pol Pot with a regime under Vietnamese control and supported by an occupation force of some 70 000 Vietnamese troops. Within months of this invasion (in February 1979), China launched its own punitive attack against Vietnam, intended to 'teach them a lesson' for invading the territory of China's principal southeast Asian ally. Of course, this brief war was a disaster for China, but since then Soviet relations with Vietnam have been elevated to a major point of contention in Sino–Soviet relations. Not only does China still resent Vietnam's occupation of Kampuchea, but they have also expressed concern about the strategic implications of Soviet naval forces operating out of port facilities at Cam Ranh Bay.

The third of the 'three obstacles' also involves the Soviet presence in a third area: the Soviet occupation of Afghanistan. Immediately following the Soviet invasion, China cancelled border negotiations scheduled for early 1980, and these talks were not resumed until 1982. For China, the invasion represented not only an example of the Soviet Union's hegemonic tendencies in South Asia but also posed a threat to Pakistan, China's major ally in the delicate South Asia balance of power.

Given these 'obstacles', what are the prospects for any progress towards their resolution? First, it should be noted that, since Mikhail Gorbachev came to power, there has been substantial movement on each of these issues. The Soviet Union completed the withdrawal of its troops from Afghanistan in February 1989. Likewise, at the time of writing negotiations are underway for the establishment of a coalition government in Kampuchea, one that would include the participation (in some form) of the major opposition groups currently fighting the Vietnamese-backed government in Phnom Penh. Vietnam claims to have completed the withdrawal of its forces as of 30 September, 1989, despite the absence, at the time of this writing, of a political settlement among the remaining Kampuchean factions.

As for the third obstacle, Sino–Soviet border disputes are by no means near resolution, nor have there been any substantial reductions in Soviet military deployments along their shared boundary. However, it appears that China has also narrowed its demands on this issue in the sense that they apparently no longer require the realignment of borders to some nineteenth century *status quo ante*. Instead, the border question now revolves around the more practical concern over the security of navigation rights along certain parts of the Amur and Ussuri Rivers (Robinson, 1987:242). Gorbachev's 1986 Vladivostok speech contained an acknowledgement of the main channel of these rivers as the border, a concession which assured China of the navigation rights it was seeking and which thereby rendered the border question 'ripe for rapid resolution', in the words of noted Sinologist Thomas Robinson. Of course, the issue of Soviet force levels in Asia has yet to be resolved. However, as we shall discuss later, prospects for movement on this matter are imminent.

While progress has by no means resolved these issues, the significance of recent movements cannot be discounted when one considers the domestic context of each nation's negotiating position. In particular, the motivations for reductions in Sino–Soviet tensions are grounded in powerful public and leadership preferences for domestic economic growth and reform, the achievement of which can most easily be realized if the resource demands of each nation's military can be minimized. Thus, a reduction in Sino–Soviet tensions will, for both nation's leaders, release for investment in domestic economic development resources that otherwise would be in demand by their respective military establishments as necessary for them to defend against the security threat that each nation poses to the other. To the extent that Sino–Soviet detente is grounded in powerful domestic economic priorities, we can expect both nations to continue serious efforts to resolve the three obstacles. Correlatively, the more urgent the tasks of economic modernization and development – for both the health of each nation's economy and the security of its current leaders's grasp on power – the more vigorously we can expect them to pursue rapprochement. It is to this matter – the domestic motivations for Sino–Soviet detente – that we now turn.

Domestic Sources of China's Changing Soviet Policy

In China, the primary policy goal of Deng Xiaoping and his followers in the reformist faction of the Chinese leadership has been and remains today the preservation of his domestic economic reform initiatives and the resulting momentum in economic growth and development. Given China's persistent shortage of human and investment capital, the pursuit of domestic economic development has necessitated the relegation of military modernization to fourth in priority among the Four Modernizations. To rationalize the low priority accorded PLA modernization, especially in the face of the unabated Soviet military buildup in Asia, Deng has been compelled to modify the official assessment of Soviet intentions in Asia, downplaying the imminence if not the extent of the Soviet threat by arguing that the Soviet buildup is directed as much at the US and Japan as it is at China. This strategy is reinforced by the cautious cultivation of limited forms of security co-operation with Japan and the US, typified by the 1978 Sino–Japanese Treaty of Peace and Friendship and by the purchase of limited amounts of military equipment from the US.

This political strategy is not without risk for Deng and his allies in the Chinese leadership. While there has been since 1978 a broad consensus among China's leaders on the validity of the Four Modernizations as a development strategy, conflicts still persist not far below the surface on programmatic details and policy priorities by which to achieve the broad goals of modernization. In particular, elements of the PLA leadership have not been satisfied with the low priority accorded to military modernization, nor have they fully accepted Deng's revisionist view on the nature of the Soviet threat. However, to date, Deng has managed to pre-empt the emergence of a coalition in opposition to his policies on Sino–Soviet relations and military modernization by, first, effectively managing the policy debate on the urgency of the Soviet threat, second, reinforcing this effort with the opening of direct negotiations on border questions, trade, scientific, cultural, and educational exchanges, and, third, (and most importantly) engineering personnel changes in the PLA leadership that have effectively pre-empted their ability to build a coalition in opposition to Deng's programme. The result has been a reduction in the level of Sino–Soviet hostility and the gradual construction of a network of interactions with the Soviets that creates a more positive atmosphere in which to negotiate the more serious 'three obstacles' that define their rivalry. Simultaneously, areas in which mutual advantage might exist (especially in the areas of trade and technological exchanges) are being identified and cultivated for the purpose of strengthening the momemtum of both nations' domestic agendas.

Until recently, there was little more than symbolic progress on the resolution of the 'three obstacles'. Agreements on trade, cultural exchanges, and the like earlier in this decade improved the atmospherics surrounding Sino–Soviet relations. However, in and of themselves they do not resolve the fundamental security issues that have divided the two nations for almost three decades. In order to maintain the sometimes fragile coalition on his domestic priorities, Deng Xiaoping carefully avoided any diplomatic initiatives towards the Soviets that might alienate the PLA leadership or provide them with an excuse to raise the political stakes surrounding the debate over the low priority assigned to PLA modernization.

Likewise, the volatile course of events surrounding Sino–Soviet relations in 1978–9 necessitated caution in his dealings with Gorbachev's predecessors because, as alluded to earlier, the actions of the Soviet Union and its clients during this period surrounding China with new loci for potential confrontations with the Soviets. Shortly after China and Japan signed their Treaty of Peace and Friendship, pledging their mutual opposition to Soviet hegemonism in Asia, the Soviets signed their own Treaty of Peace and Friendship with Vietnam, ratifying the Soviets' continued access to naval facilities at Cam Ranh Bay and providing Vietnam with the material assistance and security guarantees it needed to take the risk of invading Kampuchea. Their invasion in the last weeks of 1978 deposed the regime of Pol Pot and the Khmer Rouge whose own insurgent victory had been assisted by Chinese material support. China's own 'punitive' war against the Vietnamese in early 1979 was a military disaster for them. The sequence of events culminated with the Soviet Union's own intervention in Afghanistan in December of 1979. Thus, as China entered the 1980s, it was faced with a hostile military superpower that had demonstrated a willingness to intervene in Asia directly with its own military forces and indirectly with those of its surrogate, Vietnam. In this environment and with the PLA disrupted by the embarrassing performance in the Sino-Vietnamese war, it was politically imprudent to pursue aggressively any accommodation with the Soviet Union on the central security issues defining Sino–Soviet conflict. Therefore, China's demands on territorial issues, on Soviet force levels in Asia, on Vietnam's occupation of Kampuchea, and on Soviet intervention in Afghanistan remained largely unchanged, and little if any progress towards their resolution was achieved during the last years of the Brezhnev era or the interregnum that preceded Gorbachev's accession to power in 1985. At most, the volatility of these issues as potential catalysts of a Sino–Soviet military confrontation was mitigated somewhat by the cultivation of a wider array of low-level exchanges and negotiations on non-security matters.

Up to the time of writing, Deng has succeeded in pre-empting the emergence of a leadership coalition that could effect any substantial shifts in domestic priorities or Soviet policy, and his major strategy for accomplishing this has been to remove from leadership positions key actors from rival factions, replacing them with his own proteges. Deng himself assumed control of the Military Affairs Commission and appointed his close associate Yang Shangkun as the only permanent Vice Chairman of this critical military policy body. Party Secretary Zhao Ziyang assumed the position of first vice chairman of the Military Affairs Commission, a post that Hu Yaobang was denied during his tenure as Party Chairman. PLA veteran Xu Xiangquian was removed as Defence Minister in March of 1981, and while his successor, Geng Biao, did not last long in the position, his successor, Zhang Aiping, who had been the PLA's preferred candidate, has been no more successful in advancing PLA priorities against those of Deng and the reformers. In November of 1987, Deng, acting in his capacity as MAC chairman, issued a series of personnel appointments that resulted in the retirement of the Chief of Staff of the PLA, Yang Dezhi, 77, and his replacement by Chi Haotain, 61, who had been political commissar of the Jinan Military Command. Yu Quili, 73, was replaced as Director of the General Political Department by Yang Baibing, 66, who had been serving as political commissar of the Beijing Military Region. Yang also happens to be the younger brother of MAC permanent vice chairman Yang Shangkun. In addition, Zhao Nanqui, 52, was named to replace Hong Xuezhi, 76, as director general of the General Logistics Department (Rosen, 1988: 44). Almost all of the regional military commanders have been replaced by younger officers who, like Deng, are former victims of the Cultural Revolution. In the spring of 1985, it was announced that 47 000 PLA officers (roughly ten per cent of the officer corps) would be retired by the end of 1986, further eroding the power base of those PLA leaders who might consider mounting an opposition coalition against Deng. It was also announced that the total size of the PLA would be reduced by one million troops over the course of several years. The rationale for these changes was that a streamlined PLA led by a more professionalized officer corps could be modernized more rapidly and more extensively, and at a lower cost (Baum 1986). However, the not-so-hidden political agenda was to replace PLA veterans who might oppose Deng's priorities and programmes with younger, more technocratically trained officers who would be supportive of Deng's reforms.

Since 1985, Deng has also carefully managed a generational transition in the top leadership of the party itself, securing the retirement of most of the 'old guard' in the Chinese leadership and filling the resulting vacancies with younger, more technocratically oriented leaders. At a Party conference in September of 1985, ten of the 24 Politburo members were retired and replaced by five younger members of the so-called 'third echelon' of leaders, who are considered to be loyal to Deng and supportive of his programmes. Eight of those retired were veteran military leaders, including the venerable Marshal Ye Jianying who also relinquished his seat as the only career military man on the Politburo's Standing Committee. At the same meeting, 36 of the 162 members of the Central Advisory Commission and 30 of the 129-member Central Discipline and Inspection Commission were removed from office. Completing this wave of personnel changes, 64 members of the Central Committee, most of whom were in their seventies or eighties, were replaced by an equal number of younger officials thought to be Deng loyalists. The so-called 'veteran cadres' faction fared no better at this meeting, as only two of their ranks (Chen Yun and Li Xiannian) retained their seats on the Standing Committee, and only four others retained their Politburo seats (Peng Zhen, Yang Shangkun, Hu Qiaomu, and Yang Dezhi).[8]

The removal of Hu Yaobang, though a setback for the reformers, preceded a series of personnel moves at the thirteenth Party Congress in 1987 that further consolidated the reformers' control of key leadership positions and major policy bodies in the CCP and the state. Zhao Ziyang replaced Hu as party chairman, but conservative Li Peng assumed the position of Premier. Ten veteran members of the Politburo were retired at the Party Congress, and the Politburo was reduced in size from twenty to seventeen members. As a result, the average age of the Politburo membership dropped from 70 to 65 (Rosen, 1988: 43). Among those retiring were party elders who, to varying degrees, had been critical of certain aspects of Deng's reforms. Among these leaders were Chen Yun, Peng Zhen, and Hu Qiaomu. Zhao Ziyang was the only member of the Standing Committee of the Politburo to retain his seat, and the four new members included three vice premiers (Li Peng, Qiao Shi, and Yao Yilin), the head of the part Secretariat (Hu Qili). The new Central Committee reflected similar trends toward a younger, more technocratically oriented leadership. The average age of the 285 members and alternates dropped by 3.9 years to 55.2 years of age. The proportion of them that have a college education grew by 17.9 per cent to 209 members (Rosen, 1988: 43).

In this manner, Deng managed to pre-empt the ability of potential rivals to force any substantial change in China's strategy of cautiously rebuilding a constructive relationship with the Soviets. Mikhail Gorbachev's visit to Beijing in May 1989 symbolized the success of this strategy. To the extent that this initiative is grounded in powerful domestic priorities whose momentum has been secured by leadership changes, we should not discount their potential significance or China's commitment to them. However, the turmoil of June 1989 the fall of Zhao Ziyang and the return of many of the ageing Conservatives retired at the Thirteenth Party Congress demonstrate rather dramatically just how fragile Deng's leadership coalition is and just how vulnerable his policy strategy remains.

Domestic Sources of the Soviet Union's Changing China Policy

Similar trends in Soviet leadership politics have enhanced Mikhail Gorbachev's ability to redirect the Soviet Union's China policy in a more constructive and less overtly hostile direction. What has allowed him to do this is the unprecedented pervasiveness of the leadership transition currently underway in the Soviet Union. The ageing of the Brezhnev generation has presented Gorbachev with a unique opportunity to fill vacancies in top leadership positions in both the Party and key Ministries with younger leaders who also share his policy preferences. As a result, he appears to be consolidating his control over the policy process (including foreign policy) much more quickly than was the case when Brezhnev came to power in 1963.

When Leonid Brezhnev became General Secretary of the CPSU he was 57 years old, and the average age of the Politburo membership was 59 (Brown, 1985: 3). Thus, the major policy making body of the CPSU was already populated by other elites of his own generation. Therefore, the opportunities for patronage that are created by the normal process of attrition were not immediately forthcoming for Brezhnev. Nor were those of his generation who were already in positions of influence indebted to Brezhnev for their status. In this sense, Brezhnev's policy of 'respect for cadres' and his tendency to serve more as a policy broker among contending elites who, individually, enjoyed considerable autonomy in initiating and managing policy in their area of responsibility may have been simply his way of giving formal recognition to the political reality he faced: a collection of elites not indebted to him for their position and therefore more autonomous from him in their policy advocacy. 'Respect for cadres' and decision by consensus simply ratified the implicit compact among these elites to respect each other's institutional prerogatives and defer to each other's substantive expertise.

By contrast, Gorbachev assumed office at the age of 54 amid a Politburo that averaged 67 years of age. Of the ten voting members at that time, five were over 70 years old and three were in their sixties (Brown, 1985: 3). As a consequence, Gorbachev has had the opportunity to oversee (and manage) an almost complete turnover in the Politburo and the CPSU Secretariat.[9] In his first year in office, he succeeded in removing four of the nine holdovers from the Politburo. These included such powerful Brezhnev-era veterans as Nikolai Tikhanov (Chairman of the Presidium of the Council of Ministers), D. A. Kunayev (First Secretary of the Kazakhstan Party apparatus), Viktor Grishin (First Secretary of the Moscow Party apparatus), and Grigori Romanov (First Secretary of the Leningrad Party apparatus). Among their replacements were Nikolai Ryzhkov (Chairman of the Council of Ministers), Yegor Ligachev (Party Secretary in charge of personnel and ideology), Viktor Chebrikov (head of the KGB), Eduard Shevardnadze (Foreign Minister), Lev Zaikov (Leningrad Party chief, later promoted to a Secretariat post), Viktor Nikonov (formerly in the Ministry of Agriculture), Nikolai Slyun'kov (Deputy Chairman of Gosplan), and Aleksandr Yakovlev (formerly Ambassador to Canada). By 1989, none of the Brezhnev era holdovers remained on the Politburo, and there had been a complete turnover in the Central Committee Secretaries.

Gorbachev has been especially successful at effecting personnel changes in the party and government offices involved in foreign and security matters. Long-time Foreign Minister Andrei Gromyko was 'promoted' to the more ceremonial post of Chairman of the Presidium of the Supreme Soviet, thus effectively removing him from the day-to-day management of foreign affairs. His replacement, Eduard Shevardnadze, has gained full Politburo status and has been among the most active and visible members of Gorbachev's inner circle. In addition, the Minister of Foreign Trade, Nikolai Patolichev, was retired, along with several of Gromyko's long-time deputy Foreign Ministers. Four new deputy Foreign Ministers were appointed and one-third of all ambassadors were transferred. From his position as Chairman of the Council of Ministers, Nikolai Ryzhkov has served as one of the prime architects of Gorbachev's economic reform programme and has played an especially active role in the formulation of the Soviet Union's new joint venture laws and in the efforts to cultivate interest in such ventures among foreign visitors.

At the Central Committee Secretariat, Boris Ponomarev and Konstantin Rusakov, who had long held the two Secretariat posts dealing with foreign affairs, were retired and replaced by Anatoly Dobrynin and Vadim Medvedev. Dobrynin himself later left the Secretariat post to serve as a personal advisor to Gorbachev. The Central Committee's foreign affairs apparatus was reorganized, with Yakovlev assuming the leadership of a new commission to supervise foreign policy. As a concession to the conservatives, Valentin Falin was named to replace Dobrynin as head of the International Department. Viktor Chebrikov, successor to Andropov as head of the KGB was promoted to full Politburo membership under Gorbachev, but is not considered to be among Gorbachev's inner circle of reform advocates. In Autumn 1988, he was removed from his position a KGB and transferred to the leadership of a new Party commission supervising legislative reform, a move considered to be a substantial reduction in his power (Parrott, 1988: 31).

Following the notorious incident in which a West German youth landed his plane in Red Square, Gorbachev initiated personnel changes in the Ministry of Defence as well. Defence Minister Serge Sokolov, who had been passed over several times for full Politburo membership since succeeding Dmitri Ustinov in December of 1984 was replaced by Dimitri Yazov, who had previously served as commander of the Central Asian Military District.

To the extent that Gorbachev can use this transition in leadership to install in office individuals who share his policy preferences, he should be in a position to consolidate his control over the Soviet Union's policy making machinery much sooner and much more thoroughly than was the case when Brezhnev acceded to power in 1963. Thus, to the extent that Gorbachev has an interest in changing the direction of Soviet policy toward China, he should be in a position to overcome the inertia behind the Brezhnev policy in Asia with much less resistance than could either of his post-Brezhnev predecessors. The fact that he has managed to reshuffle the leadership of the Ministry of Defence means that he is better positioned to overcome the expected institutional sources of resistance to a demilitarization of Soviet policy in Asia.[10] And the fact that he has managed to reshuffle the top leadership in the Ministry of Foreign Affairs and the Central Committee Secretariat offices that deal with foreign affairs gives evidence of his intent (and growing capacity) to nject his 'new thinking' into the basic assumptions and operating principles of Soviet foreign policy.

Furthermore, the broad policy concerns that seem to be occupying Gorbachev's attention and which seem to be the central focus of his push for reform are also congruent with initiatives to reduce tensions with China. Clearly, the priority of the Gorbachev reforms is domestic economic modernization. Economic reforms will require a considerable investment of resources and a reordering of budgetary priorities unless new sources of revenues can be found for investment in industrial modernization, consumer goods production, and agriculture. As the urgency of domestic economic initiatives generates intensified 'guns versus butter' debates among the policy elite, one obvious source of resources for economic modernization would be the military budget, which consumes fourteen to sixteen per cent of GNP. Any diplomatic initiatives that reduce the threat to Soviet security interest and thereby reduce the resource demands of the military establishment would therefore complement Gorbachev's domestic priorities.

A reduction in tensions with China would represent just such an initiative. While arms control agreements with the US might represent a more substantial reduction in the security threat to the Soviet Union, one could argue that rapprochement with China would produce a greater savings in costs relative to risks. Despite recent efforts to modernize its nuclear arsenal, China lacks the capacity to pose a first strike or even a major second strike threat to the Soviet Union. PLA conventional forces lack both the mobility and the firepower to pose a serious offensive threat to the array of Soviet conventional capabilities deployed in Asia. Yet, to date the Soviets have continued to maintain an extraordinarily large (and expensive) contingent of forces deployed against China. Removing some of these units from border regions or reducing them to skeleton status could provide a significant savings in defence spending for the Soviets without any substantial increase in risk, given the limited offensive capabilities of the PLA. And, no doubt, any such troop reductions would occur in conjunction with the Chinese demobilization of one million troops that was announced in 1985 and which further reduced the risks to Soviet security in Asia.

Of course, such initiatives will meet with resistance on the part of the Soviet military. However, Gorbachev's ability to overcome this resistance is enhanced by several considerations. First, as alluded to earlier, the uproar followed the West German Mathias Rust's landing an airplane in Red Square presented Gorbachev with the opportunity to shake up the leadership of the Ministry of Defence and, in the process, to remove from office some of those who might oppose any demilitarization of Soviet policy in Asia. Second, the military establishment is likely to be more willing to accept reductions in Asian deployments than in its European forces that are charged with deterring NATO and maintaining the stability of the Warsaw Pact. The fact that Gorbachev felt sufficiently secure politically to announce unilateral reductions in the size of the Red Army generally and in the number and disposition (that is, from offensive to defensive) of troops deployed in Eastern Europe specifically suggest that he is certainly secure enough to propose similar reductions in Asia, where the risks of such moves would be far less. Thus, to the extent that improved relations with China can permit substantial savings in defence spending without significant risks, it would appear that such initiatives would enjoy high priority as a foreign policy complement to Gorbachev's domestic agenda.

PROGRESS IN SINO-SOVIET RELATIONS

Although progress toward any significant Sino–Soviet rapprochement was difficult and slow throughout most of this decade, an examination of the domestic context of each nation's policy toward the other would also lead one to conclude that there are powerful incentives for both China and the Soviet Union to achieve a relaxation in tensions. And the momentum toward rapprochement has accelerated rapidly since Gorbachev's accession to power.

Prior to this, significant progress in expanding bilateral exchanges had been confined largely to diplomatic exchanges, increasing economic ties, and a regular and increasing flow of educational, cultural and scientific exchanges. Beginning with the visit of Soviet Vice Prime Minister Ivan Arkhipov in December of 1984, China and the Soviet Union have forged a growing economic relationship that, in the beginning, may have carried more symbolic than substantive weight but is gradually evolving into a modest but significant trade relationship that works to the economic advantage of both nations. Arkhipov's visit resulted in a number of agreements calling for co-operation in modernizing industrial enterprises developed jointly in the 1950s, expanding scientific and cultural exchanges, and establishing a Sino–Soviet Economic, Trade, Scientific and Technical

Cooperation Commission. In addition, a long term trade agreement was signed. The reciprocal visit to Moscow of Arkhipov's Chinese counterpart, Vice Prime Minister Yao Yilin, resulted in an agreement for Soviet assistance in the construction of seven new projects and the reconstruction of seventeen older facilities, most of which were concentrated in heavy industries such as metallurgy, machine building, chemical production, and transportation. Included among these projects are some of China's most important industrial plants, such as the steel plants at Anshan, Baotou, and Wuhan as well as the showcase Louyang tractor plant (Frankenstein, 1988: 260). Bilateral trade has grown from about $160 million in 1981 to $1.9 billion in 1985, with agreements signed in 1985 calling for an expansion in trade volume to between to $17 billion and $18 billion between 1985 and 1990 (Levine, 1986:246; Frankenstein, 1988:260).

Although the volume of trade remains relatively small – the $1.9 billion figure represents only about 3 per cent of China's total trade volume and is only about 30 per cent of China's trade with the US – the prospects for growth seem promising (Levine 1986:246). At present, China is exporting agricultural products and light industrial products to the Soviet Union. Given the problems of Soviet agriculture and consumer goods industries, the Soviet Union would probably find it preferable to expand trade with China in these areas, as it would allow them to meet rising consumer demand while minimizing their dependence on Western grain purchases (with the political volatility that have characterized such purchases in the past) and on Western consumer goods. By the same token, China would be pleased to open a large new market for its products, especially one that was not subject to the same protectionist sentiments that increasingly characterize Western markets for agricultural commodities and consumer goods. In other words, each represents for the other a sizeable alternative to the West as a source of inputs for economic modernization and as a target market for the outputs of economic expansion.

Relatedly, technological cooperation in heavy industrial projects would seem to be of mutual interest to both nations as well. Such assistance has traditionally been the major route by which the Soviets have cultivated economic interdependence with developing nations. The opportunity for cultivating such ties with a nation of China's size and strategic importance would be attractive to the Soviets for non-economic as well as the obvious economic reasons. Similarly, China's industrial modernization has so far concentrated on the development of light industry producing consumer goods for domestic consumption and export markets. At some point, pressure to expand heavy industry will intensify, and by resorting to the Soviet Union as an alternative source of finance and technology for such efforts, China may be able to minimize the risks and debt problems that would accompany Western involvement in the expansion of their heavy industrial sector. Besides, Soviet assistance in heavy industry would free them to use their credits with the West to expand those sectors that have the greatest potential for export earnings from the West: that is, light industries that produce consumer goods at prices competitive in lucrative Western markets. Both nations also stand to gain by their willingness, derived from past experience, to arrange bilateral transactions in barter terms, thereby relieving some of the pressure on each nation's foreign exchange reserves that are needed to purchase technologies from and service debt to Western nations and Japan.

Amid the improved atmospherics surrounding Sino–Soviet relations that these low-level exchanges have created, there has been substantial progress on all three of the obstacles that define the crucial security issues at the heart of Sino–Soviet hostilities. Movement on these issues indicates that both nations seem determined not to allow them to prevent the reduction of bilateral tensions and the cultivation of further bilateral exchanges. The longstanding border question is, in the words of Thomas Robinson (1987:242), 'ripe for rapid resolution'. He points out that the border issue itself has never been supremely important for its own sake, as all that was really of importance was China's right to navigation along Amur and Ussur Rivers. Indeed, China had dropped references to the 'unequal treaties' in recent rounds of border negotiations, concentrating instead on the more pragmatic questions of navigation rights on the Amur and Ussuri Rivers and the size and configuration of Soviet military forces deployed along the disputed border. Mikhail Gorbachev's Vladivostok speech of July, 1986 had the effect of granting this concession by agreeing that the border should run along the main channel (see Kimura, 1987:1; Robinson, 1987:243).

The more crucial troop disposition question is, as discussed above, amenable to amelioration, as both nations have compelling domestic economic reasons to demobilize troops. In fact, as noted earlier, China has begun reducing the size of its forces and has shifted some defence industries to civilian production. The Soviets for their part have announced the withdrawal of one division (10 000 to 12 000 roops) from their contingent in Mongolia (estimated to total 65 000 roops). The 10 per cent reduction in the size of the Red Army that Gorbachev announced at the United Nations in December 1988 will undoubtedly include units stationed in Asia. Indeed, we would expect that a disproportionate share of the cuts might occur there, if only in the form of the demobilization of units withdrawn from Afghanistan. Of course, these moves have more symbolic than real value, and to date the Chinese public reaction has been less than overwhelming (see Kimura 1987:5; Ellison, 1987:24; Levine, 1986:227; Robinson, 1987:213). However, they are indicative of some movement on issues that were thought to be unresolvable only a few years ago. And the fact that the US–Soviet INF treaty also includes the destruction of SS-20s stationed in Asia and targeted against China has certainly relieved a major threat component facing China, rendering more palatable the argument within the Chinese leadership that investment in the civilian economy should take precedence over PLA modernization because the severity of the Soviet threat (especially the nuclear first strike component) has diminished.

The other two 'obstacles' – Vietnamese occupation of Kampuchea and the Soviet presence in Afghanistan – though less amenable to direct resolution because they involve Soviet commitments to third parties, have in fact moved most rapidly to resolution. The last Soviet troops left Afghanistan in February 1989. All that remains of this issue as an obstacle to Sino–Soviet rapprochement are the matters of whether the Kabul government can survive without the Soviet military and, if its collapse appears imminent, whether the Soviet Union is willing to reintervene on behalf of the current government or, alternatively, content itself with some sort of accommodation (perhaps Finlandization) of whatever coalition government might eventually emerge in the aftermath of the Soviet withdrawal.

Similarly, negotiations between Vietnam and the three Kampuchean resistance groups are proceeding along with the withdrawal of Vietnamese forces. Hanoi has announced that troop withdrawal was completed by 30 September, 1989, despite the lack of progress at that time in negotiations to establish a coalition government. As with Afghanistan, the major remaining uncertainty in this issue's role in Sino–Soviet relations is whether and under what conditions the Vietnamese might reassert themselves militarily, should the government it leaves behind in Phnom Penh prove transient. However, it appears that the financial burden of occupation imposes severe

constraints on Hanoi's efforts to revitalize its own economy and ha
imposed on Vietnam a degree of diplomatic isolation that ha
precluded its participation in the economic dynamism of th
Asia–Pacific rim. Thus, the urgency of its own domestic economi
priorities is compelling Vietnam to take actions that promise t
resolve a second of the three obstacles to Sino–Soviet rapproche
ment. The fact that Deng Xiaoping has narrowed the definition c
this obstacle by dropping demands that the Soviet Union cease its ai
to Vietnam and discontinue its naval operations out of Cam Ran
Bay indicates that he is no longer willing to have Vietnam retar
improvements in Sino–Soviet relations that could be beneficial to hi
own domestic economic initiatives (see Kimura, 1987:5; Baum
1986). Apparently, so long as Vietnam withdraws from Kampuchea
the Chinese are willing to live with the Soviet presence in and suppor
of Vietnam just as they are willing to live with the presence of th
other hegemonic power in the Pacific, the United States. Thus,
appears that neither nation has any desire to initiate a war with th
other, nor to allow crises in some third area to draw them into
confrontation or to jeopardize the cultivation of expanded, mutuall
beneficial bilateral relations.

IMPLICATIONS FOR US–JAPAN SECURITY RELATIONS

As we witness the trend towards a relaxation of Sino–Soviet tension
the question naturally arises as to what this will imply for the future c
US–Japan security cooperation in the Pacific Basin. After all, a
noted earlier, the glue that has held this relationship together despit
all the squabbling over burden sharing and trade issues has been th
shared perception of the threat posed by an escalating Sovie
presence and an activist Soviet agenda in Asia. And the majo
geopolitical factor serving to offset the substantial Soviet numeric
advantage in troops and hardware in Asia has been the counterweigh
posed by China on the mainland. If Sino–Soviet hostility is reduce
substantially and in its place emerges a flourishing, mutually bene
ficial economic relationship between the two mainland giants, th
strains that have long percolated beneath the surface of th
US–Japan security relationship could begin to surface and intensify a
a result of persistent trade friction between the two nations.

   A number of analysts have considered the prospect of Japa
gradually moving towards a more neutralist position between the U

and the Soviet Union, and usually this possibility is discounted if not totally rejected on the grounds that there are too many serious and longstanding sources of hostility between Japan and the Soviet Union for the former to ever see the latter as anything less than an enemy. However, typically these analyses do not consider as a premise the possibility of the substantial alteration in the security environment facing Japan that rapprochement between the Soviet Union and China would represent. Under such conditions, compounded by heightened bilateral tensions between Japan and the US, would Japan perhaps be more inclined to work out its own accommodation with the Soviets, redefining if not dismantling in the process the fundamental basis of Japan–US security cooperation in the postwar era? It is to this question that we now turn.

To begin with, let us place this question in its proper context. Any prudent analyst would have to argue that the prospects for a Japanese drift away from the US and toward the Soviet Union are remote at best. However, we should also keep in mind that the prospects for an Asian war, involving Japan, the US, and China against the Soviet Union, are far more remote. Yet all four nations spend billions of dollars annually trying to deter just such an eventuality by preparing to undertake it. And if the strategic balance in Asia is altered by the amelioration of Sino–Soviet hostility, then the calculus of strategic contingencies facing the Japan–US alliance would be altered in such a way as to place greater pressure on the stability of the alliance. Under such circumstances, the contingencies for which the two would have to prepare would now have to include the possibility of an Asian conflict in which Chinese forces *would not* be involved against the Soviet Union, either because China co-operated with the Soviets (a remote possibility) or, with the Soviets' blessings, chose to sit out the conflict (a far less remote possibility).

Amid the pressures created by the altered strategic environment, the prospects for a critical erosion of co-operation between the US and Japan begin to appear somewhat less remote. Thus, when assessing the prospects for a Japanese drift away from the US and towards the Soviets, one must consider the likelihood of Japan and the USSR resolving their longstanding grievances *in the context of the substantially altered strategic environment* facing Japan, one in which the conflict between the two mainland powers (China and the USSR) is being ameliorated. Only a few years ago, few analysts were willing to entertain the prospect of any Sino–Soviet rapprochement. Yet today these same analysts see the barriers melting away. If this could occur in such a short period between two nations with compelling domestic priorities but still large and powerful military capabilities arrayed against each other, can we so easily discount the possibility of a Soviet–Japanese detente, give the economic pressures Japan will face domestically and internationally, as well as its dependence on external sources for its military security and its supplies of food, energy, and other vital resources? It is with these considerations in mind that we turn to the assessment of the prospects for Japan's security policy, Caught between the two super-powers and faced with a changing security environment in Asia, will Japan feel the pressures to pursue a more independent and neutralist posture between the two super-powers in Asia?

When the prospect of an independent Japanese policy toward the Soviet Union is raised, the reflexive response is that Soviet–Japanese conflicts and suspicions are too serious and longstanding to permit such an eventuality. The most prominent point of contention between the Soviet Union and Japan has been, since the end of the Second World War, the absence of a peace treaty and the dispute over territorial claims to the four islands north of Hokkaido.[11] This historically rooted dispute has taken on the significance in Japanese–Soviet relations that comparable territorial disputes have in Sino–Soviet relations. In one sense, they appear unresolvable, at least in a formal sense. It has been argued, for instance, that the Soviet Union has refused not only to negotiate such territorial issues but even to acknowledge that they exist because to do so would be to legitimize the right of China and a number of East European nations to revive territorial and border claims of their own. However, as was noted earlier in the case of China, it appears that longstanding territorial disputes will no longer be allowed to foreclose the possibility of improved Sino–Soviet relations because compelling domestic economic and international security interests (for both China and the Soviet Union) dictate the desirability of rapprochement. Likewise, one could argue that, with the emergence of altered domestic needs and international security conditions facing Japan and the Soviet Union, both nations' leaders might be less inclined to allow territorial questions to impede the development of accommodations on more urgent economic and military matters.

Indeed, what raises the Northern Territories issue above the level of mere historical claims is their strategic value to the Soviets and, conversely, the threat that Soviet presence on the islands poses to Japan. For the Soviet Union, occupation of the islands precludes a break in the Kuril chain stretching to the Kamchatka peninsula and assures them a route of passage for their nuclear submarines that is relatively free from detection by US surveillance. To give up the islands would be to increase the vulnerability of their Pacific fleet to being bottled up in the Sea of Okhotsk in the event of a crisis. In this context the Sino–Japanese Treaty of 1978, with its 'anti-hegemonism' clause, was seen by the Brezhnev Politburo as being sufficiently provocative as to require a Soviet response. Consequently, beginning in 1978, the Soviet union began a buildup of its forces on two of the four northern islands. An airstrip was completed on Kunashiri Island and a 9–10 000 man combat force with armour, artillery, and attack helicopters was deployed there. More troops were deployed on Shikotan as well (Buck, 1981:93). In 1983, some 30 MIG-23 fighter-bombers were reportedly deployed on Etorofu (Kim, 1987:29). Relatedly, it was revealed in 1983 that 108 SS-20s with three warheads each were deployed in Asia and, according to Andrei Gromyko, specifically targeted on Japan, Okinawa, and South Korea (Kim, 1987:30). That number reportedly increased to 171 prior to the INF Treaty (Kimura, 1987:13).

The militarization of the Northern Territories dispute under Brezhnev undoubtedly made the issue even more difficult to resolve as a barrier to Soviet–Japanese relations. These developments raised the issue from the realm of historically grounded territorial dispute to that of a contemporary security issue. This perception was reinforced in Japan by the KAL-007 incident, a tragedy that intensified traditional public hostility in Japan towards the Soviet Union.

However, just as Gorbachev has signalled a redirection of Soviet policy towards China, his Vladivostok speech of 1986 and his Krasnoyarsk speech of 1988 also signalled at least the potential for a reorientation of Soviet policy towards Japan. The visit of Foreign Minister Shevardnadze to Tokyo in January 1986 and the return visit to Moscow in May of his Japanese counterpart Shintaro Abe represented the first visit by either nation's Foreign Minister in ten years. Of course, the communiques that resulted from these visits indicated no significant progress on the Northern Territories issue, the Sino–Japanese Treaty, or US–Japanese relations, all of which represent major issues of sensitivity in bilateral relations. However, as with Sino–Soviet relations, some progress has been forthcoming in the negotiation of low-level agreements and exchanges.

On the Northern Territories issue, an agreement was reached to allow Japanese citizens to visit the graves of their ancestors on these islands. On other diplomatic matters, it was agreed to hold annual consultations at the level of Foreign Minister, and both expressed a willingness to work toward concluding a Soviet–Japanese peace agreement. The Soviet–Japanese Commission on Scientific and Technical Cooperation was also revived (Kim, 1987:11). There was much excitement about the prospect of Mikhail Gorbachev's planned visit to Tokyo in January 1987, a visit that never took place, though the cancellation was not the result of any sudden rift in Soviet–Japanese relations.[12]

The most significant advances in Japan–Soviet relations have occurred in the realm of economic exchanges, as Gorbachev seems to have extended to Japan his strategy of reducing security tensions through the careful cultivation and expansion of mutually beneficial economic relations. In April 1986 a major Japanese trade mission visited Moscow at the invitation of Prime Minister Nikolai Ryzhkov. They were briefed on Soviet plans for economic reform, especially in the area of trade and foreign investment, and apparently were especially impressed by Ryzhkov's expressed desire to expand the proportion of manufactured goods in the Soviet Union's export flows and his pledge to complete a new set of laws on joint ventures (Kim, 1987: 13–15). Since then the joint venture laws have been promulgated, and more than a dozen Japanese firms (including C. Itoh, Mitsui, and Mitsubishi) have completed joint venture agreements with the Soviet Union (Kim 1987:33). In addition, Japan's Sakhalin Oil Development Corporation, created in 1972 for the joint development with the Soviets of oil and gas resources in northern Sakhalin, has proposed to resume negotiations with the Soviets concerning the revival of those resource development efforts (Kim, 1987:33).

What is especially significant about the expanding economic ties between the two nations is the changing character of the Soviet initiatives towards Japan. There has been for some time a debate among Western scholars over the nature and extent of the economic affinity between Japan and the Soviet Union. On the one hand, some have argued that, with Japan being resource poor but technology rich and the Soviet Union being resource rich but technology poor, there exists a substantial economic affinity between the two. Japan's geographic proximity to the Soviet Union and, especially, its undeveloped Siberian resources are cited as indicators of the potential for economic co-operation between the two. On the other hand, a number of scholars have recently called into question the real potential of this relationship, noting for instance that transportation problems and other costs of extraction make Siberian resources uneconomical to a Japan that has already succeeded in expanding and diversifying its sources of most of its needed raw materials (see, for instance, Smith 1987). Furthermore, as Japan's economy continues the transition away from export-led manufacturing as its base to one based on finance, high technology, and other 'post-industrial' sectors, it will have less need for raw materials to maintain economic growth.[13]

Yet, the directions in Japan–Soviet economic ties indicated by the Gorbachev initiatives seem to render this debate largely irrelevant because they seem geared toward altering the basis of bilateral exchanges from a 'raw materials for manufactured goods and technology' exchange to one based more heavily on the sale of manufactured goods to Japan and the development of the Soviet Union as a site for Japanese overseas investments (in the form of joint ventures). The stagnation of Japan's domestic economy caused by yen appreciation, increased caution in Japan's Chinese investments, and the growing protectionism in the US and Europe all serve to make the Soviet Union that much more attractive as a potential partner for Japan in economic ventures. Indeed, the argument is advanced by the Soviets that, if the import of manufactured goods from Asian NICs is part of the transition underway in Japan's economy, why not the Soviet Union as one of those suppliers? In this sense, Gorbachev's economic diplomacy initiatives seem creatively shaped to serve not only the Soviet Union's own urgent domestic priorities but also Japan's emerging needs as its economy undergoes the transition to post-industrialism.

One further aspect of recent Soviet initiatives towards Japan is the noticeable absence of sabre rattling that often characterized the clumsy initiatives of the Brezhnev era. Gorbachev's Vladivostok speech said very little about military matters, and he was especially silent on those issues in his comments directed towards Japan and China. The Japanese expressed concerns over increased deployments of SS-20s in Asia, and Gorbachev pledged to Foreign Minister Abe to seek a solution to this problem (Kim, 1987:34–36). The US–Soviet INF agreement, with its 'zero-zero' solution to the SS-20/Pershing II balance, has rendered this concern moot.

Of course, Japan's security concerns with respect to the Soviet Union will not dissolve so long as the Soviet presence on the Northern Islands persists and the Soviet force levels in Asia remain at their current levels. However, just as Gorbachev appears willing to make some concessions on these matters to ease Chinese concerns, so too could he conceivably seek to reduce Japan's concerns with some limited redeployment of forces. More generally, we can expect that his strategy for the immediate future will centre on attempting to minimize the urgency Japan's perceived sense of threat from the Soviets and to do this by gradually building a network of economic and diplomatic exchanges that build a sense of trust through growing interdependence. How Japan will respond to this will depend to a considerable degree on the status of US–Japanese trade and security relations, and it is to this question that we now turn.

US–JAPAN SECURITY RELATIONS AMID THE TRANSITION IN ASIA

To a profound degree, Japan's security posture *vis-à-vis* both China and the Soviet Union has always been determined in large part by its dependence on the US for military security, a condition with which no nation, including Japan, would be entirely comfortable. The uneasiness has been compounded in the last two decades by a series of US policy initiatives and crisis management actions that were made largely without consultation with Japan but which nonetheless placed Japan in a position of being compelled to support the US in these initiatives.[14] The news of Henry Kissinger's secret visit to Beijing was one of the Nixon shocks that shook US–Japan relations, not because it threatened vital Japanese interests but because Japan had for so long supported the US policy of isolating the People's Republic of China (arguably against Japan's own trade and security interests), only to have the US reverse this policy without even consulting or informing Japan in advance. Similar events, such as US INF proposals in the early 1980s that would have allowed the Soviets to redeploy SS-20s to Asia, all have reinforced an apprehensiveness in Japan over the potential political costs of its dependence on the US for military security. Japan is expected to support the US in its policies towards the PRC and the Soviet Union, in crisis situations in the Middle East, even when these policies may impact negatively on Japanese economic interests. There seems to be a sometimes arrogant disregard for even the common courtesy of consultation with Japan on policies that affect vital Japanese interests. US complaints over the lack of a 'level playing field' in trade matters seem to have their counterpart in Japanese concerns over foreign and security policy initiatives.

As alluded to in the introduction to this chapter, there have always been tensions underlying the US–Japan security relationship. These stem from the contradictions built into the relationship immediately after the Second World War. On the one hand, the US wished to preclude the re-emergence of Japan as a military power in Asia and, therefore, built into the Japanese constitution elements such as Article 9 that were designed to guarantee the permanent demilitarization of Japan. On the other hand, the US has vital security interests in Asia (including the security of Japan) and would like Japan to assume a greater share of the burden of protecting those interests. Similarly, there has evolved in Japan a genuine public sentiment against rearmament, and no doubt the absence of the economic burden of defence has been an asset to Japan's economic development. On the other hand, Japan's dependence on American military guarantees constrains its independence in foreign policy, as there is constant pressure to support the US position on certain issues even when Japanese national interests might dictate otherwise. With these contradictory impulses built into their relationship, the question for the two nations has always been whether they could manage the resulting tensions in bilateral interactions to the point that the long term stability of the relationship could be preserved. The question today is whether the current trade problems between Japan and the US are of sufficient severity as to raise underlying tensions to the point of causing a serious rift. The fact that the security environment that defines the *raison d'être* for the alliance is undergoing such a profound transformation renders these tensions even more susceptible to eruptions.

In recent years, security tensions between Japan and the US have centred on the US urging that Japan assume a greater share of the responsibility for three sectors of their mutual defence: (1) control of the seas south to the Philippines and Guam; (2) the ability to mine and blockade the straits connecting the Sea of Japan with the Pacific Ocean; and (3) the construction of an air defence screen across the Japanese islands to interdict Soviet long range bombers, fighter-bombers, and tactical aircraft. To perform these roles, the US estimated that Japan would need fourteen squadrons of F-15 fighters (350 planes), 25 submarines, 70 destroyers, and 125 anti-submarine aircraft (Johnson, 1986:570). Prime Minister Nakasone had on several occasions agreed to these tasks, and his defence procurement plans seemed to reflect this as his intention (Johnson 1986:570). Whether his successors will share his commitment to continue this policy building Japan's defences remains to be seen.

No doubt part of the reason for US insistence on this alteration in
the burden sharing arrangements is the current trade imbalance
between the two nations. However, Japan's assumption of additional
defence burdens in and of itself will do little if anything to offset a $60
billion trade deficit. It is important to the US more for purposes of
domestic political consumption that for either trade deficit remedia-
tion or defence burden reduction. The US trade deficit will not shrink
noticeably nor will the defence budget be reduced proportionately as
Japan assumes these new security missions. Therefore, one must ask
whether it is a wise course, for the long term, to pressure Japan into
such efforts.

There are reasons to doubt whether the Nakasone policy on
defence spending will persist beyond his tenure in office. The special
relationship between Nakasone and Reagan served to disguise
beneath the facade of personal friendship the profound bilateral
tensions that emerged during the 1980s. With the passing from office
of these two leaders, there is reason to doubt the willingness or ability
of Nakasone's successors to preserve the momentum on defence
spending. Instead, with trade problems fuelling heightened political
tensions between the two nations, persistent US pressure for Japan to
develop a greater defence capability will simply exacerbate bilateral
tensions. Objections to any violation of the traditional one per cent of
GNP ceiling on defence spending are widespread and likely to
persist. Johnson (1986:571) noted that a major public opinion poll in
1985 indicated that while 79 per cent of Americans believed the US
would come to the defence of Japan if it were attacked, only 42 per
cent of Japanese shared this belief and 54 per cent believed firmly
that the US would *not* defend Japan. US pressure on Japan with
regard to defence matters can only reinforce public doubts in Japan
about US commitments to Japan's defence, and these sentiments
could be reflected at the polls in Japan as well. Thus, Nakasone's
successors will be faced with a number of domestic political pressures
that may make them inclined to chart a path of greater security
independence for Japan, but defined in Japanese terms. More
specifically, pressures created by protectionist sentiment in the US
combined with a deterioration in public confidence in America's
defence commitments to Japan may induce a Japanese Prime Minister to explore economic diplomacy with the Soviet Union,
especially as the improvement in Sino–Soviet relations removes
China as a counterweight to Soviet military presence in Asia, and as
the Soviet Union makes unilateral concessions on certain issues
dividing it from Japan.

The new relationship that appears to be developing between Japan and the Soviet Union would create pressures against Japan continuing its military buildup. While Gorbachev has carefully avoided sabre rattling in his approach to Japan, Japanese leaders certainly are cognizant of the negative impact that a substantial Japanese buildup would have on relations with the Soviet Union, especially if that buildup is explicitly directed at the Soviet Union, as is the case with the three tasks mentioned earlier. If the US purpose is to compel Japan to assume a greater responsibility for its own defence against the Soviets in Asia, then a future Prime Minister may conclude that the more productive way to do that is to rely on tried and true Japanese methods of economic diplomacy, a strategy that would seem all the more attractive given the recent Soviet propensity for a similar 'new thinking'. Again, such a trend in US–Japan and Japan–Soviet relations may appear to be rather remote, but is it any less remote than what conventional wisdom held the prospects for Sino–Soviet rapprochement to be only a few years ago?

CONCLUSION

The purpose of this chapter has been to raise some questions that need to be addressed concerning the sometimes all-too-sanguine American attitudes about the stability of security relations with Japan. These ties have always been subject to strain created by contradictory impulses built into the relationship. And up to now, analysts on both sides of the Pacific have been reluctant to entertain the possibility of any rift in those relations because bilateral security ties have been so essential to both nations' interests in the Pacific Basin. However, as we approach the end of this century, we must become cognizant of the profound changes in the strategic environment – especially in Sino–Soviet relations – taking place in Asia, and the implications of those changes for US–Japan security relations. No longer can the shared hostility towards the Soviet Union on the part of the US, Japan, and China be presumed. If this element of the Asian security equation changes, then the strategic calculus of Japan will necessarily be altered, especially if it is faced with unprecedented economic pressure internally and internationally as well as US pressure to assume greater responsibility for its own defence. My purpose has been to sketch out some contingencies for which leaders in both the US and Japan need to plan. If they fail to do so, the altered strategic environment in Asia could magnify tensions within the alliance to a crisis point. Only by coordinating their foreign policies and adjusting the terms of their mutual security arrangements to take into account the changes occurring on the Asian mainland can the US and Japan preclude the chance of these contingencies becoming reality.

Notes

1. Chalmers Johnson (1986:561) presents an interesting rebuttal to the 'free rider' argument. He first notes that Japan has been charged with taking a 'free ride' on defence by US Under Secretary of State Michael Armacost and Secretary of Defence Caspar Weinberger, among others. He also cites Edward Olsen's (1984) argument that the American taxpayer pays for Japan's defence. Johnson then counters this argument with data comparing Japan's defence spending to that of the United States' other allies, and then presents the novel argument that, in fact, it is Japan that, through its export of capital to the US, actually financed about one-quarter of the US defence burden during the Reagan administration. The Reagan defence buildup was paid for with deficit spending and it is Japan that has financed the largest single portion of the trillion dollar Reagan deficit. For another recent analysis of the 'free ride' argument, see Fallows (1989).

2. On the politics of US–Japan trade relations, see Bergsten (1987), Krasner (1986), Cohen (1984), Destler and Sato (1984), Sato (1985), Frost (1987).

3. On the politics of US–Japan security relations, see Destler (1976), Buck (1981).

4. Recent analyses of reforms in the Soviet Union and their implications for foreign policy including Bova (1987), Gelman (1986), Hewett (1988), Hoffman (1987), Hough (1988), Laird (1987), Naylor (1988), Rumer (1986), and Tedstrom (1987), among others.

5. Among the more notable works on the evolutions and implications of the Sino–Soviet split are Lieberthal (1978), Pollack (1982), Gottlieb (1977), and Ellison (1981).

6. China has maintained that, as a result of these treaties, the Soviet Union now occupies as much as 1.5 million square kilometers of Chinese territory. For China's view on this issue, see Li (1982).

7. On the Soviet buildup in Asia, see Gayler (1979), Langer (1982). On the PRC's military capabilities, see Drayer (1983), Godwin (1985, 1986), Gregor (1984), Segal and Tow (1984).

8. For reports on the leadership changes effected at this meeting, see *New York Times* articles by John F. Burns entitled 'Chinese Retire 10 Aging Leaders in Wide Shuffle' (24 September, 1985), and 'China Appoints 5 Newcomers to Ruling Politburo' (25 September, 1985), as well as '64 Newcomers Join China's Leadership', *New York Times*, 23 September, 1985. On the thirteenth Party Congress, see Rosen (1988), Bachman (1988), Li and White (1988). For a discussion of the broader implications of leadership change that occurred during 1985, see Baum (1986).

9. Recent analyses of the extent and political implications of leadership change in the Soviet Union include Bishop (1987), Colton (1986), Friedgut (1986), Goldman (1987), Gustafson and Mann (1986; 1987), Hough (1987; 1988), and Tessendorf (1987).
10. On recent developments in the Ministry of Defence, see Herspring (1986;1987a,b).
11. For a recent treatment of the legal basis of this dispute as well as the recent politics of it, see Njoroge (1985).
12. Roy Kim (1987:25–6) argues that the reason for the cancellation of the trip was a combination of bureaucratic mishandling on both sides, including opposition within the Japanese Foreign Ministry to the idea of the visit. In addition, the fact that Nakasone would have been, in effect, a lame duck Prime Minister by the time of the trip might have led the Soviets to feel that little of substance would likely come from the visit.
13. Smith (1987) has recently raised questions concerning the economic affinity between the two nations, citing evidence on over time trends in their bilateral trade.
14. On the three 'Nixon shocks', see Buck (1981). On Japan's efforts to forge a more independent foreign policy, see Morse (1984).

References

Bachman, David (1988), 'Politics and Political Reform in China', *Current History* (September):249–52,275–7.

Barnett, A. Doak and Clough, Ralph (eds.)(1986), *Modernizing China: Post-Mao Reform and Development* (Boulder, Colo: Westview Press).

Baum, Richard (1986), 'China in 1985: The Greening of the Revolution', *Asian Survey* 26 (January):30–53.

Bergsten, C. Fred and William R. Cline (1987), *The United States–Japan Economic Problem* (revised edition) (Washington, DC: Institute for International Economics).

Berton, Peter (1986), 'Soviet–Japanese Relations: Perceptions, Goals, Interactions', *Asian Survey* 26 (December):1259–83.

Bishop, William J. (1987), 'The Gorbachev Coalition', *The Mershon Quarterly Report* 12 (Autumn): 1–11.

Bova, Russell (1987), 'On Perestroyka: The Role of Workplace Participation', *Problems of Communism* (July–August): 76–86.

Brown, Archie (1985), 'Gorbachev: New Man in the Kremlin', *Problems of Communism* (May–June): 1–23.

Buck, James H. (1981), 'Japan's Defence Policy', *Armed Forces and Society* 3 (Fall): 79–98.

Cohen, Stephen D. (1984), *Uneasy Partnership: Competition and Conflict in US–Japan Trade Relations* (Cambridge, Mass: Ballinger Publishing Co).

Colton, Timothy (1986), *The Dilemma of Reform in the Soviet Union* (second edition) (New York: Council on Foreign Relations).

Destler, I. M. (1976), *Managing an Alliance: The Politics of US–Japanese Relations* (Washington, DC: Brookings Institution).

Destler, I. M. and Hideo Sato, (eds)(1982), *Coping with US–Japanese Economic Conflicts* (Lexington, Mass: Lexington Books).

Dreyer, June Teufel (1983), 'China's Military Power in the 1980s', in R. C. Bush, (ed.) *China Briefing, 1982* (Boulder, Colo: Westview).

Ellison, Herbert J. (1987), 'Changing Sino–Soviet Relations', *Problems of Communism* (May–June): 17–29.

Ellison, Herbert J., (ed.) (1981), *The Sino–Soviet Conflict: A Global Perspective*, (Seattle, Wa: University of Washington Press).

Fallows, James (1989), 'Let Them Defend Themselves', *Atlantic Monthly* (April): 17–24.

Frankenstein, John (1988), 'Chinese Foreign Trade in the 1980s', *Current History* (September): 257–60, 272–5.

Friedgut, Theodore H. (1986), 'Gorbachev and Party Reform', *Orbis* (Summer): 281–296.

Frost, Ellen L. (1987), *For Richer, For Poorer: The New US–Japan Relationship*, (New York: Council on Foreign Relations).

Gayler, Noel (1979), 'Security Implications of the Soviet Military Presence in Asia', in Richard Solomon, (ed.), *Asian Security in the 1980s: Problems and Policies for a Time of Transition* (Cambridge, Mass: Oelgeschlager, Gunn & Hain).

Gelman, Harry (1986), 'Gorbachev's Dilemmas and His Conflicting Foreign Policy Goals', *Orbis* (Summer): 231–47.

Godwin, Paul H. B. (1985), 'Soldiers and Statesmen in Conflict: Chinese Defence and Foreign Policies in the 1980s', in Samuel S. Kim (ed) *China and the World: Chinese Foreign Policy in the Post-Mao Era* (Boulder, Colo: Westview).

Godwin, Paul H. B. (1986), 'The Chinese Defence Establishment in Transition: The Passing of a Revolutionary Army?', in A. Doak Barnett and Ralph Clough, (eds), *Modernizing China: Post-Mao Reform and Development* (Boulder, Colo: Westview).

Goldman, Marshall (1987), *Gorbachev's Challenge* (New York: Norton)

Gottlieb, Thomas (1977), *Chinese Foreign Policy Factionalism and the Origins of the Strategic Triangle* (Santa Monica, Ca: Rand Corporation).

Gregor, A. James (1984), 'Western Security and the Military Potential of the PRC', *Parameters* 14 (Spring): 35–48.

Gustafson, Thane and Dawn Mann (1986), 'Gorbachev's First Year: Building Power and Authority', *Problems of Communism* (May–June): 1–19.

Gustafson, Thane and Dawn Mann (1987), 'Gorbachev's Next Gamble', *Problems of Communism* (July–August): 1–20.

Herspring, Dale R. (1986), 'The Soviet Military in the Aftermath of the 27th Party Congress', *Orbis* (Summer): 297–315.

Herspring, Dale R. (1987a), 'Gorbachev and the Soviet Military', pp. 42–53 in Robbin Laird (ed.), *Soviet Foreign Policy*, (New York: Academy of Political Science).

Herspring, Dale R. (1987b), 'Gorbachev, Yazov, and the Military', *Problems of Communism* (July–August): 99–107.

Hewett, Ed (1988), *Reforming the Soviet Economy*, (Washington, DC: Brookings).

Hoffman, Erik P. (1987), 'Soviet Foreign Policy from 1986 to 1991: Domestic and International Influences', p.p. 254–71 in Robbin Laird (ed), *Soviet Foreign Policy* (New York: Academy of Political Science).

Iough, Jerry F. (1987), 'Gorbachev Consolidating Power', *Problems of Communism* (July–August): 21–43.

Iough, Jerry F. (1988), *Opening Up the Soviet Economy* (Washington, DC: Brookings).

ohnson, Chalmers (1986), 'Reflections on the Dilemma of Japanese Defence', *Asian Survey* 26 (May):557–72.

.im, Roy (1987), 'Japanese–Soviet Relations Under Gorbachev', presented at the Annual Meeting of the International Studies Association (Washington, DC).

.imura, Hiroshi (1987), 'Soviet Focus on the Pacific', *Problems of Communism* (May–June): 1–16.

.rasner, Stephen D. (1986), 'Trade Conflicts and the Common Defense: The United States and Japan', *Political Science Quarterly* 101 (Winter): 787–805.

.aird, Robbin F. (1987), 'The Gorbachev Challenge', in Robbin Laird (ed.), *Soviet Foreign Policy*, (New York: Academy of Political Science).

.anger, Paul F. (1982), 'Soviet Military Power in Asia', in Donald Zagoria (ed.), *Soviet Policy in East Asia* (New Haven, CT: Yale University Press).

.evine, Steven I. (1986), 'The End of Sino–Soviet Estrangement', *Current History* 85 (September):245–8, 279–80.

.i Cheng and White, Lynn (1988) 'The Thirteenth Central Committee of the Chinese Communist Party: from Mobilizers to Managers', *Asian Survey* 28 (April): 371–99.

.i Huichuan (1982), 'The Crux of the Sino–Soviet Border Question', *China and the World* (Beijing: Beijing Review Foreign Affairs Series, No. 1).

.ieberthal, Kenneth (1978), *Sino–Soviet Conflict in the 1970s: Its Evolution and Implications for the Strategic Triangle* (Santa Monica, Ca: Rand Corporation).

.ason, T. David (1986), 'Sino–Soviet Relations Amid the Transition in Leadership', *Korean Journal of International Affairs* 17 (Autumn):23–72.

.orse, Ronald A. (1984), 'Japan's Search for an Independent Foreign Policy: an American Perspective', *Journal of Northeast Asian Studies* 3 (Summer): 27–42.

.aylor, Thomas H. (1988), *The Gorbachev Strategy: Opening the Closed Society* (Lexington, Mass: Lexington Books).

.joroge, Lawrence, M. (1985), 'The Japan–Soviet Union Territorial Dispute: An Appraisal', *Asian Affairs* 25 (May):499–511.

.lsen, Edward A. (1984) *US–Japanese Strategic Reciprocity: A Neo-Internationalist View* (Stanford: Hoover Institution Press).

.arrott, Bruce (1988), 'Soviet National Security Under Gorbachev', *Problems of Communism* (November–December):1–36.

.ollack, Jonathan (1982), *The Sino–Soviet Rivalry and the Chinese Security Debate*. (Santa Monica, Ca: Rand Corporation).

.obinson, Thomas W. (1987), 'The New Era in Sino–Soviet Relations', *Current History* 86 (September):241–4, 303–4.

.osen, Stanley (1988) 'China in 1987: The Year of the Thirteenth Party

Congress', *Asian Survey* 28 (January): 33–51.

Rumer, Boris (1986), 'Realities of Gorbachev's Economic Program *Problems of Communism* (May–June): 20–31.

Sato, Hideo (1985), 'Japanese–American Economic Relations in Crisis *Current History* 84 (December):405–408, 435–435.

Segal, Gerald and Tow, William T. (ed)(1984), *Chinese Defence Polic* (London: Macmillan).

Shao Huaze (1982), 'A Reliable Guarantee for Socialist Construction *Honqi* in *FBIS-CHINA*, 17 March.

Smith, Gordon B. (1987), 'Recent Trends in Japanese–Soviet Trade *Problems of Communism* (January–February): 56–64.

Tedstrom, John E. (1987), 'On *Perestroyka*: Analyzing the Basic Provisions *Problems of Communism* (July–August): 93–8.

Tessendorf, Martin (1987), 'The Changing Soviet Elite', pp. 32–41 in Robbi Laird (ed.), *Soviet Foreign Policy*, (New York: Academy of Politic. Science).

Zhang Aiping (1983), 'Several Questions Concerning Modernization c National Defence', *Honqui* in *FBIS–CHINA*, 17 March, 1983.

Appendix 1
The Dimensions and Significance of US–Japan Trade and Trade Frictions
Joseph Kvasnicka

The 1980s represent a watershed in the US global trade relations. After decades of surpluses in the country's current transactions with the rest of the world, the accounts plunged into a deep deficit. By mid-year 1986, the trade deficit reached an annual rate of $170 billion.

This single figure embodies a mass of problems that the trade deficit has brought to the US economy: millions of workers displaced from their high-paying jobs in a number of manufacturing sectors; massive losses and bankruptcies in a large number of exporting and import-competing US industries; hardships and foreclosures in the nation's farmlands. In addition, the trade deficit has resulted in the dissipation of the nation's international wealth that has been built up throughout this century, turning the United States into the world's largest international debtor.

All these developments have had, and for years will continue to have, profound impact on the economic lives of all US citizens. The nation's frustration over these developments appears to have focused on the single largest component of our trade deficit – our deficit in trade with Japan. In 1985, that deficit (at $43 billion) accounted for some 35 per cent of our total deficit – far exceeding our deficits with any other nation. Our trade relations with that country came under the closest scrutiny and criticism over the past several years as our overall trade deficit deepened and associated domestic problems multiplied. The economic friction and conflict between the United States and Japan has become the most critical issue facing the two countries since the cessation of the Second World War hostilities.

And – to the extent that the conflict involves the free world's two largest economic super-powers, which, between them, account for one out of every three dollars' worth of goods and services produced in the entire free world – that conflict has become the most critical issue facing the entire world economy, with profound economic, strategic, and geopolitical implications for the world at large.

A rational resolution of this conflict appears essential for the continuation of growth in global trade and cooperation on which virtually every nation in the world depends to maintain its security and well-being. Such a rational resolution requires, in the first instance, an objective evaluation of the underlying causes of the conflict. The economic data presented in chart form in this appendix is an attempt to contribute to that process. The charts were

193

prepared as a supplement to a paper presented at a conference on the US–Japan trade friction, organized by the Mississippi State University, and were designed to highlight some of the major underlying trends that have shaped the economic developments in the two nations, and thus their interaction via their trade.

Appendix II

Joseph Kvasnicka

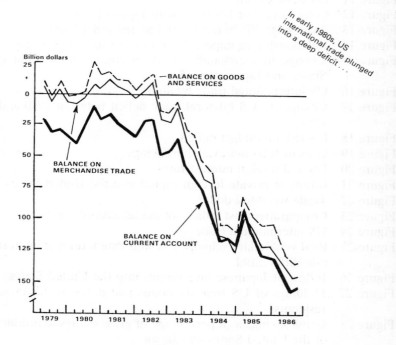

Figure 1 US international trade balances (1979–86)

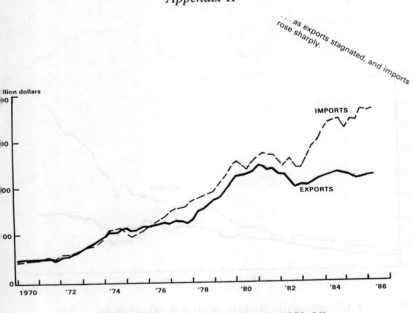

Figure 2 US merchandise trade (current dollars) (1970–86)

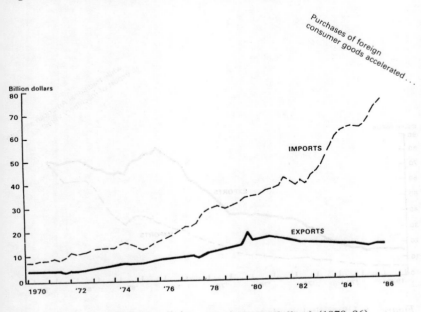

Figure 3 US trade in consumer goods (current dollars) (1970–86)

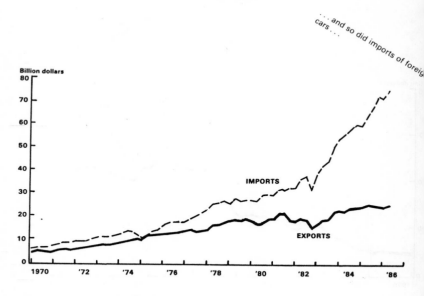

Figure 4 US automotive trade (current dollars) (1970–86)

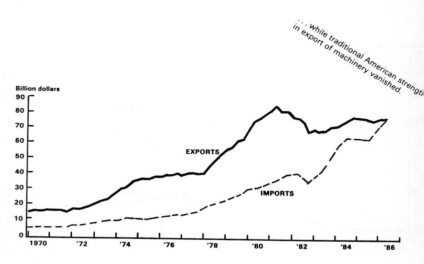

Figure 5 US capital goods trade (current dollars) (1970–86)

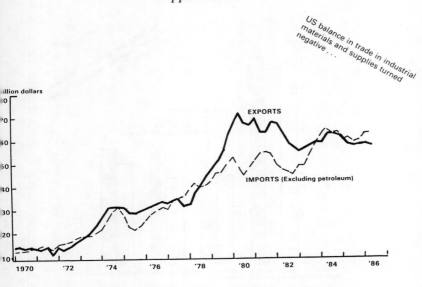

US balance in trade in industrial materials and supplies turned negative . . .

Figure 6 US trade in industrial supplies (current dollars) (1970–86)

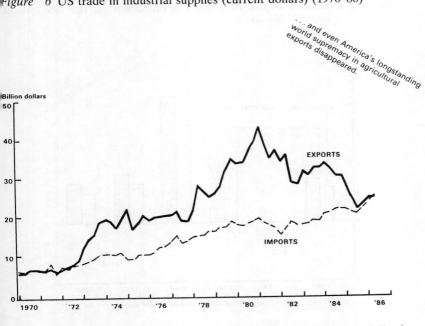

. . . and even America's longstanding world supremacy in agricultural exports disappeared.

Figure 7 US trade in foods, feeds and beverages (current dollars) (1970–86)

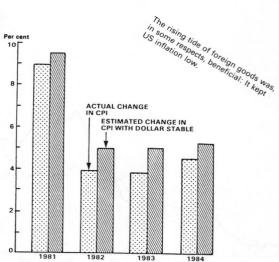

*Based on estimates derived from multi country econometric model, with dollar remaining at the
end of 1980 level relative to major currencies.

Figure 8 Estimated impact of dollar's appreciation on the US rate of
inflation (1981–4)

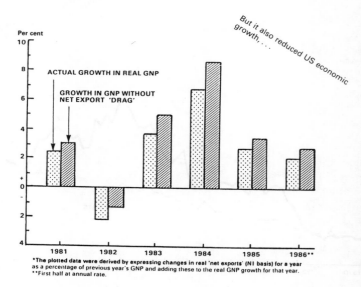

*The plotted data were derived by expressing changes in real 'net exports' (NI basis) for a year
as a percentage of previous year's GNP and adding these to the real GNP growth for that year.
**First half at annual rate.

Figure 9 Estimates of foreign sector's 'drag' on US economic growth
(1981–6)

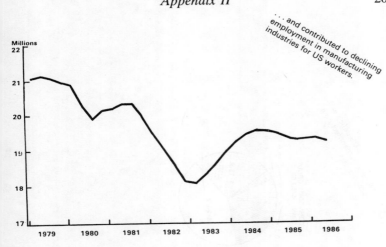

... and contributed to declining employment in manufacturing industries for US workers.

Figure 10 US manufacturing employment (1979–86)

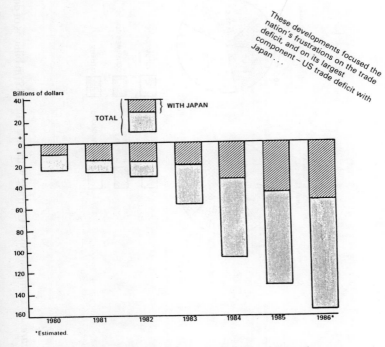

These developments focused the nation's frustrations on the trade deficit, and on its largest component – US trade deficit with Japan ...

*Estimated.

Figure 11 US trade deficit (total and with Japan) (1980–6)

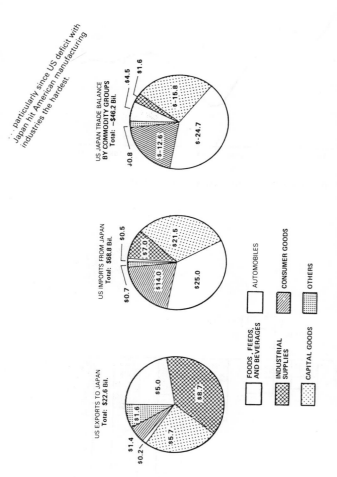

Figure 12 Composition of US trade with Japan in 1985 (in billions of dollars)

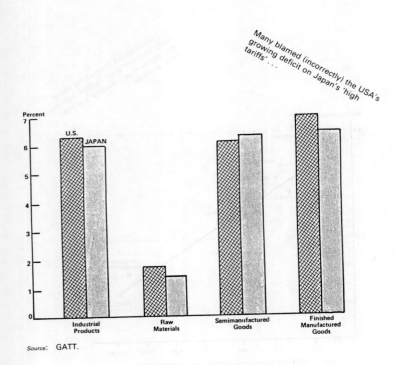

Many blamed (incorrectly) the USA's growing deficit on Japan's 'high tariffs'...

Source: GATT.

Figure 13 Average tariffs in the United States and Japan (simple average of rates)

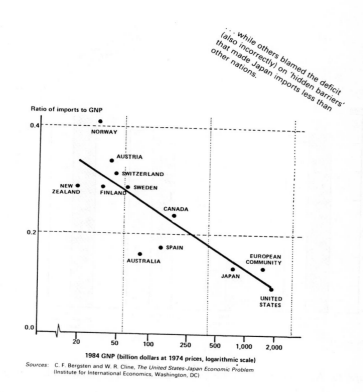

Figure 14 Relationship of import–GNP ratio to size of economy

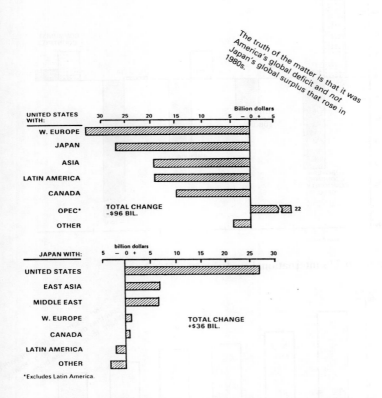

Figure 15 Change in merchandise trade balances of the United States and Japan, 1981–5

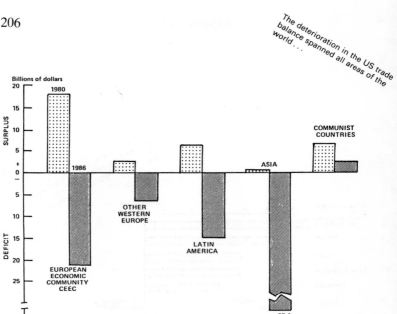

The deterioration in the US trade balance spanned all areas of the world . . .

Figure 16 US international trade by area (1980–6)

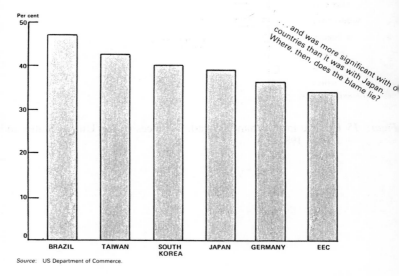

. . . and was more significant with other countries than it was with Japan. Where, then, does the blame lie?

Source: US Department of Commerce.

Figure 17 Changes in US bilateral trade deficit between 1980 and 1985 (as a percentage of US trade with each country)

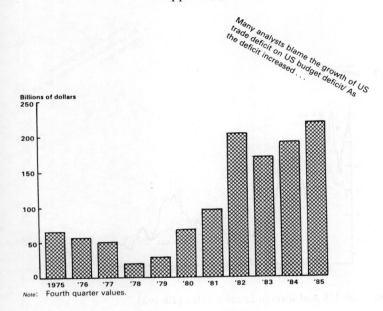

Many analysts blame the growth of US trade deficit on US budget deficit/ As the deficit increased . . .

Figure 18 US federal budget deficit (1975–85)

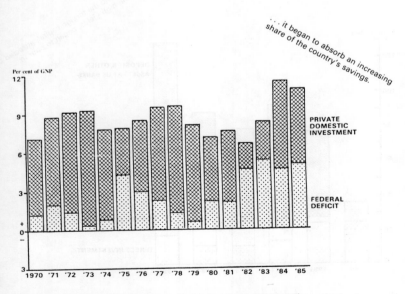

. . . it began to absorb an increasing share of the country's savings.

Figure 19 Uses of total net available savings (1970–85)

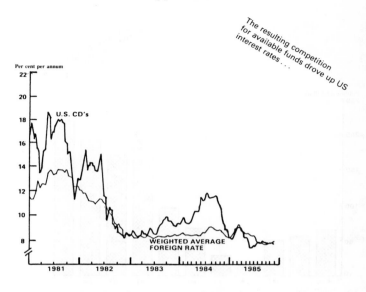

Figure 20 US and foreign interest rates (1981–5)

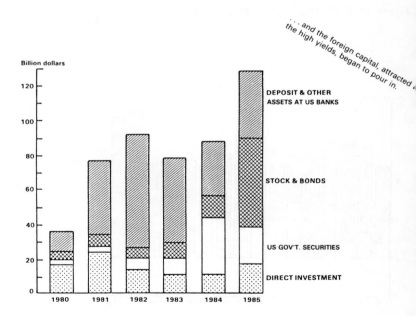

Figure 21 Inflow of private foreign capital into the United States (1980–5)

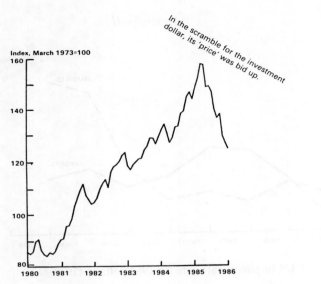

Figure 22 Trade weighted dollar (1980–6)

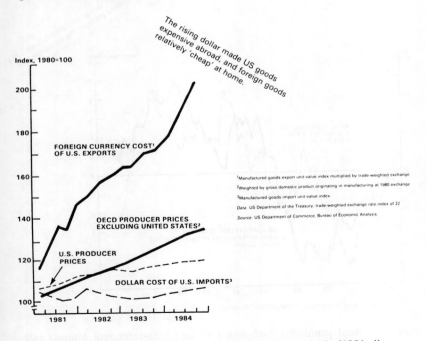

Figure 23 Comparative cost indices of manufactured goods (1981–4)

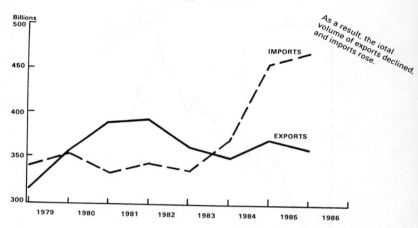

Figure 24 US international trade (in 1982 dollars) (1979–86)

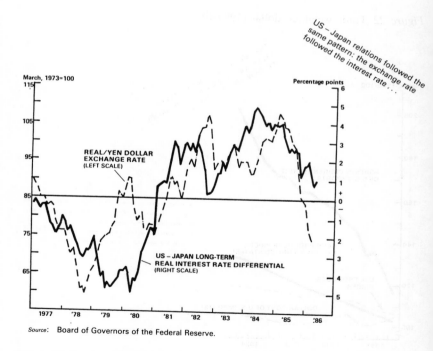

Source: Board of Governors of the Federal Reserve.

Figure 25 Real yen/dollar exchange rate and long-term real interest rate differential (1977–86)

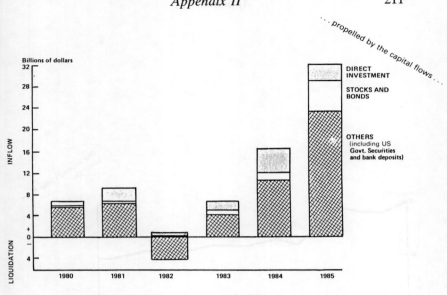

... propelled by the capital flows ...

Figure 26 Inflow of Japanese investment into the United States (1980–5)

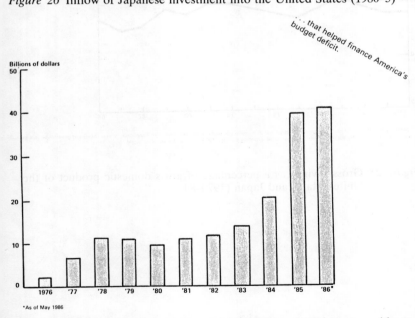

... that helped finance America's budget deficit.

*As of May 1986

Figure 27 Holdings of US treasury bonds and notes by Japanese residents (1976–86)

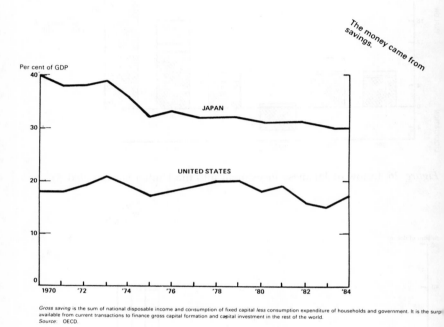

Gross saving is the sum of national disposable income and consumption of fixed capital *less* consumption expenditure of households and government. It is the surpl available from current transactions to finance gross capital formation and capital investment in the rest of the world.
Source: OECD.

Figure 28 Gross savings as a percentage of gross domestic product of the
United States and Japan (1970–84)

Part of that saving was attracted to the United States, boosting the dollar . . .

JAPAN (Trillion of Yen)	SOURCES	UNITED STATES (Billion of dollars)
¥92.4	Total gross private saving	$ 674.8
36.5	Of which: Households	168.7
3.5	Corporate	91.0
43.0	Depreciation	415.1
	Corporate $253.9 Noncorporate $161.2	
8.5	Government	–

	USES	
44.5	Business Investment	416.6
14.2	Residential Housing	181.4
1.6	Stock (Inventory)	64.1
23.1	Government	101.5
	Federal $−170.0 State & Local $+ 68.5	
+ 8.7*	Shortfall (−) (Made up by borrowing abroad) OR Surplus (+) (Invested abroad)	−90.7

Note: Totals may not add up because of rounding and statistical discrepancies.

Source: US Department of Commerce, OECD Japan Economic Survey 1985.

Figure 29 Sources and uses of savings in the United States and Japan
(sample year: 1984)

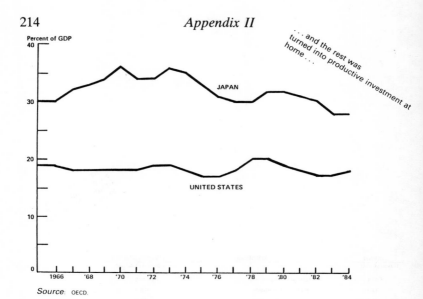

Figure 30 Gross fixed capital formation as a percentage of gross domestic product of the United States and Japan (1966–84)

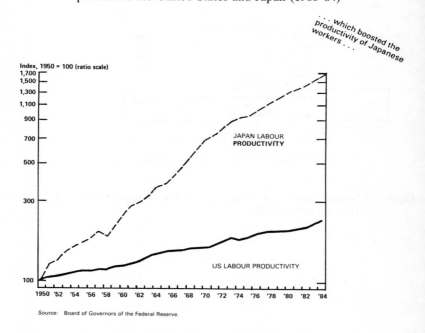

Figure 31 Output per hour in manufacturing (1950–84)

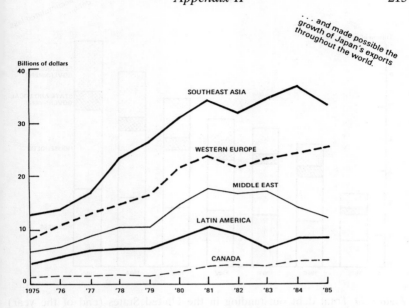

. . . and made possible the growth of Japan's exports throughout the world.

Figure 32 Japan's exports by area (in US dollars) (1975–85)

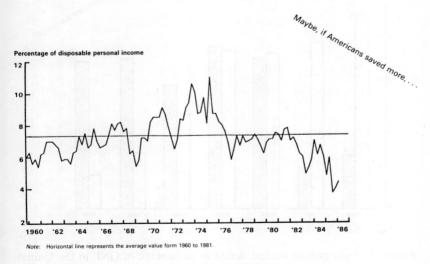

Maybe, if Americans saved more, . . .

Note: Horizontal line represents the average value form 1960 to 1981.

Figure 33 US personal savings (1960–86)

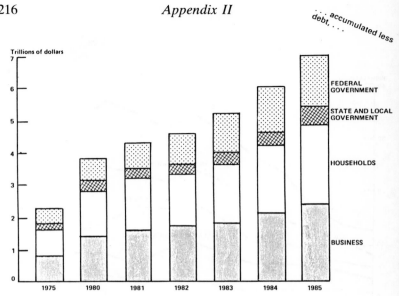

Figure 34 Total debt outstanding in the United States (end of the year) (1975–85)

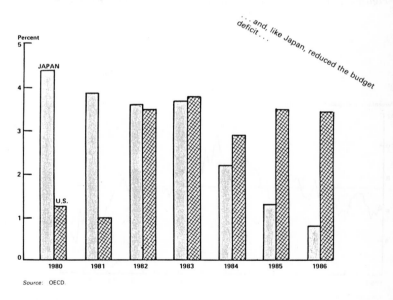

Figure 35 Government budget deficit as percentage of GNP in the United States and Japan (1980–6)

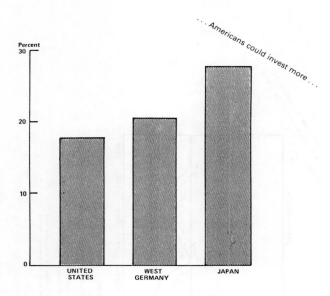

Figure 36 Gross fixed capital formation as a percentage of GDP in 1984

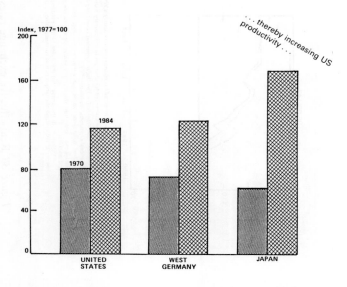

Figure 37 Output per man-hour in manufacturing (1970 *v.* 1984)

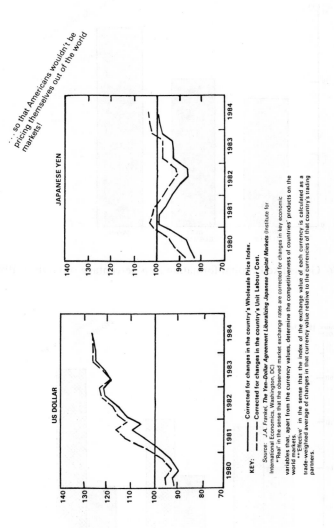

KEY: —— Corrected for changes in the country's Wholesale Price Index.
      - - - Corrected for changes in the country's Unit Labour Cost.

Source: J.A. Frankel, *The Yen–Dollar Agreement Liberalizing Japanese Capital Markets* (Institute for International Economics, Washington, DC)

**'Real' in the sense that the observed market exchange rates are corrected for changes in key economic variables that, apart from the currency values, determine the competitiveness of countries' products on the world markets.

***'Effective' in the sense that the index of the exchange value of each currency is calculated as a trade-weighted average of changes in that currency value relative to the currencies of that country's trading partners.

Figure 38 Real effective exchange rates of the US dollar and the Japanese yen (1980–4)

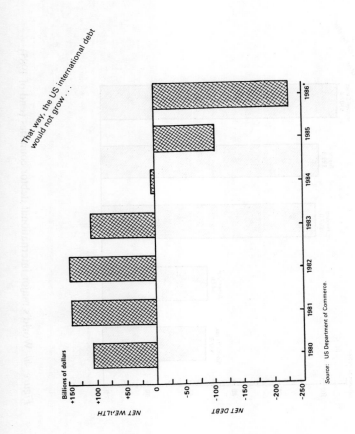

Figure 39 Net international investment position of the United States, 1980–5

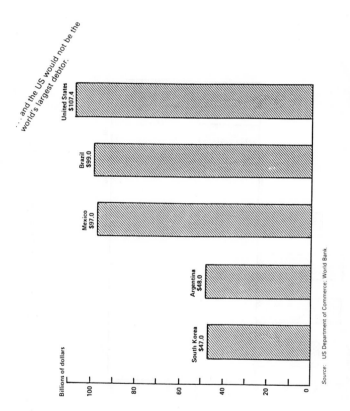

Source: US Department of Commerce; World Bank.

Figure 40 World's major international debtor countries (end of 1985)

Index